Indie Book A

Thank You for p...

child abuse is teen p...

Love,
James Mill...

PIECES OF VICTORY

JENEEN MILLER

Copyright TXu 1-949-625

WGA WEST Registration #1779009

ISBN # 9780692539026

This is a non-fiction memoir of my childhood events, however,
I used pseudonyms to protect survivors as well as the perpetrators in this book.

Senior Editor: Phil Shapiro

Junior Editor: Rosemary Zetts

Graphic Design:

Front/Back Cover - Damonza.com - Alisha

Front Cover - Black & White/Color - Ryjin Pearson

Graphic Design:

In Memory of... - Jeneen Miller

Foreword

How does one claim victory? By definition, *victory* is an act of defeating an opponent in battle, game, or other competition. In life, there are many victories. Most are hard-fought battles. While reflecting on my many years of friendship with Jeneen, two words come to mind: survivor and compassion. While reading *Pieces of Victory*, these words shine through. Her harrowing life experiences have caused her survival instincts to kick in which she has adequately articulated to the page. Jeneen's compassion brings awareness and hope which in essence gives a voice to the forgotten, abused and voiceless.

I fondly recall meeting Jeneen in Los Angeles while we were working on *Cult of Torture,* an episode of season 2 on *Haunted.* After a very long day on the set, we made plans to freshen up and meet at the hotel restaurant. We communicated all the time through social media and phone. Due to the distance between us, we rarely had the chance to talk face to face. We chatted for hours, laughed, shed a tear or two and discussed plans for the future.

Jeneen always brings her "A" game. She has knowledge of the troubled teen *camp* I was sent to, as I do with the one she was forced to attend.

There is a kindred spirit that survivors of this type of abuse share. Even with unspoken words… we understand one another.

It is with great pride I congratulate my dear friend, Jeneen Miller, on yet another *piece of victory* for allowing us to read her words of life. You will have many victories in the future.

— James Swift

I dedicate this book to the boy who saved me when I was hiding from the world. Drake was my guiding light who gave me the hope to survive the mental and physical torment I was forced to endure. His spirit gave me the strength and courage to move forward because he promised me that things would get better. I held on to that hope as a means to travel through the darkest times of my life.

Contents

Foreword iii

Dedications ix

My Higher Self. xix

Piece One - C:\Jeneen\Hell\Victory\Jade.doc 1

Piece Two - C:\Jeneen\Hell\Mother\Blame\Guilt\Parakeets.doc 7

Piece Three - C:\Jeneen\Hell\Mother\Unloved\Unworthyofreceivinggifts.doc 9

Piece Four - C:\Jeneen\Hell\Dad\Unloved\Nosecondchances.doc 13

Piece Five - C:\Jeneen\Hell\Father\Unloved\Dentist.doc 17

Piece Six - C:\Hell\Jeneen\Myfirsttamponexperience.doc 21

Piece Seven - C:\Jeneen\Hell\Dad\Low Self-Esteem\Modeling Career.doc 25

Piece Eight - Have You Ever. 29

Piece Nine - C:\Jeneen\Hell\Victory\Parents\Unloved\Abandoned\Thebigbetrayal.doc   33

Piece Ten - C:\Jeneen\Heaven\Drakemccallister\Firstlove.doc 45

Piece Eleven - C:\Jeneen\Heaven\Love\Drake\1stdatesince8thgrade.doc 55

Piece Twelve - C:\Jeneen\Heaven\Love\Drake\Jumpingoutofbed.doc 61

Piece Thirteen - C:\Jeneen\Heaven\Love\Drake\Theaddiction.doc. 67

Piece Fourteen - C:\Jeneen\Heaven\Drake\Ragingwaters.doc 71

Piece FIfteen - C:\Jeneen\Heaven\Drake\Mycloudoftrust.doc 79

Piece Sixteen - C:\Jeneen\Heaven\Drake\Hitops.doc 85

Piece Seventeen - C:jeneen\Heaven\Drake\Homecoming1987.Doc. 95

Piece Eighteen - C:\Jeneen\Heaven\Love\Drake\Christmas.doc 103

Piece Nineteen - C:\Jeneen\Heaven\Drake\Movienight.doc. 107

Piece Twenty - C:\Jeneen\Heaven\Drake\Positivereinforcements.doc 111

Piece Twenty One - C:\Jeneen\Heaven\Love\Drake\Thepiano.doc. 115

Piece Twenty Two - C:\Jeneen\Hell\Victory\Howigotoutofgr.doc. 119

Piece Twenty Three - C:\Jeneen\Hell\Victory\Thestagnantpiano.doc 129

Piece Twenty Four - C:\Jeneen\Hell\Christiancounseling.doc. 133

Piece Twenty Five - C:\Jeneen\Hell\Victory\Qc'smanifestations4us.doc 139

Piece Twenty Six - C:\Jeneen\Hell\Victory\Dogleash.doc. 145

Piece Twenty Seven - C:\Jeneen\Hell\Victory\Mouthsealedshut.doc. 153

Piece Twenty Eight - C:\Jeneen\Hell\Victory\Ontheroadagain.doc. 159

Piece Twenty Nine - C:\Jeneen\Hell\Victory\Religionbashing.doc 167

Piece Thirty - C:\Jeneen\Hell\Victory\Dreaming.doc. 171

Piece Thirty One - C:\Jeneen\Hell\Victory\Hardlabor.doc 177

Piece Thirty Two - C:\Jeneen\Hell\Victory\Searchraid.doc 185

Piece Thirty Three - C:\Jeneen\Hell\Victory\Careysun\2ndtimearound.doc 191

Piece Thirty Four - C:\Jeneen\Hell\Victory\Abomination.doc 197

Piece Thirty Five - C:\Jeneen\Hell\Victory\Goatpile.doc 203

Piece Thirty Six - C:\Jeneen\Hell\Victory\Offbuddy\Isolation.doc 209

Piece Thirty Seven - C:\Jeneen\Hell\Victory\Careysunescapesvictory.doc 213

Piece Thirty Eight - C:\Jeneen\Hell\Victory\Firstvisit.doc 219

Piece Thirty Nine - C:\Jeneen\Hell\Victory\Lackofappetite.doc 227

Piece Forty - C:\Jeneen\Hell\Victory\Thanksgiving.doc 231

Piece Forty One - C:\Jeneen\Hell\Victory\Exercise.doc 235

Piece Forty Two - C:\Jeneen\Hell\Victory\Laborversuseducation.doc 241

Piece Forty Three - C:\Jeneen\Heaven\Drake\Mr. L\Theraven.doc 245

Piece Forty Four - C:\Jeneen\Heaven\Positivereinforcement\Mrs.t.doc 251

Piece Forty Five - C:\Jeneen\Hell\Theillusionofmydreamhouse.doc 255

Piece Forty Six - C:\Jeneen\Heaven\Drake\St.julie'sanaheimtrip.doc 271

Piece Forty Seven - C:\Jeneen\Heaven\Drake\Juniorprom.doc 277

Piece Forty Eight - C:\Jeneen\Heaven\Drake\Orion'sbelt.doc 283

Piece Forty Nine - C:\Jeneen\Hell\Father\Proveit.doc 289

Piece Fifty - C:\Jeneen\Hell\Mother\Runaway.doc 297

Piece Fifty One - C:\Jeneen\Hell\Mother\Holyoil.doc 305

Piece Fifty Two - C:\Jeneen\Hell\Victory\Happybirthday.doc 313

Piece Fifty Three - C:\Jeneen\Hell\Victory\Christmas.doc 323

Piece Fifty Four - C:\Jeneen\Hell\Victory\Laundryhelper.doc 329

Piece Fifty Five - C:\Jeneen\Hell\Victory\Mynervousbreakdown.doc 335

Piece Fifty Six - C:\Jeneen\Hell\Victory\7monthvisit.doc 341

Piece Fifty Seven - C:\Jeneen\Hell\Victory\Separation\Breeanna.doc 347

Piece Fifty Eight - C:\Jeneen\Hell\Victory\Jadeandthegoodsoldier.doc 351

Piece Fifty Nine - C:\Jeneen\Purgatory\Theprodigaldaugherreturns.doc 359

Piece Sixty - C:\Jeneen\Purgatory\Parents\Drake\Emptiness.doc 365

Piece Sixty One - C:\Jeneen\Purgatory\Lifeaftervictory\Wakingup.doc 369

Piece Sixty Two - C:\Jeneen\Purgatory\Lifeaftervictory\Mynewgpa.doc 375

Piece Sixty Three - C:\Jeneen\Purgatory\Lifeaftervictory\Mycollegeapplication.doc . . 381

Piece Sixty Four - C:\Purgatory\Lifeaftervictory\Bonnie&Clyde.doc 385

Piece Sixty Five - C:\Jeneen\Purgatory\Lifeaftervictory\Pinkfloyd.doc 391

Piece Sixty Six - C:\Jeneen\Purgatory\Lifeaftervictory\Thegift.doc 395

Piece Sixty Seven - C:\Jeneen\Lifeaftervictory\Rayoflight\Pepperdine.doc 401

Epilogue 409

In Memory Of Michele Ulriksen 413

Dedications

In Memory of Dr. Roy Adler, Professor of Marketing at Pepperdine University, respected by many, including myself. He was my mentor while I worked alongside him in the business division. He was down-to-earth, humble and I enjoyed his quick wit. Roy D. Adler and Alexis Bonnell are the authors of Get Your Dream Job! I can truly say that his passion was serving as Fulbright Professor at Pepperdine University and he loved his students. His unconventional creative marketing made him unique, and as an end result, captured students' attention. I had the honor of auditing a couple of his classes. I worked diligently with Dr. Adler on his Fortune 100/500 projects during the time I spent in the word processing department, HAC. I am so fortunate that I reached out to Dr. Adler right before he passed and told him how much he impacted my life. You are my angel and are truly missed.

The business division family encouraged me and contributed to the biggest part of my victory. I can truly tell Dr. Adler that I have my dream job — writing while sitting on my towel on the sandy beach, with my laptop, listening to the sounds of the waves.

Both Dr. Banks, Ph.D in Clinical Psychology and Dr. Adler, licensed psychologist, took the time to show their support by providing additional tools in coping with my childhood memories and the loss of my grandparents. They both played a big part in building the strength I carry today.

To my friend and filmmaker, Ryjin Pearson, for being there

during my hardest emotional times and bringing wine when you visited! You are the best! Visit my talented friend: Ryjin Pearson - Dark Fujin Productions!

To Phil Shapiro, thank you for your diligence in editing Pieces of Victory. This book will be a powerful tool in helping to prevent abuse in teen programs. Thank you for being part of the change.

To Rosemary Zetts, thank you for putting a nice *ribbon* on my book project. You really tied everything together and you are truly a *grammar bulldog* who could *sniff out* grammatical errors. Thank you for wrapping up my beautiful book.

To Barbara Waite & *Schoolboy* Carl! You have been there for me over the years and are like family. I'm so proud of your success with Projects Your Way! I am extremely busy with writing, working, and other projects. I needed to be able to delegate some of it to an outsource Marketing/Business Development Specialist. Projects Your Way fits the bill!

Jennifer Huse, thank you for your encouragements and support. Jennifer is a Certified Holistic Life Coach, a Certified Stress Management Coach and an Energy Healing Practitioner. She is also in the midst of working toward obtaining her certification as a Holistic Health Practitioner. Education: Masters of Science in Counseling. Visit: www.mindfultransformationslv.org.

Colin Huse, I'm looking forward to having your production company set up another platform for my book. Signing Pieces of Victory will be a door opener for the deaf community. Visit: Colin Huse!

To Dr. Jere Yates and Regan Schaffer who made the Pepperdine University Business Division welcoming by always going the extra mile to accommodate students and faculty. Both professional and nurturing, I would always see students gravitating to their office for guidance. Regan, in my eyes you were the "mother hen" and the glue that held the Business Division together. Thank you Dr. Baim, Dr. Seshan, Dr. Summers and Dr. Whitney. It was a pleasure working with you. You made me feel like a key player to the division.

To Jim Archibald who spent time encouraging and building the confidence that molded me into a professional woman. You gave me valuable tools to climb up a ladder of success at Pepperdine University. You told me that I was talented and I would never have a problem getting any position I sought. Well, I believed you… Your strongest characteristic is your encouragement of others. Thank you Darlene Kirtz who was a team player while working in the Word Processing Department, HAC. Your comedy kept my spirits high every day! I enjoyed working with you. You both were great mentors and played a very important role in building my self-worth, creating the strong woman that I am today.

To Jing Redfern, I will never forget our long talks while walking along the track at Pepperdine. Our discussions were not only therapeutic but also good exercise! Reflecting on the past, I realize now more than ever how appreciative I am for the quality time we had during our lunches together.

To my dearest friends, Dick Womack, Paul Reilly and Joe Schooler, you have been my support through some of my darkest times. Dick Womack, my personal Enrolled Agent/Tax Preparer, I'll never forget our lunchtime breaks at Pepperdine when you worked in Financial Services! I have so many fond memories of our friendship. You understood loss and you specifically told me that time heals. Well, you were absolutely correct. Paul, I'll never forget you telling me about the position available at HAC. You helped me on my journey to get to the next level. You were my loyal friend who was there for me every day when I felt alone. Your friendship was key to my healing. Joe, I'll never forget our pizza run to the homeless in Santa Monica. Thank you Dick, Paul and Joe for being a rock in my life during a time when things were not exactly pieced together.

In memory of Grandma, you were my escape almost every weekend when I was a lonely seventeen-year-old. You were there for me during my darkest times and I will always treasure hugging you during my surprise visits. The Florentine Garden dances, the spaghetti and meatball dinners and your nurturing energy kept me grounded. Your spirit will always be a part of me.

In memory of Grandpa, thank you for all of your support and being there for me when I needed you the most.

In memory of Michele Ulriksen, the author of "Reform at Victory: A Survivor's Story." Unfortunately, Michele's story is far from an isolated incident as other stories just like hers travel, like a fatal disease, spreading throughout the United States. Thank you for using your book as a tool, raising awareness, in order to prevent child abuse. In 2011, our strong leader of the survivor community sadly took her own life. I will keep Michele's fire alive and pass her torch forward to help prevent child abuse in teen programs. She is my guiding light and her spirit is with me always. Please visit: "Reform at Victory: A Survivor's Story."

In memory of Chelsea Martinez, a survivor who was recently brutally murdered. Thank you for being brave and telling your story on Keen TV. You truly will be missed. I know your spirit is there on this journey to help prevent child abuse in institutions. You are my angel of light, leading me on my path to prevent child abuse.

In memory of Shaun Grepiotis, you were my entrepreneurial mentor and my love. You taught me everything I needed to know about real estate, having my own business and metaphorically riding the next wave to success. You will always be my inspiration to take advantage of opportunity. I know you are my angel guiding me always.

In memory of Junior (Robert) LaSpada, Graduate from Pepperdine School of Law. Your ambition motivated me and I felt that you could reach all walks of life with any business venture. You were an entrepreneur, a real-estate angel and my good friend. I truly miss you.

Rock LaSpada, Financial Advisor, Real-Estate Agent/Broker, you have been a source of constant stability during any circumstance in my life. Your loyalty is something I can count on during my journey. Thank you for living out your name, Rock. It suits you.

In memory of Scott Donaldson, I'll never forget the Eagles concert we went to at the MGM. I cannot believe you wore my necklace to work! When your mom told me that story, I laughed. I also realized how brave it was to wear something feminine (rose quartz heart with pearls over it) as you greeted guests in the casino. It was then that I realized the value of our deep level friendship.

To Henson Aviation, Joyce B. and Jeri Davis. Thank you so much for encouraging me when I was seventeen years old to compose a letter to my congressman, senator, and Social Services of San Diego in order to close down Victory Christian Academy in Ramona, CA. You were my support system at a time when I was trying to unravel my darkest demons. Henson Aviation was my door to opportunity and the stepping stone to several positions at Pepperdine University.

Thank you Professional Massage, Inc. for giving me the flexibility I needed in order to write this book. You are my vehicle to a number one best seller!

To Chris, my business developer. We have been friends and business partners for over two decades. Looking forward to this new journey on raising awareness! Your optimism and positive attitude are contagious and I'm excited to have you on board the Pieces of Victory team!

To Juanita Feamster, you gave me the opportunity to work with you at Carpenter's Insurance. You taught me so much and gave me the administration skills to become successful in the workplace.

To Mrs. Thee and Mr. Louis, thank you so much for taking the extra time, going above and beyond the call of duty as teachers. Both of you have been influential in almost every aspect of my life.

Michael and Hannah Rogers, who helped with the synopsis, formatting style and Piece One of this book. Thank you Michael for encouraging me to put my emotions and passions on paper, especially when I wrote about Victory Christian Academy.

Carol Workman, for reading this book over hot coffee and getting excited about the developments of my teenage love story. Your enthusiasm and encouragement for this memoir mean the world to me.

Nick Gaglia, survivor of a straight program, director, producer and filmmaker (*Aaron Bacon*) was there for me with every chapter and participated in the developmental stages of my cover. Michael and Nick encouraged me to keep writing for a solid year. Allen Bradshaw and Chris Biehl, who encouraged me to take photos and videos on the property of Victory Christian Academy for my book and documentary. Thank you Daniel Berube for your input on my front cover as well!

Theresa Gaglia Peña, thank you for sharing your story of your unfortunate time in a lockdown straight program. Your book, *Run*, is truly captivating and I could not put it down! Much success to you!

Theresa Kent, you inspired me to speak in front of Capitol Hill in DC. There was something about your energy that day that encouraged me to give my speech to prevent child abuse in teen programs!

Tere Earl, you made me laugh in DC. Your sense of humor is what carries you through any obstacle that is in your way. It is your strength and your gift.

Survivors of Institutional Abuse (SIA), your organization empowers me because it is filled with survivors who make a difference. Thank you Jodi Hobbs, the founder of SIA, who is also a survivor of Victory Christian Academy. You have really created strengths by connecting survivors and making a difference in preventing child abuse in residential programs.

To all the survivors from Victory Christian Academy: Angela Bennett, Jennifer Berl, Carey Dunn, Margaret Harris, Jodi Hobbs, Gianna Johnson, Haley Johnston, Elva Martinez, Faith Nelson, Christie Niznik, Sara Sherry, Michelle Hearn Thibodeaux, Heather Tierney, Michele Ulriksen, Trisha Vasquez, Kimberly Williams and all of the other brave survivors.

For Kidnapped for Christ, David Lawrence Wernsman. Thank you for coming forth and sharing your story and making it accessible on Showtime and iTunes. You can purchase his documentary at *Kidnapped for Christ*! (I appear at the end of the documentary!)

For former husband, Troy, who stood by me during the sleepless nights when I suffered post-traumatic stress disorder (PTSD) while making this book happen.

For KEEN-17 TV, a Christian station based in Las Vegas that supports survivors of institutional abuse all over the country. A big thank you goes to KEEN-TV for dedicating their time and efforts to spread awareness and contribute to justice being served in Louisiana. Thank you Dale, Renee and William, and to Simone Jones, Silvia Henry McMillan, Teresa Fry, Joanna Wright and Tara Cummings for supporting Jennifer Halter's emotional journey back to Louisiana, the birthplace of Jennifer's abuse at New Bethany Home for Girls. Visit this site for further info: The New Bethany Home for Girls story…

To Mark Levine, thank you so much for volunteering your time to the survivor community. You have interviewed survivors on MarkLevineTalk, organized protests with SIA in DC and encouraged us to use our strong voice to prevent child abuse. You have helped empower survivors of teen programs in so many ways and I am truly grateful.

To Kim Holt and Rhonda L. and every New Bethany survivor (See above).

Thank you for being brave and telling your story. Please read New Bethany, by Roger Kiser.

To all the survivors who felt abandoned and trapped, there are organizations to help you in your healing process. Visit: SIA-Now.org. You don't have to suffer silently. Please know that you are not alone.

I dedicate this book to my childhood friend, Jennifer Sue Harris (Jenny Penny Poo). She taught me what it was like to be loved by a mother by showing me her nurturing mom. I spent many days at her two-bedroom apartment and we would talk for hours. She was my escape from my abusive household. I'll never forget running away to her place and have such great memories of our special bond. Through Pieces of Victory, I hope to reconnect with her and be a part of her life again. I pray this book will find her.

I dedicate this book to Krystal Dolan, who went the extra mile to override a so-called preacher's sermon. She turned it into a Bible study which strengthened my spirituality.

I dedicate this book to Dolores Parrish who finds her spirituality through Buddhism. She has inspired me to reach a higher level of self through finding the positive within my pain. I am excited about creating a video/sign language platform for this book with her.

To Steven Kimbrough, thank you so much for the media work you have put together regarding Survivors of Institutional Abuse and Pieces of Victory, spreading awareness through social media. You have taken my book to the next level and I am truly grateful. For more info, visit: PodBrother.com.

Thank you Samantha Fenner for your support and love. It was so much fun reminiscing about our double date from the past and then writing about it. You brought back many memories of *Hi Tops* and our sunset beach excursion. I'll never forget the bike ride to your grandmother's house, the slumber parties and all the choreographic dance routines that your father videotaped with his camcorder from the eighties. Many memories!

To the Poserinas, Bill, Judy, Kara and *Hammy*. Thank you so much for taking me into your home for six months without any strings attached. I needed that stability in order to become an independent woman at the age of seventeen.

Chris Meske, thank you for Pink Floyd, the long drives and the therapy along a desolate road leading to the Pacific Coast Highway.

For the lunch group of good friends at Newbury Park High: Amy Nesbitt, Dorothy Peters, Tami Carter and Brenda Stoffregen.

To my angelic Angelique de Wolfe! You are a healer and a guiding light assisting others to self-heal. I know you will be an asset to the survivor community, helping those who suffered and survived to self empower.

Thank you Matty from Chicago for your generous donation towards my book trailer, Pieces of Victory.

To Lisa Loitwood... Thank you so much for reconnecting with me in Newbury Park as we strolled down memory lane. It helped me fine-tune a piece in my book!

Your help with the details of the horse program and the waterfall trail in Sycamore Canyon was invaluable.

Thank you *Drake McCallister* for supporting my book and helping me highlight child abuse in teen programs. You were my inspiration for writing Pieces of Victory.

This book gave me hope in finding love and passion for life again — passion that I thought was robbed from me at Victory Christian Academy. It was not taken but buried deep in the recesses of my soul. I have extracted these demons, accepted and released them for the world to see.

My Higher Self

If the human mind can be said to be like a computer, then memories are like individual files. Groups of related memories are then like directories holding these files for future reference and study. I often refer to my memories and experiences this way as the part of the hardware that is my mind. After I left home at seventeen, I allowed my second ear-piercing to close up, sealing the skin so well that the exterior damage to my so-called hardware almost vanished. I no longer wanted visible proof of young love to be found on the surface, subconsciously pulling up compartments of subdirectories. I forbade the constant reminder of iridescent jewelry pieces reflecting the memory of what was taken from me.

Two decades had passed when I decided to begin meditating, reaching a deep alpha/delta meditation level, and started to channel. I reached my higher self and tapped into a memory of Drake and of feeling loved again. I reached in and grabbed the content that was trapped in that corrupted file and created a new one. I suddenly had an urge to get in tune with my act of love. I envisioned that I would have to reopen the second ear hole, inflicting pain on myself as a necessary part of the process. I cringed, imagining the many layers I had to go through in order to open that part of me again. The stud I pierced it with, after dousing it with alcohol, came through on the other side of my skin as if there were no barriers. It was only a thin layer.

For many years, I wanted to forget about the memory of Drake. If I could override the memory or bury it so deep, the pain would dissipate. If I bring it up to the surface, however, there is a chance I could feel love again in spite of the obstacles I would have to face. It took me thirteen years, but in 2001, I took a giant step forward and dove in, practicing self-hypnosis and risking many damaged applications in order to find the treasures that were locked up inside my root directories.

In 2012, I started to write Pieces of Victory.

PIECE ONE

C:\Jeneen\Hell\Victory\Jade.doc

IT IS ALMOST 8 pm as I stare into the face of that timeless mechanism and notice the ticking hands that barely move. The red moving mechanical part that indicates the seconds only reminds me of the minutes, hours, days, weeks and months ahead. I can almost hear the sound of a rhythmic audible tap as it drives me a little mad. I sit frozen as I find myself idly sitting on my bunk bed. I fight the urge to panic as I feel the darkness slowly beginning to suffocate me. In this room, the walls are bare, except for the motion of shadows, without so much as a window for light. I am not sure if I could stand to see outside though because I am certain it would only serve as a reminder of my imprisonment.

"This is awful," I think to myself. I close my eyes and begin to imagine the wondrous things that could be going on outside, miles away from this hellhole. I tilt my head up and scan the room for anything that could anchor me to the outside world but all I can see are brick walls. I notice that my cheeks feel wet and I suddenly realize that I have been crying. Odd, considering I feel dead inside.

"Ladies, gather up. We are having a *roast night* in about ten minutes," Alexandra shouts, loudly enough for the girls in both dorms to hear.

"What's *roast night*?" I ask, discreetly wiping my eyes. At this point, I am looking for any kind of distraction from the monotony that I could find.

"You'll see!" Alexandra replies with a creepy cheeriness.

I cling onto my Bible like a security blanket as I follow a mob of girls dressed in their nightgowns to where *roast night* is to be held. I follow closely behind Alexandra without questioning further. As I make my way farther into the hall, I can see the girls begin to form single file rows.

"This feels strange," I mutter under my breath.

Alexandra stops walking abruptly and I almost collide with her as I try to stop as well. The room in which I find myself standing is very brightly lit. Squinting, I feel a sense of pain as my eyes strain to adjust from the much darker hallway. I hear a stifled commotion coming from inside the room and I move through the crowd to get a better look.

I am horrified. Ahead of me in the distance, I see a young girl bound to a school chair. Her crying is muffled by the duct tape over her mouth and a pair of reflective shiny silver handcuffs bind her hands behind her back. She struggles to free them but is unsuccessful in her attempts. Her glowing pale skin and bright reddish hair seem set ablaze by her fearful eyes as the girls circle around her.

Oh my God, what is going on? Why isn't any of the staff doing any-thing about this? I try to process what I'm seeing but my mind, my CPU and motherboard, can't process this. Like looking at a blank radar screen, I can't find any way to help. I conceal my emotional turmoil for good reason; it would be a disaster if any of the staff or *Helpers* notice my concern.

I look over towards the wall and spot a conservatively dressed, dark-haired woman. She would appear fairly normal except for the wicked smirk on her face. I recognize her immediately as Ms. Arizona.

Breaking her silence, she shouts like a drill sergeant, "Okay, girls, I want you to say how you really feel about Jade. Let's start with the *Helpers!*"

Elizabeth raises her hand and shouts, "Jade is a loser and she is evil!" Another girl raises her hand and yells, "Jade is a Heathen!" Corey raises her hand and says in disgust, "Jade is rebellious and she is a disgrace to the Lord! God is puking at the gates of heaven at her and she is a terrible example for the other girls!"

As I sit quietly in the circle, I search for any reasonable explanation that would help me justify this staff-sanctioned cruelty. Deep within me, I feel that the girls who are raising their hands and shouting these horrible things about Jade are just venting the pent up rage they possess because they are forbidden to speak their minds or display emotion. This is their only chance to let it out.

These judgments are not the teachings of Jesus. I cannot believe this is happening at a 'Christian' institution. I mutter quietly. *What crimes had she committed... Were they the same ones I had? Did any of us deserve this kind of horrible injustice?*

I cannot take it anymore. My anger bubbles up like a blister ready to pop and I involuntarily take action to prevent the pain and infection from spreading any further inside this chamber.

I raise my hand and everyone turns and looks at me. "Yes, Jeneen, go ahead," Ms. Arizona chimes pleasantly.

"I like the way Jade smiles in the hall and how she is always nice to me," I voice fearlessly. At Victory, there are consequences for thinking outside the box. If you think differently than your superiors or state your opinion, it is grounds for isolation in the *Get Right* room tantamount to being an inmate stuck in solitary confinement. Generally, this is every girl's worst nightmare, but at this point, I am determined to put an end to this evil.

"That's what I like about you, Jeneen. You always find the good in everyone," Ms. Arizona chides with a crooked smile as every girl in the circle agrees with her in a robotic fashion.

What a revelation! I thought sarcastically. *Isn't that what Jesus teaches?* Losing their interest in me, the mob continues on with their attack, cheerily led by the judge, jury and executioner that is Ms. Arizona.

I close my eyes for a moment to drown them out and find shelter. I find myself wondering how such a place could possibly exist — a place where people are filled with such hate but somehow see it as a righteous foundation of God's love. I can't decide what I would rather endure — the emotional, mental, and physical abuse that we girls experience every waking moment at Victory for the supposed sake of the greater good or life as my uncle's *underaged whore*. I am all but certain that living in New York with that dysfunctional situation would at least seem easier at times than this. At least I was something special, as long as I gave my uncle what he wanted, and perhaps a bit freer.

Here it does not seem to matter what I do or do not do. I am just not good enough. I am being put on trial every day by their endless sermonizing and I'm always guilty as charged. I am frightened every day for a million, horrible, inexcusable reasons and I want it to stop. I hate the way Ms. Arizona curses Jade and forces the other girls to participate. It sickens me to have to watch her suffer helplessly for fear of this ungodly woman's wrath if I refuse. I despise the fact that I cannot take the duct tape and handcuffs off of Jade. I hate being forced to sit in this fucking circle with a Bible in front of my face! How is this hateful mob the work of a loving God? Where in the Bible is this justified?

I could never believe in this. This is the real evil. Not the shit we were sent here for. I cannot figure it out. Girls have left this so-called 'Christian' school before. How is it that these people have never been reported? I mean, this is against the law, for God's sake! You cannot handcuff a girl to a chair and torment her like this...

As my inner rant continues, a sickening feeling sweeps over my body, like death, as the obvious answer comes to me: They have never been reported because anyone who leaves here is brainwashed. The girls all inevitably lose their identities and are released back into the world in a robot-like state with no will of their own. Without hesitation, this circle of zombies obeys Ms. Arizona — terror encapsulates my body as I wonder how long it will take for me to be programmed like them.

I look back at Ms. Arizona with horror and contempt. She returns my wide-eyed stare with a wicked smile. "You're not going anywhere," her eyes seemed to say. I gulp and bow my head.

God? Hello?! I am desperate and you need to answer me! I want to die tonight and I'm not fucking joking! Slowly, a single tear falls down my cheek as I fight the urge to scream out loud. I shut my eyes and wish with all my heart to never have to open them again.

Post Traumatic Stress Disorder

I always compare the human brain and memory to a computer using file names as a means of compartmentalizing memories and experiences. I've created subdirectories (recalls) located in my hippocampus (the region of the brain in which memories are stored) of good, horrific, angry, defeated, joyful, distraught, helpless and empowering moments in my life. Sometimes, people delete files (recollections), replacing them with something better. This is my coping mechanism. Occasionally, files randomly pop up to the forefront, interrupting my processor and make me think, "Didn't I just delete/replace this?" This is my *virus* — PTSD (Post Traumatic Stress Disorder) in my head and… this is my book on paper. Each *piece* in this book is a subdirectory that has been *created in my mind,* either by myself or someone else.

My name is Jeneen Miller and this is my story…

PIECE TWO

C:\Jeneen\Hell\Mother\Blame\Guilt\Parakeets.doc

WHEN I WAS nine years old, I had two green and yellow feathered parakeets that dwelled in my family's warm laundry room. Their cages sat next to the water heater in our duplex. It was the warmest quarter in our home — so warm that it made Death Valley feel like the universe allowed a draft from an open refrigerator door to grace its existence.

My daily responsibilities included feeding them, filling up the water and changing the paper. I loved those little dinosaurs and I spent a lot of time training, petting and cuddling them. I was pulled in so many directions as a child. I multitasked all the time combining my responsibilities with play. I would frequently start a project only to get distracted and then begin a new one. My tireless mind continued to pull me in many directions as an adult. Eventually, I learned to channel it to my advantage and focus — transforming myself into a young entrepreneur.

One day I peeked in the cage to see how my tropical companions were. Sadly, they were on the bottom of the cage, lying still. I started crying so hard and called my mom over just in case she knew how to wake them up again.

My mother cried in hysterics, "They are dead! They are dead!"

We both started sobbing but then soon after she started yelling at me. "It's your fault they are dead. You didn't give them enough water! You didn't give them water! It's all your fault."

I never really felt loved by my mother. She would yell at me all the time, as if it were part of her DNA. Her vocal chords had the power of a bullhorn; if she was yelling at me on aisle five at the grocery store, aisle twenty-five could feel her wrath.

PIECE THREE

C:\Jeneen\Hell\Mother\Unloved\ UnworthyofReceivingGifts.doc

WHEN I WAS nine years old, I had hair growth above my upper lip. I'll never forget the first time inspecting my complexion. I used my light-up vanity mirror in order to check for acne. As it turned out, an unexpected surprise rose to the surface as I stared in horror at my magnified follicles only to find thick black hair above my Cupid's bow. I screamed. I screamed again feeling a bit perturbed that my parents had me believing for years that I was a little girl. I screamed so loudly our neighbors most likely thought a homicide was taking place right next door to their duplex. *Was there a mix up at the hospital regarding my gender? Did my parents neglect to inform me that I am male? How much testosterone do I have?* It is common for an Italian but at the time I thought I was the only adolescent who had this problem. No one told me otherwise so I didn't know any better. My mother said I couldn't get rid of it because I was too young. Refusing to buy into her outlandish response to my *tweener* crisis, I was aware that I was far too young to have this problem…

My grandmother once embarrassed me by pointing it out saying it right in front of my brother. I was teased about it in school as well and I wanted to do something about it.

My Aunt Sylvina told me about Neet Hair Removal. Aunt

Sylvina lived in New York and would call us frequently. Her beautiful dark-brown curls accentuated her flawless complexion. When I would catch a glimpse of her profile, I could not help noticing her thick, black, curled lashes. She wore seventies fashions, stylish bellbottoms and complementing bell-sleeved blouses. This made her an expert when it came to hip trends. I had been emulating her since the age of five. Intuitively, I knew she could relate to my traumatic ordeal and would come to my rescue. She would rectify this matter and make me look feminine once again.

When my mom and I went to the store, I thought it was the perfect opportunity to get a miracle cure to make my masculinity disappear once and for all. When I nervously placed the *magic potion* in the shopping cart, I almost hesitated because my mother would yell at me if I were to ask for anything, even something as little as strawberries. We were always on a budget and that was putting it lightly. I was never allowed to manipulate the thermostat when it was freezing in our house. "Don't touch that. You are not allowed to adjust the temperature! Put on a sweater and bundle up!" my mother would suggest as a means of coping with our cold home.

My mother had a short fuse and I remained reluctant to ask for something I needed because she would humiliate me in public calling me a spoiled brat. This time I didn't care; I was desperate. She saw it and yelled, launching like a rocket into explicit detail of the product and how I was too young. Her obnoxious New York guttural slang wouldn't seem so shrill if only she could control the venom that she spewed towards me, like an out-of-control cobra. "We don't have enough money and I'm not going to buy it for you. Put it back... NOW! I already told you, you are not old enough!" At that point in time, everyone in the drug store knew about my upper-lip facial hair. I was so humiliated; I wanted to disappear. Everyone was looking at me. I ran out of the store and waited in the front of Save-On.

An elderly woman with white shiny hair coiled in a bun noticed my tears and told me not to cry trying to comfort me. She wanted to make me feel better. I think she heard my mother yell at me. "It's okay, honey. Don't cry little one," She said, protecting me from the atrocious snake that attacked me without remorse. The nurturing grandmother-figure stood nearby like an energy shield from my poisonous reptile of a parent. Maybe she was on aisle one hundred and heard the screaming? Eventually, she gave me fifty cents and vanished, abandoning me in the middle of a treacherous jungle. She left me as vulnerable prey to my slithering enemy. The feeling of being loved swept by me all too quickly, caressing my saddened face, only to leave me stranded right in front of a drugstore.

I felt the quarters in my blue jean pants pocket and thought of the many items I could choose to purchase: Cracker Jacks, Boston Baked Beans, a double scoop of German chocolate cake ice cream… I thought about the faded, blurry vision of the little old lady — a complete stranger who cared enough to stop the wet, salty droplets from sliding down my flushed cheeks. It made me smile. I knew, deep in my soul, the coins that jingled as I walked were never going to fill the emptiness that threatened to strangle me as I fought for survival. I just wanted a mother who loved me.

PIECE FOUR

C:\Jeneen\Hell\Dad\Unloved\NoSecondChances.doc

WHEN I WAS nine years old, I chipped my tooth at the Hollywood Girl's Club.

The non-profit organization was a safe-haven for children providing art classes, drama, swimming, basketball, gymnastics and various other activities to keep us busy over the summer. I'll never forget the ballads played in the drama room and watching teenagers dancing to a compilation of seventies love songs. It was at that moment that I realized I couldn't wait to fall in love. As I watched the energy of love, people intertwining and moving slowly to *How Deep is Your Love* by the Bee Gees, my heart raced with excitement! My best friend, Jennifer Paris, caught a glimpse of my happiness and smiled at me. The half Caucasian and half African American girl had an exotic skin color that gave her the perfect sun-kissed tan. She was beautiful. We were friends since I met her at Santa Monica Elementary School in second grade. Was it Jennifer's Mickey Mouse afro puffs that I was drawn to or was it her self-confidence? She carried herself with the utmost self-respect. In my opinion, her mother Sandy was responsible for this outcome. She would speak of her mother in such high regard that it made me want to live in her home. Although I was at her apartment often enough, you would think I was a permanent fixture. Jennifer continuously wanted the best for her single mother because she knew how hard she worked.

Sandy balanced providing financially and spending quality time with her daughter.

Jennifer and I would spend every waking moment with each other — We were inseparable. She had a collection of Judy Blume books that I would always borrow from her library. *Are You There God? It's Me, Margaret* was my all-time favorite.

My summer rituals consisted of watching the *Twilight Zone* until Jennifer arrived. She would walk from her apartment complex to my house so we could take a stroll to the Girl's Club together. Jennifer was bright, educated, quick witted, organized and studious. We would spend most of our time laughing.

One time in ballet class, we noticed our teacher had her hair in a ponytail but it was sticking straight up from the crown of her head. It made Pippi Longstocking's hair look relaxed. Maybe she didn't want bangs or any hair getting into her face as she sashayed across the dance floor. My uncoordinated dance moves became the center of attention in this ballet class. However, I was primarily there to support Jennifer since she was the one who enjoyed the class.

I caught another glimpse of our performing arts educator's hair and I started shaking, trying to be inconspicuous, but sadly not succeeding. The more I thought about trying to control myself, the more I started shaking, until laughter coughed out of my mouth like I had a bad cold. I ran out of the class because I didn't want to hurt my instructor's feelings while drawing attention to myself. I already had enough eyes planted on me during the class, like laser rifle sights on my dance wear, as I tried to be graceful in First Position while transitioning to a Plié… but *The Force* was not with me. A couple of times I almost tumbled to the ground. My face was flushed from embarrassment as I left with Jennifer following me out. As soon as we were out of earshot, we burst into laughter. We were always on the same page.

"I have to use the restroom. Come with me!" Jennifer said, giggling, still in the same state she was in after leaving ballet.

"Jeneen, there isn't a lock. Can you hold the door for me?" she asked, in desperate need to have me guard her privacy.

As I held the door secure for her, I started getting impatient, my mind accelerating about a hundred miles per hour, and I needed to move on to a new idea. I wanted to play a joke on her so I climbed on the door. I didn't realize it swung open and it hit me in the mouth. As an end result, I lost half of my front tooth.

Jennifer saw that my lip was bleeding and then said, "Oh my God, half of your tooth is gone!"

My heart sank and I realized that I'd rather have my hair sticking straight up in a stupid ponytail as opposed to having half of a tooth missing!

Jennifer walked me home and then walked back to her apartment that night. I knew I had to tell my father and I was hoping that he could find a solution to my problem. I ran as fast as I could to find him. He was in the bedroom reading the Holy Bible. He paused and stuck a piece of napkin to hold his place, taking a break to look up at me.

"Dad, look at my front tooth! It's broken! What can we do to fix it?"

"Is that your second tooth?" he asked, seriously not knowing the answer. I sheepishly replied, "Yes."

He said, "Then you don't get a second chance."

He was fuming, and angrily said "I don't have dental insurance for you. You shouldn't have been horsing around! It's a shame because that is your second tooth!"

I felt like I committed a heinous crime after speaking to him about my predicament. My tail hung in last position between my legs and I almost face-planted on the ground. There wasn't going to be any resolution or hope that it could be fixed in the future if he had money. He didn't try to find a way to make it better and left me with half of a tooth for several years. I felt ugly and unworthy of being cared for.

PIECE FIVE

C:\Jeneen\Hell\Father\Unloved\Dentist.doc

THE FIRST TIME my father took me to the dentist was at the age of twelve. I had been in severe pain for two straight days and had begun to involuntarily cry out. My dad's defense for not taking me to the dentist was the mere fact that dental coverage wasn't part of his work benefits. Sitting at the dining room table trying to chew what was on my plate was an agonizingly difficult task. Time was dragging like honey dripping in slow motion into a hot cup of tea. The white plates with etchings of a golden brown flower pattern reflected my image. I saw myself wondering how I managed to endure this ruthless existence without immediate medical attention. While watching me fight the pain, spaghetti twirled and wrapped neatly around my fork, my father joked, "I can get the pliers and take it out myself." He laughed, feeling like the comedian of the year, oblivious to the obvious fact that he was the only one at the table giving himself any applause. No one was laughing. In fact, wet droplets were once again sliding down my fleshy cheekbones. *This* was his way of somehow lifting my spirits? So he had an umbrella to catch my downpour but he refused to acknowledge my complex challenges. I do not remember getting anything, not even aspirin or Ibuprofen, to kill the pain — maybe some alcohol around my gums.

I cried from the pain for a couple of days, providing an undoubtable indication that I needed care. Finally, my father decided to take me to see his dentist who was located in Fairfax. "Okay, I'll take you tomorrow and you can see Dr. Steinberg," he said, surrendering this battle in the war of basic fathering.

Most children hate dentists but when my dad told me he would take me, I was thrilled! It turned out that I had gums growing over my tooth which explained why I was in so much pain. The dentist was going to surgically remove it. I didn't know what to expect. My father did not sit down and explain with a soothing choice of words, such as… *"Once the dentist gives you Novocaine you will no longer feel pain…"* My anxiety was similar to that of a captive wild animal. Dr. Steinberg saw this and expressed to me that it was going to get better. Although my father was in the next room, I could sense his indignation at having to spend money on this. I wish my father would have been the one to reassure me that the excruciating discomfort would subside but he was too wrapped up in how this was a financial burden — how I was a hardship.

During an intermission of work on my teeth, I overheard the dentist telling my father that he could fix my chipped tooth. The drywall in the procedure room did not reach the top of the ceiling, leaving an ample amount of space for me to hear their conversation through. I was so excited that it could actually be repaired! I never knew it could because my father never told me. The only comforting words he mustered up when I was nine years old were *"I could not get a second chance."* He made it seem as if it were impossible and now, I knew the truth.

The commotion in the next room grew louder and my father's temper escalated as did my restlessness. He continued shouting at the dentist for wanting to give me fillings because he didn't want to pay for them. "You are a shyster!"

"She has eight cavities and if you do not have me fill them now, it could lead to serious and lasting complications!" The dentist barked back with authority and concern for my well-being.

I became fixated on the repetitive sounds coming from my menacing father, not wanting to restore what was destroyed, seeming like a broken record.

He yelled again, reiterating facts, "I cannot afford it and I do not have insurance!"

My protector and stabilizing rock of our household made it crystal clear that dental work was not on the agenda for his daughter. He would become irate if anyone tried to force him to do the right thing. I think the dentist finally told him that he had no choice as it would be considered neglect if he didn't. I'm not sure what went on...

However, shortly after that heated moment, it got quiet. Dr. Steinberg had resolved the issues at hand.

I was so happy to have a front tooth that wasn't split and to look pretty again!

Somehow... I never really got in tune with it. At that time, I could not grasp the concept that my dad didn't want to make any efforts to keep something that he should value above all else in good condition. The dentist hands me a shiny piece of glass and I gaze at what was missing for years in the reflection. My father said that he was poor and currency was at an all-time low but it was never about the lack of funds. To my twelve-year-old self, it was about how he made me feel when he chose not to help me or to even inform me that a dentist could rectify the problem in the future. He did not reassure me or offer any optimism. The outcome was that I carried the guilt of being unwanted cargo on his train going nowhere. Deep down, perhaps, he did want to help but he never conveyed it, so it will always leave a question mark on my hard drive.

PIECE SIX

C:\Hell\Jeneen\MyFirstTamponExperience.doc

THE ANGRY WOMAN heading towards me possessed shoulder-length, dark, curly brown hair. She appeared dreamlike, distorted and faded. I sat upright on our artistically intricate decorative oriental rug, supporting my back against the studio couch in the living room. The abrupt interruption startled me while I was reading *Then Again, Maybe I Won't* by Judy Blume. My boisterous Italian mother had a way of alarming me like a Molotov cocktail used by the Viet Cong during a surprise attack. Her mood swings were at a high today, shifting in my favor. She carried an upbeat melody at this moment in time and I had the feeling of shell shock as I saw the twenty dollar bill being placed in my palm. *Is this a booby trap?* I pondered if the weapon of choice today would be a side-closing Panji. "I need you to buy us Kotex at Sav-On Drugs. Call Jennifer and find out if she can walk you to the store!"

I was forbidden to walk by myself anywhere because we lived in a rough neighborhood. My mother installed this program on my hard drive at a very young age of how dangerous it was and that I could get propositioned, stabbed, kidnapped, raped, or worse... murdered. I never dared to test the waters by going against this rule. This fear crept up sporadically, showing its ugly head in random access memory like an annoying infomercial. My mother said to me numerous times that if a stranger approaches me to pretend that the nearest vehicle was my father coming to pick me up and to run swiftly. This was my so called mace, my protection against a jungle filled bristling with unexpected traps.

The yellow rotary phone rested on a table located in the hallway near the dining room. I inserted my index finger into the indented circle and dialed, number-by-number, impatiently watching it spin around. "Jennifer, I need you to walk with me to Sav-On Drugs. What are you doing right now? Could you come over?" I asked, eager to spend quality time with her, escaping to a different life filled with laughter, confidence and adventure.

My charismatic, intellectually educated girlfriend soon arrived at the Spanish-tiled complex home and patiently waited to escort me to the store. "Jeneena, are you ready!" she sang through the screen door, remembering what my grandmother called me, imitating her Italian accent and sounding a lot like Sophia Loren.

"Yes, give me one moment, Jennifer! I'll be right there!" I excitedly shouted, wondering what sort of literature my friend had brought for me today! I opened her *Hello Kitty* backpack to find another teen book about self-exploration her mother bought for her.

"Is this the book you were telling me about, Jennifer?" I asked, wondering if this was the instruction guide on how to achieve a strong, euphoric feeling of excitement and pleasure.

"Yes, that's the one!" Jennifer chimed with enthusiasm, willing to share the taboo ingredients of an untapped recipe.

As we made our way to Sav-On by crossing the 101 Ventura Freeway overpass, we watched the traffic going by. I squinted as the sun was beginning to set and caught a glimpse of the flashing brake lights in single files, noting the complicated bumper-to-bumper cluster, but only for a brief moment. It was rather difficult to shift my focus away from the upbeat and intriguing conversationalist beside me. I appreciated the way I could confide in Jennifer about everything. She would never judge but simply return the favor. Her unconditional love was not a conscious effort on her part; it was just there for me to grab anytime I wanted. It stood, always loyal, like a book on a shelf, whether it was in mint condition or worn out and covered in years of dust. It was constant and I could pull it off the shelf and hold it in my hands at any given moment.

We purchased the bulky pads (that remind me of diapers) for my mother and I realized there was enough money left over for tampons. I was twelve years old and I had read somewhere that tampons are cleaner than pads and I wanted to try them to determine the difference. This particular item had come from part of my studious bookworm's collection. I read a lot about teen sexuality, health and wellness. Sandy purchased these books for my beloved, inquisitive comrade who then loaned them to me. I bought the tampons but was concerned my mother would yell at me for spending money on something extra.

When I arrived at my supposed safe-haven, I noticed the porch had chipped pieces of red paint. The withered step was my welcome into a disconsolate dwelling. I said goodbye, waved to Jennifer and marched past the screen door — the squeaking noise revealing its old age and lack of upkeep. I handed my mother the pads and then had to explain why there was less money left over.

"Where is the rest of the change?" my mother barked with a suspicious tone.

"I bought tampons for myself with it. I want to try them," I said, keeping it simple because my honesty was always in the forefront.

Anger arose and she screamed so violently… I thought a knick-knack would tumble off the mantel. Our next door neighbors, Ray and Ace, definitely got the lowdown when they heard, "You must not be a virgin! You went against me and were only allowed to buy pads. If you can put a tampon inside, you must not be a virgin!"

I ran so fast to hide myself. I sprinted down the hall, through the door that divided the duplex that my father constructed and frantically searched for a cocoon in my room to keep me hidden from predators. I looked for a covering to envelop my body and somehow managed to find some silk to swaddle in. I had taken shelter in my closet... It was dark around me and I fought my way in, feeling with my hands, but I embraced it because I didn't want anyone to see me. I wanted to die. My tear ducts were working overtime without compensation and the end result was uncontrollable raindrops sliding down my rosy complexion. I was humiliated and certain the next door neighbors heard my mother's announcement. I scrambled around again and all I could imagine was being surrounded by vegetation that blinded my sight of the enemy. Fear of poisonous snakes and wildlife put me on extreme high alert. Before I could catch my breath, I fell into a pit that held a treadle board. The booby-trap turned and I tuned into the excruciating pain that jabbed me as the spike end struck my face and chest. I tried to climb out...

I stayed in this treacherous jungle for hours because I was so absorbed with shame... *Now my family thinks I'm a whore.*

PIECE SEVEN

C:\Jeneen\Hell\Dad\Low Self-Esteem\Modeling Career.doc

THE COLLECTION I had built up of *Teen* and *Seventeen* Magazines had made its way into a basket in the corner of my room. The articles, filled with relationship, fashion, beauty and health/fitness advice, inspired me to explore my creativity with cosmetics and fashion. My father, who worked for the City of Los Angeles as a sanitation engineer, would find the magazines in the waste containers on his one-of-many mundane daily routes. I took what he gave me and reconstructed my personal library, filling it with valuable treasure.

I peeked out my vintage Jalousie window. The louvered glass panels from the 1950's remained as an unaltered fixture in my rede-signed 1980's bedroom. I opened the once transparent contraption which was now stained with mineral deposits that, unfortunately, the sharpest razor blade could not remove. After using the lever to open this ancient holdover, I had a vision of myself as a gullible nine-year-old child standing in my own backyard near a hungry wolf. I was completely still from terror. Thinking of myself as that little girl made me cringe because I was aware of her tendencies to trust the wolves that lived in the thick, dark forests of her life. She wanted to believe that behind the pointed teeth they use to wound and kill prey, their glowing, amber-lit eyes were an invitation to look into their soul. She neglected to acknowledge the numerous prior attacks she had suffered. The carnivorous predator has used its back molars to crush her fragile bones and its small front teeth to nibble and pull at her delicate skin. She flat out ignored all warning signs of a repeat scenario and asked the savage beast if she could ever model high fashion for a magazine.

After asking the ferocious endangered animal the question that would reassure her of her outward appearance, the answer was not forthcoming. Perhaps he took his time because he could sense her heartbeat and was calculating when the element of surprise would best allow him to pounce. She could hear the birds nesting in the avocado tree and the sound of buzzing bees swarming around the Lantanas. The homing pigeons making cooing sounds from their barricaded habitat distracted her from reality. As she looked into their cage, she flashed back to a drive with her dad on the 101 Ventura Freeway, heading north.

She remembered him showing her the area where Busch Gardens was once located in the scorching hot San Fernando Valley. He told her how he put tags on pigeon legs. No matter how far he would take them, they would always find their way home. She was impressed... Her father occupied his time on those trips by demonstrating how to drive a stick shift. She was never behind the wheel but every time he put his foot on the clutch, she knew precisely which gears to switch into.

The little girl comes back from her daydream only to find herself still alone with the wolf. The vicious canine foamed at the mouth. He was infected with a serious disease caused by the responsibility of caring for his pack. He tossed blame about like devoured carcasses. The pack was always reminded of the strenuous hard labor he endured on their behalf and how it took its toll on him physically. She still awaited his answer.

The furry demon hesitated for what seemed like an eternity and said, "No, I don't think so. I used to be a photographer and I know you can't be a model. You have too much peach fuzz on your face and it will show up in the pictures!"

Unaware of the fact that this unrefined beast comes from a line of animals governed by malicious survival instincts, she opted to stare at the ground, growing uncomfortably numb. She focused on the bald patches of the lawn, in order to distract herself from the loud gnashing sounds of her flesh being ripped apart. She wondered why this wild monster would attack something that he should have taken pride in. Maybe he just didn't have the means.

Back in my room, I suddenly had the urge to become one spirit with the frightened little girl, to rescue her from the wilderness. I scanned over the homing pigeons and wondered how much coin has gone into that hobby. I looked at my chipped tooth in an imaginary mirror inside my mind. I focused on the facial hair that I couldn't get rid of because my mother did not want to purchase hair removal cream for me. I thought of a girl at school who thinks I have an ugly face.

I did not shed a tear and I just remained frozen like an icicle hanging from the ceiling of a cold, dark cave. I was no stranger to this type of reaction from that uncultivated animal and it appeared that nothing could violently shake me anymore.

Oh my God! Is my father right? After all, he was a former photographer before working for the sanitation department! His final stamp of disapproval left me feeling humiliated once again. *How could I have imagined that I could catwalk on the nearest runway... that anyone would think I was pretty enough... anyone?*

I looked back into the pigeons' so-called prison and wondered why on earth, if they had a chance to fly so far away, they would continuously return to this...

PIECE EIGHT

Have You Ever...

HAVE YOU EVER felt your heart actually shatter into a million and one pieces from a breakup? The aching feeling is chronic, and worse, no medical doctor can perform a surgical procedure to fix this dreadful ailment. You wake up every morning with an emptiness in your core because the person you loved is no longer in your life. You wish with all of your might that this is just a horrifying nightmare and that you'll soon awake. When you come to your senses and accept that the unpleasant dream is real, not just an illusion, all hell breaks loose. You start to perspire, the moisture seeping through your pores, your hands clammy and you feel yourself slipping into a zombie-like state. Now, you are just one of the walking dead, going through the motions. You are in limbo, a ghost, a mere reflection of your own past memories. The horrendous physical discomfort pricks and throbs; you are in a pit of sorrow. You imagine this burden heavy in your stomach. Anxiety rises in you, shattering your consciousness, leaving you with barely more than a pulse. You feel nauseated and your survival becomes a mundane chore as opposed to an art. Your appetite for food has ceased. Fighting to keep composure, you make painstaking efforts to hide your tears when you go out among the living. Romantic songs, the couple on the corner kissing, the enveloping intimacy around the holidays and everything that is couple related is accentuated to the tenth power. These flashes are constant reminders that everyone and everything is moving forward… but you stand still, frozen in time. You are hoping and waiting to see if the magnetic attraction that brought you together can, after he has explored other relationships, bring you back together again.

When I hear someone say to a teenager, "You are much too young to be in love," I cringe. Those sharp words cut me like a blade because my love story is well-preserved, stored layers deep, in a highly secured subdirectory on my mental hard drive. I reminisce about this time when I was so in love because it was magical, with no emotional anchors weighing me down, with nothing keeping me on military alert and always on guard.

I truly felt like a princess in a fairy tale and it was the greatest chapter I experienced in my lifetime. I would never misinform a teenager with the fictitious rubbish conjured up by the jaded. I have personal knowledge that there is no specific number of years required for the experience of the heart. Love is a pure, clear feeling and adolescence should not deny one the privileges of existence.

There was a time when I couldn't wait to spring out of bed at the break of dawn and make myself beautiful for the boy I loved. I recollect a time when I didn't hit the snooze button several times because I didn't want to delay meeting my handsome prince. I would spend two hours getting ready. I was only fifteen years old; with utter confidence my heart told me I had found my soulmate. Was I naïve or just in love?

There was a time when I pierced my ear for my knight in shining armor. I wanted him to think I was pretty. Performing an act of love, I decided to get some ice and, numbing myself, poked a silver post through… twice! Now I had two earrings on each lobe and, in the eighties, it was a little daring. It was during a time when Drake made me feel on top of the world. I believed in him wholeheartedly. It was like Romeo and Juliet and all of the passion in my soul became manifest.

I was a wild mare running freely beside her stallion; he was my first love. He would unexpectedly appear at my window, his tapping startling me at times. We would spend countless hours conversing about everything and nothing. I knew he loved me because I felt his being enveloping mine like a quilted blanket on a rainy day. You know when you are loved when you can feel it penetrating every fiber of your being… and I did. I really felt it.

There was a time when he gave me multicolored roses from his mother's garden (and perhaps the neighbors' as well) breaking up the monotony of his ritual. He carefully snipped a floral arrangement, risking being pricked with thorns, just so I could have something meaningful to put on my table. The intent was to demonstrate the depth of his passion. I had no doubts about his strong affection. It wasn't blind or selfish; it was just there for me to reach at any given moment. I could always pull it up into my RAM. No matter how corrupt my memory files became, Drake's love for me remained pristine. It would be impossible to destroy no matter how worn or outdated my processor would become.

There was a moment in this universe where I hurdled the fiery pits of hell in order to be with my one true love. I managed to cut through the obstacle course, galloping at full speed to the height of heaven. It was the most enchanted time of my life.

Christmas

Although you couldn't put a price tag on what Drake and I had, our love increased in value like diamonds. Every day was like Christmas because he gave with his heart and it penetrated my soul. His gifts were like a conglomerate of tiny snippets of artwork coming together to form a treasured masterpiece. Maybe it was so deeply layered to me because I never experienced love and nurturing from my parents. He filled the empty shell I had for so long with happiness and I will always be grateful for the experience. Finding its way back to the forefront of my mind, after years of being hidden, the memory remains intact — a foreshadowing of my present.

PIECE NINE

C:\Jeneen\Hell\Victory\Parents\Unloved\
Abandoned\TheBigBetrayal.doc

As I COMPLETE my Junior Year of high school, my parents finally deliver the unexpected news that they will take me to get counseling. I am satisfied and appear a bit calmer at this point, positive that there will be changes. I ponder what influenced my parents to make a decision in my best interest. I know they do not want to be scrutinized by a psychologist's magnifying glass. *Do they fear skeletons rising up from some dark, secluded passage? Do they fear burning under that lens as the light of truth shines through it?*

It is July, 1988. As I practice my normal morning regimen, I open my closet door to view my limited selection of teen clothing. I take note of a long, white dress with its white eyelets running throughout the fabric. I feel the soft cotton material and recall the way it conforms to my body, ruffling at the bottom. Taking advantage of my employee discount, I purchased this summer's fashion statement at the clothing store I work for at the Jans Mall in Thousand Oaks, California. As I'm getting ready, I think about Drake and my heart begins to pump faster than normal. The adrenaline rush makes me feel as if I were running on a treadmill. We just celebrated our one-year anniversary and I long to see his bright, exuberant smile. My beautiful sweetheart — his eyes an aqua as deep as the ocean — an ocean whose depth matched the intensity of his soul. His fair skin is soft and supple, inviting my touch and it glows with the radiance of his affection. I'm dressing for him just in case we happen to see each other this evening. His spontaneity always keeps me on my toes, always catching me off guard. When he comes to my house unexpectedly, it leaves me euphoric because it indicates that he wants to see me more often than our planned rendezvous.

I take a deep breath and mull over the counseling session ahead of me. Drake will be so relieved when I tell him that my parents changed gears and decided to send me to therapy!

I get into our boxy Ford Fairmont. It reminds me of a family-sized boat, launching off a dock rather than a curb. Looking up, I skim over my mother's multicolored gazanias growing against the front hilltop and giving life to our gloomy, drab home. My father is driving for what seems like hours. My mother is in the passenger seat. I begin to wonder, *Why are we going so far?* These unfamiliar freeway interchanges are nerve-wracking and multiple red flags instantaneously begin signaling for my attention.

Why couldn't they find a psychiatrist close to home? This is odd, shuffles through my mind. I become fatigued from the tiresome drive so I decide to lie down in the back seat. I drift into a fog-like daydream of dancing with Drake. We sway in slow motion to *Run to You* by Bryan Adams, the music softly echoing throughout Sequoia Middle School's auditorium. I can almost smell the warm, spicy amber of his fragrance, leaving its imprint on my skin as his cheek slightly caresses my face. I fall into a slumber, resting my head against his chest, shutting out my worrisome assumptions. I feel safe.

My mother coos for the first time, "It's best that you are lying down because it is going to be a long drive."

I awake to my mother's annoying screeching and jump up. Thoughts are now flooding my mind like being on the Pacific Coast Highway during a downpour.

Would they possibly be taking me to the so-called *nunnery* that

BreeAnna was forced to attend? I can hear the sound of my heart beating in overdrive. According to her description, its fiery gates lead to torment and everlasting punishment. This thought escapes my mind like dust blowing in the wind, taking this toxic idea with it. I reassure myself with the logic that I am doing exceptionally well in school and not using drugs and override my paranoid hypothesis. I cannot fathom how my parents could make such a ludicrous choice.

My father asks me, "What do you want to eat?" I reply, "How about McDonald's?"

He drives us to McDonald's and little did I know… it would be my *last supper*.

I immediately lift myself up, my hands propelling my petite structure upward.

I see a fence that has barbed wire on top of it but I am looking at it from inside the property as opposed to the other way around. The electric gate closes, making loud clanking and buzzing noises as it rolls shut, trapping us inside. My body trembles and I become anxious.

The prison-like structure surrounds the vessel that transported us to this dark, foreign territory, but I don't focus on that as much as the farm-like house in front of me.

I process this all silently, my fight-or-flight response ready for my protection — *Is this where the psychiatrist has his office… in the middle of nowhere?* It finally hits me like a ton of bricks that just fell off a New York skyscraper. *This is the place where they sent BreeAnna Stafordson!* I panic, my emotions taking off like a rocket bound for another solar system.

I step up to the office noticing the white country cottage curtains. My parents remain expressionless beside me. The first person I meet is a *preacher* that appears to have risen from the demonic dark crevices of the underworld. His thick, coke-bottle glasses are windows leading to an untapped, caliginous dimension.

"Hello, Jeneen. I am Brother QC and your parents have decided to place you in my care. They have had enough of you giving them nothing but grief by causing trouble!" he spews angrily, as if he were in the middle of a fire and brimstone sermon. I watch saliva fly from his mouth.

Immediately I play back in my mind an Oprah show that I had seen, like a recorded video on my family's VCR. The story aired last year and was about AIDS hitting a small town in Williamson, West Virginia. The community and family of Mike Sisco shunned him because of their lack of education on the virus. Fighting for his life and having to deal with being an outcast, unworthy of his family's nurturing, it caused him to feel trapped by their ignorance. I remember that story a little too well, especially the part when a venomous audience member yelled, "Let's just put them all on a reservation!" The poison awakens in me after replaying the social death that took place in that *godly* town. Now I realize that I am an *untouchable* because my unidentified disease is too gruesome for my parents to bear. I look at them with disgust for giving up their parental rights to a complete stranger.

I see the wetness glistening on my arm, remnants of the preacher's wrath. Fear and panic strike me like an incurable plague and I take a few steps back. I'll be damned if I get showered with QC's airborne maladies.

I ask, "How long will I be here?"

"You are here for one full year."

In slow motion *one full year* runs through my processor, taking up so much space that my computer is about to crash. I pull up a picture of Drake in my mind and it suddenly blinks uncontrollably until it fades into nothing. Beautifully painted files holding snippets of an art gallery are now on the brink of corruption. Suddenly, I see a bold warning sign — TAMPER DETECTION — flashing lights on my screen. Like sand running out of a broken hourglass, I do not have time to encrypt my valuable data. My only option is to shut down my operating system altogether. I'll set aside this grueling, tedious process for a later period. This is an emergency and this is merely a *quick fix* to protect my complex mechanism.

"What? Are you kidding me?" I bark so loudly that I assume other girls in the next room could hear my cries.

My parents are not defending me from anything this minister from the dark side is saying.

I shout, my rage laced with a heavy dose of arsenic from the sting of betrayal, "How can you do this to me?"

Repeatedly, I shout again, "How can you do this to me?" unembarrassed by my hot, flushed cheekbones. I don't want to give the enemy any form of satisfaction.

Besides, once Drake finds out, he will come and rescue me, I silently babble to myself, trying to ease the pain of the poisonous bite. My blood is boiling, spilling over the top; my anger flows like oil into a fire, threatening to engulf me. Miraculously, I curb my temper and the impulse to slam my fist through the drywall in his office. I contain my emotions, analytically weighing out the consequences. I do not want to succumb to the barbaric reaction they are expecting from this *troublesome child.*

Ms. Arizona lures me in by holding her arms out and speaking with an angelic voice, "Come with me, I'll get you situated and show you where everything is. You are going to love it here!" she smiles, displaying her perfectly straight teeth. It was if she were on some sort of commercial trying to convince me to buy the leading brand of toothpaste.

I follow the staff members Ms. Arizona and Ms. Josella as we pass a kitchen. I observe the lengthy formica cafeteria-like countertop. I inhale the smells of foreign flavors and breathe out with utter disgust, their toxins filled with wrongful judgments. I am led to a girl's bathroom that is equipped with showers. The yelling of both staff members alarms me and the once angel-like voice dissipates as the wicked one creeps to the forefront. "Get into the shower...

NOW!" Ms. Arizona shouts, while they both rummage through my personal belongings.

What are they looking for… drugs?

They hand me some medicine to kill lice and tell me to wash my hair with it.

I don't have lice so why the shampoo? Why don't they inspect me?

They leave, finally giving me some privacy but only for a short time.

Before they walk out the door, I get another message, "Your mother bought you a dress and some underwear."

Wow, she never did that when I was living with her. Now that I'm locked up in prison, she splurges and treats me like a princess? I have a cigarette burn on my favorite dress. My father found this treasure in the trash on one of his routes. I would complement my outfit with shoes that were not my size. The burn on my favorite dress was overlooked. I focused on the way it fit my form, the metal beads it had and the way Drake looked at me when I wore it. *It's unfortunate to have to throw such a nice dress in the trash because of one lousy cigarette burn!*

Ms. Arizona speaks in an informative tone, "Your mom went shopping and packed your bags with all new clothes. When you get out of the shower, pick out culottes and a shirt."

I replied, "My mother wouldn't buy me any clothes when I was at home! Now she is splurging?"

"Watch your attitude!" Ms. Josella snaps at me like a drill sergeant. It is the last time I am permitted to voice anything negative about my parents, even if it's truthful.

There is a window in the bathroom. I peek out becoming spellbound by the long, desolate dirt road in the front. *Was it the road to freedom? It's too bad there is a twelve-foot fence with barbed wire on top barricading me like an unruly animal.* I'm like a tiny bird trapped in a cage wanting to fly away. In my mind, I fly away to escape what is in store for me.

I rummage through the suitcase and I see three pairs of culottes, three shirts and bloomers for underwear. *My mother hated my bikini underwear. She thought they were trampy.* I snatch something quick without any concern of committing a fashion faux pas. After all, Joan Rivers is nowhere to be found in this lockdown; she would never be caught dead in this place! I sadly come to the realization that my creativity and appreciation for the clothing industry is of no use to me now.

When I look at the suitcase my parents had hidden in the trunk of the car, I remark, "I can't believe my mom went shopping for me! Where was she when I came home with a report card that any other mother would have loved to hold in her hands? Where was my shopping extravaganza for going the extra mile? Oh, I see... My gift, representing positive reinforcement for my behavior, is a reform school! At this point, a dog biscuit would have been a better choice!"

"Didn't we tell you to watch your attitude?" Ms. Arizona reiterates in an authoritarian manner.

"Yes, but this is a good attitude considering I have been forced, against my will, into prison without having committed a crime!" I shout back, hoping someone could identify with my justifiable rage.

"Do you want me to take you to *the Get Right Room*?" Ms. Arizona says scornfully, spittle flying as it had from Brother QC.

I visualize an umbrella to protect me from the unidentifiable fluid getting on my skin... or worse, in my mouth! The thought of it is just downright gross!

"Yes," I reply without hesitation.

I couldn't wait to get to *the Get Right Room*. I had somewhat of an inkling of what this tiny closet was because my friend, BreeAnna, was forced into confinement at Victory for doing drugs and hanging around a *bad crowd*. I thought what they did to her was horrible and I saw how brainwashed she was after her time here. She truly believes that she deserved it all and that Victory was the best thing for her. She almost had me convinced.

I am crying hysterically, my high-pitched sobs amplified and reflected off the washroom walls. I transform into a nun by putting on my brand new conservative garments. A potato sack with a sash around my waist would have been more risqué. The painful awareness of my loss of freedom and feelings of uncertainty overwhelm me and I am overcome by trepidation. *I will never see my childhood heartthrob again — my Drake, my love and my everything!*

As if reading my mind, Ms. Arizona and Ms. Josella yell, "We told you if you keep it up, you will get sent to *the Get Right Room!*"

"What exactly is *the Get Right Room?*" I say in a voice that hides my fear. "You'll see," Ms. Josella chuckles with a smirk and a sadistic undertone.

In this moment... I am willing to do anything to get away from these people so I can have some time to process what is happening.

So I shout, holding back my fear, "Go ahead and put me there! I want to go!"

I want to be in isolation as opposed to being scolded by these Nazis for voicing my justifiable rage. I want to get there immediately so I can think about what my parents did to me.

Ms. Arizona grabs my wrist until it hurts, pinching my pale flesh and drags me to a secluded room in Dorm Three. I glance at my wrist — the skin is turning red. It's as if her touch was fire, scarring me. I touch it gently, my anguish like a tattoo on my psyche. On the way, I pass by Dorms One and Two. They are dark and gloomy, perfectly matching my mood. I blink, noticing my hard contact lenses are dry. I must have cried out all my tears and strained to view the blue brick walls that are in Dorm One. There are wall-to-wall bunk beds. All of the girls are fixated on me as I am forcibly pulled by Ms. Arizona. Not a soul utters a single word and the silence soon grows eerie.

"Keep your eyes to yourself, girls," Ms. Arizona sternly demands.

In an instant I am sitting on the floor, confined in a pint-sized, isolated room and begin to stare at the tiny peephole. The strong feeling that I am being watched makes me feel naked, stripping away my sense of privacy. I start banging my head against the plain, white drywall and then realize that it will not accomplish anything more than causing a headache. I start thinking about Drake. I silently reassure myself, *He is going to find out what my parents did to me when he calls or visits my house. He will notify his parents immediately and the whole family will rescue me, including his dog, Droopy! His parents are going to flip out when they realize that my parents would stick a child inside a reform school... especially one who is studious, works hard, is an overachiever, attends a private Christian school (by choice) and voluntarily attends church/youth group several times a week! They know I don't have any behavioral issues with any adults other than my parents. They know my situation.* Wet, salty raindrops start streaming, one-by-one, down my lifeless face. *Good thing I chose the tan culottes my mother packed.* They are now taking the place of Kleenex.

I have a feeling I will be in this secluded matchbox for a long time but I don't give a rat's ass. It is obvious to me at this point that I am forbidden by trained soldiers to express how I really feel. This *Cracker Jack box,* unfortunately, seems to be the only free place where I can troubleshoot a way out of this hellhole. I'm so good at tuning things out. My only form of companionship in *the Get Right Room,* other than my own thought process, is the raging lunatic screaming on the cassette tape recorder.

Cornerstone Christian School starts in September. In less than two months, one of my teachers is going to raise holy hell about where my parents took me! Someone is bound to get me out! I am mainly counting on Drake but that is my second fantasy. More tears start heading for my tan culottes.

Several scenarios started flooding my mind. *My parents lied and told me I was going to receive some sort of psychotherapy but instead they put me in a high security prison camp for troubled teens. They constantly called me a liar but THEY deceived ME by trickery into getting me in this reform school! My brother had a low C-, bordering on a D average and HE wasn't in a military academy! I didn't think he deserved some-*

thing like this… so why me? Why me? At this moment, I don't care how many streams of despair come pouring down my face. My tan culottes are soaked. Who am I going to impress? Ms. Arizona or QC?

I start fantasizing about a third plan. *My counselor, Bolivia, will get me out. She is well-aware of my situation at home and when she gets wind that I'm in a school for the wayward, she will definitely do something about it.*

I start imagining what Drake would say to my parents when he learns of the damage they caused on this warm, sunny day. What an ending to my summer of happiness.

He's on the protective side and he wouldn't tolerate anyone hurting me. He's my rock. He's going to tell them that I need therapy.

My guard dog *Helper*, a student aide, remains still outside the door. This hidden masterpiece was built by the hands of QC and according to the sermons on this disturbing tape, the girls at the lockdown. My ear catches cruel glimpses of what to expect at Victory on the never-ending cassette. It is a preview of the torment in store for me at this *fun-filled boot camp.*

The *Helper* continues to watch me through the miniature circular lens to make sure I don't kill myself. Kill myself… with what? One of QC's recorded sermons? They could possibly be substantial evidence in a criminal court case.

Again, there is no logic with these people. I finally start to listen intently to the tape, hearing the dysfunction that awaits me outside this *Get Right Room.* I listen for eight hours to the sounds of an angry man *shedding the light of the Word of God* to the girls at this so-called *Christian* school. I allow the introductory sermon to hit my fragile eardrums. He shouts to the students during this *biblical lesson,* calling them Jezebels, thieves, alcoholics, heathens, sluts, manipulators, home-wreckers and liars. The vocabulary list is backed up by the Bible and I hear shouts of "amen" from the robotic acolytes, all in agreement with this critical master. I have never heard the head of the church speaking to his congregation in this particular fashion.

Like the contents of my father's garbage truck, I have been dumped in foreign territory. I feel like the hero of a spy novel — drugged and kidnapped. When finally coming to, I feel the weight of chains and realize I am a prisoner in another country without the decency of basic human rights.

The tape continues to play and I hear QC interrogating a young girl about her weight, making her feel shameful in the eyes of God. I can hear her weeping. Horror strikes me like lightning in the middle of the night, startling me enough to make me jump out of bed unexpectedly. I expect to hear the loud beads of water tapping relentlessly against my window, alerting me to the serious disturbance of the elements... I wonder how many hours have passed. I need to drown out this psychotic clergyman by thinking of something else. It amazes me that my parents said I was going to see a psychiatrist but instead, I'm in a cult-like dungeon of the deranged. Like them, I will go off the deep end if I don't distract myself. I'll think of Drake...

PIECE TEN

C:\Jeneen\Heaven\DrakeMcCallister\FirstLove.doc

I FIXATE ON the coin-sized eyehole, staring at it until it becomes blurry; even a dream would be more clear. The constant ridicule spewing from the *man of God* diminishes until it evaporates into the chilled atmosphere. I glance at the continuously turning spools and observe the direction of the tape movement. In my relaxed meditated state, I inventively create a portal to another dimension. I force my spirit out of my body and send it beyond the glass of the spy-hole.

I start drifting into a realm far from this dumping ground... My voyage begins slowly, first escaping this armpit of hell intended for the purification of lost souls.

Soon I'm traveling at mach speed, zipping past lights and feeling the wind against my face. I can feel the pressure of the wind, distorting my cheeks, contorting my facial expressions and making it difficult to breathe. In this state of mind, Space Mountain seems a bit on the sluggish side.

The inevitable crash landing catches me off guard but I find myself at ease and on familiar ground. The year is 1987 — a hot July in Southern California. I was fifteen years old and had just returned from living for a year with family in New York. It had been only three hours since I had been home and my mustard-colored luggage remained untouched sitting in the corner of my room. My friend

Samantha St. Thomas told me about a dance that was being held at the St. Julie Catholic Church. She said she would come by in an hour to pick up my brother and me. Samantha is my childhood friend. I met her in eighth grade at Sequoia Junior High. Her wavy blonde hair shimmered in the sunlight and her blue eyes sparkled with her zest for life. We had a full year of catching up and I couldn't wait to see her.

My brother, Giovanni, was a natural-born skater. He dressed fashionably, choosing a blue OP shirt and matching shorts. You couldn't help noticing his perfect teeth, the direct result of a diligent and disciplined use of his retainer. The blonde highlights in his hair were mother nature's way of thanking him for spending countless hours outdoors. The sun's accents spread throughout the light-brown hair that he parted on the side. Giovanni patiently gave me hundreds of skateboarding lessons and showed me how to pick up his board *"like a totally bitchin' skater!"* as he would say. I mastered these techniques through determination and what was left of my tomboyish childhood. Giovanni came rushing into my room. Feeding off the excitement of attending the St. Julie's dance, he showed off his mock attempt at a skateboard trick called the *butter flip*. I was so excited to be spending some time with my brother! I was already dressed for the dance in the beautiful midnight blue dress that my aunt bought me. The flowing movement of the chiffon made me feel like a confident runway model. The lightweight mesh material displayed the many layers of sheer, loose fabric as the gentle breeze picked up the trail behind me. I felt free.

The sound of the beeping horn startled me, signaling that my best friend was out by the mailbox waiting for me. I peeked out my bedroom window to see Samantha's silver van as it sat patiently waiting to take us all to the dance! She had three other male companions. My mother made comments implying that she was *boy crazy*. Of course that was putting it lightly because I knew what she really thought. My mother came from a generation and an upbringing that couldn't fathom the opposite sex being friends. My mother found a way of making Samantha into a floozy that day.

"Jeneen, why does Samantha have a lot of boys in the car?" she asked, without having to explain her other thoughts.

I avoided that question, hoping it was rhetorical.

I hugged Samantha. I was so happy to be back with her, especially because we had spent so much time together in eighth and ninth grade.

When we arrived at the St. Julie's recreation room, out of the corner of my eye, I saw my junior high school sweetheart, Drake McCallister. He was a lanky five feet, eleven inches and his sandy blond hair stood out in the dim light inside the dance hall/theater. He was just as I remembered, except he was more mature-looking. After all, it had been two years since I had seen him. His braces were gone and his complexion had a glow that I noticed right away. I was only thirteen years old and Drake was fourteen when we went on our first date — chaperoned, of course. I can still remember his dad, Gram, and my parents sitting in the back row watching our every move at the United Artists Movie Theater inside the Thousand Oaks Mall. I'd seen my share of punk rockers, stoners and valley girls occupying this hip teen's hangout spot. In fact, Samantha and I once rode our bikes three miles to get there one summer. If you were going to categorize which stereotype we were, it would be valley girls, hands-down, because our teen vernacular consisted of: "*Oh my God! Totally dude! Like, like, like, like, totally awesome! That's so rad!*" Drake took me there to see *Rambo* during Sylvester Stallone's prime. Despite the fact that we had three Doberman pinschers on guard in the back row, I touched and caressed his hand and kissed his smooth skin. I envisioned the carnivorous scavengers devouring popcorn and other treats, keeping the attention off of us. On our way out of the mall, we passed by Casa Escobar. The authentic Mexican, fine-dining restaurant had been in Southern California since 1946 and decided to grace our neighborhood mall with its presence! I enjoyed their use of fresh ingredients in everything they prepared. My family would take us there on special occasions.

"Drake, what do you think of this restaurant? The food is flavorful and I would love to take you there on our next date!" I said, mentally counting up the babysitting money I had socked away. We skipped with excitement, followed closely by our canine guards. It was like they were walking us instead of the other way around! I bumped him lightly, trying to bring his attention to the arcade named Tilt! "Balloon Fight, Jet Set Willy, Ice Climber, Lazy Jones, Knight Lore, Montezuma's Revenge, Centipede, Pac-Man, Ms. Pac-Man, Defender and Asteroid — Oh my!" I shouted, like Dorothy on her way to Oz, sporting my knowledge of video games to impress my boyfriend.

"Yes to dinner and video games at the arcade!" he said, enthusiastically!

"Which pinscher do you want to bring with us on our next date? I'd rather have your dad! I think he'd be happy to see his son on a date as opposed to my nervous guard dogs. In their paranoia, they will only assume I will get pregnant if you breathe on me the wrong way!" I said, matter-of-factly. He laughed.

He was the first boy I ever held hands with and the first boy who kissed me. I mean *really* kissed me. It wasn't just a peck on the lips, a shy brush of flesh against flesh — it was much more complex. We kissed on the *Adventure Thru Inner Space* ride at Disney's Tomorrowland. It was the best experience I ever had!

We raced through Tomorrowland holding hands as we tilted our heads up in unison to view the *People Mover*. The excitement of the park ran through me as I watched passengers in the cars on the track above. They were up in the sky, soaring through a land of science and technology, promising a miraculous future.

We waited in a long wrap-around line talking about school, our goals and the ride to come, passing the time until it was our turn to get on. The rows of people soon dwindled as we neared *the shrinking experience.* We took note of the giant-sized microscope. I noticed the images of the candy, apple-shaped, blue buggies, sitting at an incline, being reduced into tiny forms. They were in motion, seen through the clear front of the scientific instrument, and I wondered how they managed that high-tech special effect.

We stepped onto the conveyer belt and rode to the transports that would take us on our adventure. It was unexpected but I knew the time would come for my first kiss. I was worried that it would happen when one of our guard dogs was behind us.

(Traffic Controllers) „Atommobiles approaching snowflake specimen…" "All phases stand by to verify resolving power…" "Phase blue, phase blue: Light wavelength approximately .5000 millimeters. Definition excellent." "Phase green: resolving power decreasing…" "Phase green, increase hue angle… verify…" "Phase green: Hue angle increased to 14 degrees, 29 minutes. Atommobile definition excellent." "All phases hold hue angle until forward units reach crystalline stage of snowflake."

It was dark and I suddenly heard the haunting voice of Paul Frees. He started our tour with this introduction, *"I am the first person to make this fabulous journey. Suspended in the timelessness of inner space are the thought waves of my first impressions. They will be our only source of contact once you have passed beyond the limits of normal mag-ni-fi-ca-tion."* Echo! Echo! Echo!

Drake wore braces and I was worried about getting my lips caught in the metal but the thrill superseded any fears. It lasted the whole ride; we couldn't stop kissing each other. I was addicted. I took a brief break from Drake's pillowy lips only to be startled by the all-seeing eye looking at us through the *master microscope!* If it's not our parents watching us every minute, it's some scientist on a ride conjured up by *imagineers!* I jumped! Drake pulled me in again, protecting me. The ride was shrinking us more and more and I caught glimpses of the giant-sized snowflakes. The experiment of love was a tangible force pulling us through the dark. We were breathing as one, our passion for each other accompanied, the entire time, by the sound of the same narrator from the *Haunted Mansion*. I hear the storyteller's deep mesmerizing voice again, "Nothing is as solid as it appears!" Drake held me tight and I gently kissed him. His kisses were soft, gentle and exploring all at once. My heart was racing so fast I thought I was still on a Disney ride even as we stepped off the *atommobile*. I touched my skin to feel the residue of his energy imprinted on my lips.

I caught the different smells of corn dogs, the buttery popcorn and Mickey Mouse pancakes as we made our way past Main Street, USA. Drake placed his arm around me, enveloping me with his warmth, and led the way to New Orleans Square. The sound of Dixieland jazz was in the air and we were caught up in the romantic atmosphere as we gallivanted through the French Quarters. Drake grabbed my hand and interlaced his fingers with mine. His gentle touch made me smile. Occasionally, when a pole or a small child would separate us momentarily, he would say "bread and butter!" I could have sworn I had visions of pixie dust flying between us as our auras separated for a few seconds until we reconnected, meshing both of our beings back as one. He was a bit corny but, then again, I had magical particles flying around us — it was all part of the romance package!

After my daydreams about Drake and our eighth-grade graduation at the *happiest place on earth* ended, I came back to the dance at St. Julie's. I placed my head on his warm shoulder and drifted once more. There was a sort of self assurance about Drake that attracted me like a magnet. A couple of files popped up from their various subdirectories and I thought of the eighth-grade dance at Sequoia Junior High. In a flash, my mind took off like a Saturn V rocket again. This time, I found myself at a different dance, held in a different school auditorium. I went with my friend, BreeAnna. She had dark short hair, glasses and her best feature… voluptuous lips.

Back then, Drake was just an annoying fourteen-year-old boy sporting camouflage gear. He chased me around, tugging my Strawberry Shortcake bra strap, thinking it was cute! I remember the blue lockers and the tall, lanky boy beside them, waiting to pounce... As soon as we were in his sight, he chased BreeAnna and me like a hunter seeking his prey. I dreaded every day we had to walk by him and his comrade, Kurt.

One time, as BreeAnna and I left Biology Class, these two boys were around, causing nothing but trouble. They were experimenting with an action-packed plan to court a lady and going about it as if we were playing *Soldier*. I was flabbergasted that I didn't get drafted on the way to Art Class. Although, it wouldn't have surprised me at all if I had found a draft notice in my locker! It's interesting how arrogant boys are when they're in packs. The lanky one pointed out my upper lip hair as it was clear in the bright sunlight. I wished I waxed at that time. I was so horrified that my peers could hear him!

Shut up, you bloody bastard! My prospect for the eighth-grade dance might hear you! I said this in my mind since I was too shy to defend myself at the time. Kurt, for his part, was just following orders from his out-of-control captain and truly believed this method of wooing two young ladies was the best.

"BreeAnna, these boys are complete jerks. Just ignore them," I whispered in her ear.

I clicked my heels three times and found myself back at the dance with BreeAnna. I was wearing a simple white cotton, spaghetti-strapped mini-dress just in time for spring. It was the same dress I wore to my sixth-grade graduation!

"Oh my God, BreeAnna... there he is! Ugh! I want to run!" I gasped, wanting to dart quickly for cover, preferably underneath the punch bowl table. There he was, dressed up, a smirk across his face, with his best pal, Kurt. I wondered if I needed binoculars because I imagined a look of victory on his face. His apprentice, Kurt, had straight light-brown hair and thick *Coke-bottle* glasses. Drake immediately got into my space and I feared that he would pull the pin out from a grenade and that the explosion would be too much to handle.

"Would you like to dance?" he asked. It was as if he were a different boy — one who just completed his first year of finishing school in Switzerland!

Before I could answer, he grabbed my hand and pulled me gently onto the dance floor. I almost hesitated because I was uncertain of which Drake this was. We danced all night. We danced to Bryan Adams' *Heaven*. I felt concerned for BreeAnna being alone but when I looked across, she was dancing with a boy named Quinn. We later double-dated, celebrating our eighth-grade graduation at Disneyland! It was so hard for me to fathom that I was dancing with the same *captain* that conjured up that childish army game by my locker. I had dreaded going to get my books out, not wanting to deal with his countless, tiresome interrogations. He held me tight as if the past incident didn't happen. He shook with nerves and it made me feel that either he was interested in me or *he was afraid I might retaliate!* He answered that question by asking me for my phone number.

"BreeAnna, do you have a pen and paper?" I asked, positive that she carried in her purse the essential tools for matters of the heart. I scribbled with handwriting that makes a doctor's signature appear legible. I wrote my phone number on the pretty pink stationery and handed it over to him. *It was like night and day! Why was the same boy who tormented me daily interested in my number?* The confusion baffled me but the fascination of the opposite sex superseded any doubts.

I blinked my eyes five times and I was back from my trip through my memory and in the present day of July, 1987. I finally settled in and nestled my head underneath Drake's neck. I was on my tiptoes! I took hold of his waist and wrapped my arms around him, feeling his back and he purred in my ear like a happy kitten. A more upbeat song started — Samantha Fox's *I Surrender*. We managed to rock the night away in the recreation room at St. Julie's. I put my feet on top of his to increase my height and he held me tight as we moved to the music together for hours. In fact, this was the beginning of the only slice of heaven that I experienced in my teenage years.

The next day, I asked my brother to become for me what my Jewish friends called a *yenta*.

"Giovanni, could you do me a favor and call Drake to see if he is interested in me because I would love to start dating him again! I can't take the rejection and it would be so much easier if *you* meddled instead!"

A short while later, Giovanni gently hung up the receiver on the rotary phone as I crossed my fingers. "Well, what is the outcome?"

"He said that he doesn't want to get hurt again!"

You see, when I was thirteen years old, we were dating all summer long and then before I started ninth grade, I ended our relationship. I was young and I wanted to enter the ninth grade without any commitments. Now a mature fifteen-year-old, I loved the qualities that Drake possessed. He was nice, smart and a talented piano player. I was looking for a good guy in my life because I didn't want anything less. I wanted quality and Drake McCallister fit the bill. I already knew his family and his dogs, Lady (a cocker spaniel) and Droopy (a basset hound). They were obviously named after the cartoons. It was a perfect fit — My brother had to get us together!

Eventually, Drake and I gave it another shot…

PIECE ELEVEN

C:\Jeneen\Heaven\Love\ Drake\1stDateSince8thGrade.doc

THE FOUR KNOCKS at the front door told me that the light of my life was here.

There was no doubt that this door was the passageway to my happiness. My heart went into overdrive and if a physician had used a stethoscope on me right then, he might be the one to have a coronary!

"It must be Drake!" I thought to myself.

I inhaled and exhaled slowly as I turned the knob and pulled open the country-style door. There he stood, with Boney Mountain as a backdrop, my first love — holding a vibrant, hand-picked floral arrangement. He was smiling, his perfectly aligned teeth the handiwork of an outstanding orthodontist. I smiled… We were ready to go on our first date since the eighth grade and my enthusiasm was obvious. He leaned over and kissed me, softly brushing my lips and cradled my head with his palm, pulling me into his energy field. You didn't have to be psychic to see how we felt about each other.

I stood on my tiptoes because I am only five feet, four inches tall and I wanted to match his level. I reached up and embraced him, the warmth of our two bodies joining together.

I was surprised by how affectionate he was, considering that just yesterday he told my brother he was reluctant to reconnect… and for a good reason. He had recapped the end of our summer romance that we had right before Freshman Year — how I left him and shattered his trust in order to find a new path.

This time, I was ready. I had my new experiences, and quite frankly, it was all a bit overrated. I thought about the old, mustard luggage still sitting against a wall in the corner of my room. I had no intentions of opening the unorganized tangled mess. At least not yet…

I didn't want to think about anything except starting over with Drake. I decided to climb onto his shoes to make it more convenient for myself. It was another passionate kiss just like the ones we experienced at Disneyland. I could smell the nutmeg, lavender and clove of Drake's cologne. I gently touched his neck with my lips, following the alluring trail of the scent on his flesh. I was becoming addicted, once again, to his affection.

He escorted me to his silver Mazda, parked right in front of my house. My home sat right across from Sycamore Canyon State Park. It was filled with eucalyptus trees, quarter horses and coyotes. Growing up in the city left me completely unprepared for the cries of coyotes at night. What a shock to learn that they sounded nothing like they did in the cartoons!

Drake opened the passenger-side door for me, closed it and walked around to the driver's side after getting me situated. I smiled and unlocked his door, figuring it was only fair.

His mother taught him chivalry and how to treat a lady with respect! I thanked her silently.

Drake started the car and immediately I could hear *Heart* playing in the air.

He quickly turned down the volume before my father could hear it and complain. Apparently, Drake was blasting *Barracuda* all the way down Reino Road.

I was wearing a hot pink ruffled miniskirt that I had carefully chosen. Like a greeting from the universe, I suddenly felt the warmth of sunshine graze over my knees. I opened the window and inhaled the sea salt breeze and exhaled the thrill of being alone with my jewel. This time, the *Mafia* wasn't trailing behind us. After all, I am Sicilian and the thought did cross my mind. The Pacific Ocean was only seven miles from my house. Drake took the winding, twisted road called Potrero, heading us towards paradise.

Barracuda was a little bit rough for my taste in music... but because Drake enjoyed it so much, I never changed the tape and learned to appreciate this new genre. The next song that came on, *These Dreams*, was a little bit easier on the ears. I enjoyed the beautiful lyrics allowing the poetry to form new memories on my hard drive. Little did I know, there would be an association with *Heart* that would serve as a keepsake, forever etched in my soul. Drake and I conversed for hours about New York, religion, his parents, our goals and our dreams. I poured out everything imaginable to him... and then some. The hours escaped us and it seemed like only minutes had passed. I told him how I wanted to attend a Christian school because I wanted the one-on-one attention. We spoke of my eagerness to attend college and really make something of myself. I told him that I somehow convinced my mother to send me to Cornerstone Christian School in the fall. I knew that my last two years of high school at a private institution would prepare me for higher learning.

He drove through Point Magu and we finally parked alongside the Pacific Coast Highway in front of Leo Carillo Beach. I packed dinner and a blanket into a grocery bag so it would be easier for me to carry. We strolled along the beach and I could feel the wind rummaging through my hair as if it were looking for some sort of treasure. Soon, I slid off my white summer sandals and stood there with my arms wide. I loved the sensations of warm sand caressing my feet as I walked out into the mysterious patterns of waves. The tide brushed the salty water over my feet, energizing me. It was ice cold! I started skipping around. Immediately, I jumped into Drake's arms, my legs wrapped around his waist and I started kissing him, slowly at first. I did not care about the glare of the sun because my only focus was the soft lips that were gently caressing mine. I felt his tongue with mine and we stayed interlocked for a very long time. It was an intense exploration of each other's feelings of desire, more intense than any fire. The bursting pressure of a firehose couldn't extinguish the wild spread of flames. I remained uplifted for what seemed like eternity. The light breeze showered us with sprays of salty droplets that I could taste when he pressed his lips against mine. It made me feel... alive.

He gently put me down and I ran into the unpredictable swell. He chased me down and tagged me and then I was *it*! He grabbed me and passionately kissed me again as if it were the last time we would ever see each other. It's hard to fathom that this was the same boy who kissed me when I was in the eighth grade. This was like living the story of a magical romance in a far-off land.

My heart was racing and I knew I was falling in love. He held me tight as we watched the waves crash against the sharp, enormous rocks. The sounds of seagulls and the sea against a concrete and stone cliff was our personal soundtrack played by nature just for us; the sun painted splashes of colors behind us. It looked like a watercolor painting. This moment in time was so beautiful that it was almost surreal.

The sun was heading down and soon the chill in the air would require me to have a light jacket or sweater, but I was a tad unprepared.

"Are you cold?" Drake inquired.

Without waiting for me to respond, he put his arms around me to keep me warm. He rubbed my arms to provide heat. He was a real gentleman now and I remembered again the eighth-grade Drake playing army captain to impress me. It is a comical recollection that we could tell our grandchildren in the future.

We ate our picnic dinner reminiscing about Sequoia, chaperoned dates and our mutual friends. Soon, we had covered all of the last two years and now we were here, wrapped up in each other's thoughts about the future.

We proceeded to go back home, speaking intimately about where our relationship was going.

He looked at me and said, "You are my goddess and you are so beautiful!"

It was something that your average sixteen-year-old wouldn't say today. He made me feel I was on top of the world because he put me there. I had so many butterflies. The fluttering was uncontrollable every time I saw his blue-gray eyes. It was almost as if he was peeking into the depths of my psyche when our eyes locked. In his presence, my spirit was exposed and he could see right through me.

He whispered softly in my ear, "Your eyes are the windows to your soul."

PIECE TWELVE

C:\Jeneen\Heaven\Love\Drake\JumpingOutofBed.doc

THE NEXT MORNING, I awoke and immediately began to relive my perfect date.

Like a shooting star, Drake graced the darkness with his presence, illuminating my dreams. As I played last night back, I realized there were more memorable scenes to come. I catapulted out of bed, as if shot from a gun. I didn't need a good cup of cappuccino as an incentive to get me out of bed back then. I thought about

Drake and our wondrous date and I couldn't wait to get started! As I prepared myself for my first job interview, I selected my most professional attire. On that hot day in July, I landed my first tax-paying job at, ironically, the McDonald's on Wendy Drive. A man in his late twenties who closely resembled Weird Al Yankovic, interviewed me. His name was Rick and he hired me on the spot. I lied in order to work the register, telling my supervisor that I was sixteen years old. I figured I could go to confession at a later time. *Oops, my mother switched us over to born-again Christian. They don't have a booth there! Damn it!* My job was close to home but definitely not walking distance. My parents would have no other recourse than to drive me.

This position entailed packing food to go or placing *Happy Meals* on a dine-in tray. We also cleaned the plastic carriers and were in charge of the fryer. As I sprinkled salt over the hot potatoes, I could hear my mother lecturing us like a live broadcast in my mind. Her guttural, high-pitched screeching about how unhealthy salt is was etched into my mind like grooves on a record. She lectured us about how anything fried was a big caloric catastrophe... but she did not use those particular words!

Our household was filled with a constant obsession about weight. My father fixated on my mother's weight after having children and that's how it all started. They attended Weight Watchers together and discovered butter and salt were a big *no-no* on their popcorn so we began air popping. In fact, when they were on a no red meat kick, we all were. So we had pasta with re-fried beans (from a can), crispy pasta (leftovers), pasta with oil, garlic, parsley, clams (from a can) and Italian bread as our side dish. My father would make a vegetable soup from scratch with chicken and pasta. That was my favorite meal as long as it wasn't served too frequently. As leftovers, it immediately wore out its welcome. Mother would make an occasional side salad on Saturday and Sunday when their friends Nita and Anakin visited. Those were more balanced meals. In fact, they were completely different. Overall, we ate so much spaghetti that I vowed never to incorporate that into my nutritional program as an adult.

So... no red meat, no fried food (except when you tossed leftover pasta in olive oil in a pan), no pop and absolutely no cookies, pastries or sweets except on special occasions. All-you-can-eat carbs, however, were the golden ticket to skinny at our house. I hardly ate and Drake was concerned. He said he thought I was undernourished and started giving me vitamins. I was starting to stress out that my mother would find them. She was so paranoid and would immediately assume they were drugs and I knew she wouldn't bother to find out what they really were.

I wasn't anorexic — I was merely... repulsed. I was searching for better nutritional choices. My mother's low-calorie frozen food was starting to appeal to me but I was forbidden to eat it. "You can't have that! That's my diet food!" she yelled, warning me. The smells permeating the air when she warmed it up in the microwave drove me crazy.

My mother's constant bragging about her diet expertise became so overwhelming that once, while visiting me in New York, she couldn't stop herself from commenting on my weight. She pointed out that I was getting chubby but then softened her tone by telling me that I filled out. I would like to use alcoholism as the reason for her lack of sensitivity, however, my non-nurturing *mother bird* didn't even consume red wine.

I stared at the lights on the deep fryer at McDonald's, waiting for the batch I was cooking to be done. Somehow, all of the nutritional lectures were put by the wayside like the trash my father collected. I was so excited about the fact that I could get a free meal on every shift and have all-you-can-drink sodas. I justified it because I had a high metabolism and hiked frequently. Besides, I was starving myself at home. I was unaware of the repercussions of eating a lot of fast food, but at fifteen, it was pure bliss. In the breakroom, I gobbled up the highly-processed junk food out of pure desperation and to exert my own free will. The music in the background, Nena's *99 Red Balloons* (the German version), mixed with thoughts of my sweet Drake and the smell of the burger, made me so happy. One would think I was on a sandy beach soaking up the rays on a Caribbean Island.

I worked the opening shift from 4 a.m. until 1 p.m. and then Drake and I would spend our time together.

I took Drake out to dinner after work. There was a Japanese restaurant in the Jann's Mall called Akio's. As it was my first time eating Japanese, I played it safe and ordered tempura. This consisted of lightly fried shrimp and vegetables with a warm soy sauce based dipping sauce. I thought of what my mother would say but this was a special occasion. The free ticket my metabolism gave me would only last so long, I knew. My father told me he used to be skinny like me until he hit the age of twenty-seven. He warned me how it went downhill for him at that point in his life.

Japanese food was a chance to experience something new. My well-mannered boyfriend loved it. We skipped the sushi, because at the time, raw anything simply grossed us out! We had teriyaki chicken and rice instead.

"Jeneen, this was a good idea! Thank you so much!" he exclaimed as our kimono-clad waitress handed us our bill. The intricate floral stitching on the delicate material, along with the chopsticks in her long straight hair, made her look like a work of art. I grabbed the check and demanded to pay it.

"This is my treat. I have the money since I'm working at least five days a week!" I said, my radiant smile expressing my love. "That's what I like about you, Jeneen. You compromise with finance. You are the best girlfriend I've ever had!" He genuinely cheered. I racked my brain for any mention of girlfriends besides me and nothing popped up on my hard drive.

Drake drove me all over the place and buying dinner was the least I could do for him; I simply wanted to make him happy. He drove me back to my house on Potrero Road. It was a somewhat busy street used by runners, bikers and hikers exploring the state park and drivers using the back roads to the beach. In the evening, however, all you could hear was nature. It was nearing 10 pm and Drake and I found ourselves in front of my house. I looked at his face in the moonlight as I stroked my hand across his soft, shaved skin. He pulled me close and gave me a tender kiss.

He said, "I love you."

It was the first time I heard those words from a boy. The butterflies in my stomach started acting up again, and this time, they were completely out of control.

"I love you too, Drake," I whispered softly in his ear, brushing my lips against it. Honestly, we didn't have to voice our love for each other. The soft caresses of our lips spoke the words. It was our personal language of love. Every brush and sweep added another layer of deeper meaning that one couldn't deny. It wasn't artificial or superficial but the most intense expression. I could still feel the tingling sensation on my lips. His touch lingered along with his scent and I carried it with me. I never felt alone, even in his absence. I took his spirit with me everywhere I went.

He handed me a love letter and I gave him mine, filling his palms with my words and sealing it shut with his fingers. Every time I received a letter from Drake, it was equivalent to receiving a Christmas present from Tiffany's, but to the one hundredth power. I never knew what he was going to say with his poetry but I knew it was something about our love. His letters were, in essence, magical literature that kept me alive and nourished. It left me full.

PIECE THIRTEEN

C:\Jeneen\Heaven\Love\Drake\TheAddiction.doc

I WASN'T A drug user by any means. I never *puffed the Magic Dragon*, popped E or drank an ounce of demon rum! I did, however, have an addiction that was so difficult to shake, not even the Betty Ford Center could help. I had swallowed the love pill, all right. It hit me the first time his hand gently touched the side of my neck. I remembered the delicate hold that first captivated me back in the eighth grade.

Like a hound dog, I caught the scent of my boyfriend's love in the wind. His exotic, refreshing, woody fragrance matched my inner intensity. I was lost in the Bermuda Triangle but I had to try and stay grounded. Focus, Jeneen...

I heard the doorbell ring. The sound stopped me, frozen in my tracks. I could feel my heart pounding like I was a racehorse at Santa Anita Park. I would give up any possession just to have my fix. Materialistic items were no longer of interest. All I really needed was the passion of our love. I was, in plain English... finally content. I didn't need meaningless belongings to fill the void in my life. Drake's soul satisfied that for me. He was an open book, meant to be read by only me. As I peeked inside, I saw myself kept in pristine surroundings. It was my nest and my safe-haven with him always there to protect me.

My fix was here and because I hadn't seen him all week, my hands started trembling. I was going through withdrawal and knew I had it bad! My palms were sweaty and I felt warm with fever. I skipped through the hallway yelling, "I'll get it!"

"Who is it?" I asked, knowing very well who it was. "It's Drake!" he said in a low distinctive voice.

I turned the rounded brass handle and pulled open the door, allowing the sunlight to warm my chilled home. His beautiful, angelic face sent goosebumps down my spine. He leaned over to softly touch my lips, playfully teasing. I grabbed his shirt, pulling him closer to let him know I meant business. His chest had sprinkles of hair and I did not want to yank too hard. The last thing I wanted was to ruin this intimate moment.

We were ready to pick up Mike Kane and Samantha and started to make preparations. The journey along the Pacific Coast Highway awaited us.

Drake suggested confidently, "Let's stop at Albertsons and pick up chicken, Hawaiian sweet rolls and other side dishes to bring with us."

"That's fine. Let me search the linen closet in the hall for a blanket."

I carefully selected a lovely quilt for this special occasion. I grabbed Drake's hand and caressed it. It seemed as though time slowed down as we headed for the Mazda; molasses would have dribbled faster.

We drove up to Samantha's house and I was impressed with the size of her new home. She was no longer around the corner from my house but remained only about a mile away. There was a nice cut lawn in the front with enough flowers to open a flower shop! The garden was filled with roses, gardenias and hibiscus in all colors. It looked like it rained Skittles the night before and the beautiful floral smell permeated my dress. I glanced over the well-manicured landscaping and rang the doorbell.

"Are you ready to go, Samantha? Drake is keeping the engine running. Where's Mike?" I asked excitedly.

"He's getting some towels," Sam said breathlessly.

She looked like she had been running around, getting everything ready for our day at the ocean. She was probably used to it by now, being on the cross country team at Newbury Park High School.

Drake, once again, drove down the twisted, winding road called Potrero. Laughter filled the car and Samantha's high-pitched enthusiasm kept our energy charged. I saw Mike steal a couple kisses from Samantha.

"They are such a cute couple," I thought silently.

Drake looked at me, smiled and reached for my hand, caressing it softly. I paid attention to his touch, not missing a moment, absorbing everything as if it were our last encounter. The electricity and the magnetic connection was palpable.

We parked at Point Magu and decided to set up our romantic picnic. Drake pointed out the cuts and shapes of the rock formations. The continuous motion of the waves was mesmerizing as we listened to the tide's enchanting music. Beethoven couldn't have orchestrated it any better. The astonishing backdrop, mixed with good company, was the perfect recipe for a great evening. I could hear the power of the water beating against the rocks. I tasted the salt air on Drake's lips when he reached over to kiss me sweetly.

Samantha and I spread the blanket that wrestled with the unpredictable wind.

Eventually, the hand-stitched masterpiece fell perfectly to the ground. We looked for silverware or plasticware but couldn't find any in the grocery bag.

"Drake, where are the forks and napkins?" Samantha asked curiously.

"Did we forget the essentials? *Only on Tuesday!*" Drake responded with his usual corny phrase. "Let's improvise! Hey, did you two bring Martinelli?"

"Yes, but we didn't bring any cups or a bottle opener," Mike replied disappointedly.

"Any ideas?" Sam asked.

"Let's try to open it with the hubcap of Drake's economical vehicle," Mike said playfully.

Before we could blink, Mike comes back with an open bottle of Martinelli, suds overflowing from the top. We shared the bottle and passed it around. "Mmm, this chicken is good," Drake said with his mouth half full.

"Only on Tuesdays!" I mimicked facetiously.

Everyone laughed. The sun was beginning to set and the sky was filled with beautiful colors. Orange, magenta and red created a natural show for us of such magnificence that the naked eye couldn't grasp it.

I could see Mike leaning over to give Samantha a passionate smooch. Drake looked at me desiring the same. My heart skipped a couple beats and I pressed my lips against his. It started out tender at first and then erupted into passion that rivaled the show in the sky. In between our kisses, I held his chest against mine. I felt so secure in his embrace. It enveloped my being and I felt waves of *agape* love. My hand traveled down his back and I started massaging his lower lumbar. I could tell he liked it by the look of pure pleasure on his face. It was perfect against the canvas of the sky.

PIECE FOURTEEN

C:\Jeneen\Heaven\Drake\RagingWaters.doc

MIGUEL AND FLORENCE Martinez were our youth group leaders at First Christian Church located on Knollwood Drive. For weeks, they had been organizing a Raging Waters field trip for us. It was a hot July and I couldn't wait to be with our friends and have an action-packed day at the waterpark.

Drake and I had another date planned, and this time, it wasn't Disneyland. I woke instantly and launched out of bed with excitement when my alarm rang. I hit the *off* button on the annoying gadget in order to keep the dead from rising. I knew it was going to be a perfect day! I hastily grabbed my swimsuit and headed for the bathroom.

I glanced over the navy-blue and white polkadot bikini and involuntarily flashed back to the time in ninth grade when I bought a swimsuit with money that I earned babysitting. The pattern of green, blue and purple with ties on the bottom, were etched in my mind the minute I purchased it. Getting something new was a rarity for me and I was thrilled that trash had never touched its silky material. I enjoyed the untouched garment until my mother confiscated it and burned it… or at least that is what she told me.

She screamed like I committed the cardinal sin of the century, "That swimsuit is too revealing! Not for you!"

"Mom! You can't do that! I bought that with my own money

that I worked so hard for!" I cried wondering why my life seemed so unfair.

"Tough, I'm burning it!" she spewed with a vengeance.

My purchase was a typical eighties-style two-piece without a trace of being risqué and now it's classified as rubbish. *Was I trashy as well?* It was the last time I saw my swimsuit and I was also out the hard-earned cash. Couldn't I have returned it and then purchased another item? At the time, I didn't focus on that logical plan; I was too busy dwelling on my shame.

Suddenly, I was back, continuing my morning regimen, fixated on my positive day ahead. I had a similar swimsuit this time and for some reason, my mom didn't seize this one! It was from my mother's friend, Nita. The forty-year-old woman with a Kentucky accent had straight black hair with a pageboy flip for a more professional look. She took care of her skin with products from the Estée Lauder counter at the Thousand Oaks Mall. I knew if I took care of my complexion that I would stay young looking. She was living proof and made me feel more confident about facing the aging process. I'll never forget the time she gave me her polka-dot bikini. The vintage seventies style was appealing to me. I invented an imaginary fashion show runway and made a catwalk over the bathroom rug heading towards the mirror. *Nita has good taste in swimsuits!* In the blink of the eye, my burnt swimwear was *dust in the wind.*

I concentrated on my date with Drake. In a New York minute, my heart was pumping love beats like a drum set. I washed my hair, put my customized ensemble on and then applied my makeup. I made sure I outlined my lips with fuchsia lipstick and applied a gloss made specifically for smooching. It had a cherry taste and scent that left my lips feeling supple. It was necessary to get my lips in the perfect pucker condition for the upcoming kissing marathon. It took me a long time to style my hair. It was 1987 and every strand in the front had to be teased with a ton of a hairspray called Aqua

Net! The results left my hair sticky but everything was set in place and going nowhere. It's a good thing that I woke up at 5 am.

Drake rang the doorbell at 7 am. I gave him a quick kiss on his cheek and then he pulled me close.

"You look sensational," he whispered in my ear.

I held him in my arms and then he kissed my forehead. He handed me flowers from his mother's garden and in return, I kissed him again.

He looked at me and informed, "We better go. Everyone is waiting for us at the church."

"Mom, we are leaving now!" I shouted so she could hear me. My mother replied, "Have fun!"

She knew I wouldn't be home until curfew. That was 9 pm on weekdays and 11 pm on the weekend. Drake always kept us on time. He was by far every parent's dream of a teenage boyfriend for their daughter. He was an honor roll student, played the piano, was polite to my parents, well-mannered, affectionate, responsible, sensible and treated a woman with the utmost respect. He didn't have any tattoos and the *goth* look wasn't for him. In other words, my boyfriend was a nerd but I loved him. He liked to make machine gun noises and play Dungeons and Dragons with his buddies on a Friday night. Again, he was my geek and I loved every bit of him. I liked the intellectual nice guy who treated me like a queen. Besides, I was always interested in learning new things and I knew he had the capacity to take me to a different level. I always thought he would make a great teacher because of his never-ending patience. He was my knight and I was his lady and together we were going to hop into his silver chariot and head to Raging Waters.

My brother attended the youth group with us and we were all going together. Giovanni sat in the back and I of course was in the passenger seat next to Drake. Giovanni and I were at the age where we shared the same friends; I enjoyed the morale it brought to our household. His buddy, James Garcia, flagged him down as soon as we stepped out of the car.

I heard Tami Cartier calling my name. "Jeneen, come quick. I need to talk to you!"

Tami had long, wavy, luxurious red hair that was so striking. The freckles on her face complemented her and lent a bronzing glow to her complexion. We were both attending Christian Cornerstone in Camarillo in September. She wanted to talk to me about a guy she has had a crush on for some time. While at first preoccupied with the conversation, I tilted my head up and caught Drake looking at me. The butterflies returned and I almost lost track of what Tami was saying.

"Jeneen… Jeneen, are you listening to me?" Tami inquired, making certain she still had my attention.

"Sorry Tami, I was a little distracted by my boyfriend," I said, smiling. She gave me a wink and said, "You make a darling couple."

"I'm falling more and more in love with him everyday!" I said, without hesitation.

Miguel cleared his throat to announce, "All right everyone… gather up. I want everyone to get in a circle. Let's all hold hands and pray before we go on our venture."

"Dear Lord, I just want to thank you for the good weather that you provided for us. Please guide us today in building friendships and bond us as a Christian family. In your name, I pray."

While all of us wanted a positive light to bless our day, I couldn't help being happy, holding hands in a circle with everyone I love. I appreciated how special this camaraderie made me feel. It was a nice teen support system and I hardly ever missed a meeting. It was during a time that I felt self-assured and confident in my religious beliefs.

We took the bus that had the words *First Christian Church* painted on it. We all jumped aboard and all I could hear were the happy conversations of young adults discussing what they wanted to do first at Raging Waters. I was determined not to go on anything scary. I already had enough excitement with Drake.

On the course of the lengthy bus ride, Drake spent time conversing with Frank and James. I could have sworn I heard machine gun noises but the chatter from all the girls discussing romance overrode the sound. It was my favorite topic.

I told Susie and Andrew about one of my dates with Drake. I'm surprised that no one had been irritated with me because that was the only topic I wanted to talk about. It was my obsession! I turned my head to talk to Tami. "I have to tell you about our date last Saturday. I invited Drake over to have a picnic. I decided to get a soft wool blanket which I spread underneath the eucalyptus tree on our front lawn. Our scenic view for the afternoon was Sycamore State Park." I shouted with enthusiasm.

I had cooked lunch for us that day, which was a rarity. My mother was at work and my brother was home. It was a good thing she was because my mother didn't like me preparing anything in her kitchen.

When I was ten years old, I would find activities to keep myself occupied during the scorching summer days. I grabbed a cookbook my father found in the trash on his daily routes. I wanted to learn how to make muffins. I started reading the ingredients that I needed. We didn't have all of them so I improvised. I substituted spices that we had for the ones we didn't have. I delighted in mixing everything together in order to create something spectacular. I pre-heated the oven and then started scooping my homemade batter into the muffin tray. I set the timer and watched the alchemy begin. I loved seeing the muffins rising. It was an amazing transformation and the two ingredients that remained constant were my love and effort. I shut the oven off and let everything cool down. I could hear my father's white Ford Maverick pulling into the driveway and I was eager to hand him my unorthodox creation.

I gave him a big hug and said, "Dad, you have to try this!"

He spun me around and said, "That is really good — a little salty, but really good!"

It made me feel special and confident that he enjoyed my work of art. His reaction made me want to explore more recipes and continue my growth as the "little chef" of the family! Shortly after, my mother came home and I was hoping I would get the same reaction.

She started scolding me as if I killed another parakeet, "Why were YOU in the kitchen? You know you're not allowed, especially when I'm not home! Get to your room! You are forbidden to turn the oven on!"

I ran to my closet, searching frantically for solace. I hid from her and cried in private.

One week later, there was a chrome lock on the pantry door. That clamp represented the end of a creative outlet that I wanted to pursue. I could no longer learn new techniques and cuisines. I couldn't expand my horizons. I was stuck in my mother's ignorance. It was in that moment I told myself: *I will never learn to prepare and present nice food! I do not know how to cook! If I'm in the kitchen, my mother will yell at me. If I'm in the kitchen, my mother will yell at me. If I'm in the kitchen, my mother will yell at me.*

The negative reinforcements were building up on my processor. This file was called, *I Cannot Cook!* It was loaded with bad data and I vowed never to click on that corrupted area ever again.

"Jeneen… Jeneen, what happened next? You drifted off somewhere," Tami said, frustratedly assuming I was a space cadet.

"I'm sorry, so where was I… We just had a nice sunset picnic on the front lawn and he loved my dinner extravaganza. He was impressed because I made Mexican. As usual, we kissed and called it a night." I said with a lovestruck expression.

Conversation ended with the halting of the church bus. Everyone was ready to have a great time at Raging Waters. I looked up and examined the daredevil ride called 'Drop Out'. I was happy to say, I was not planning on participating in this near-death experience.

'Drop Out' is seven stories high and it only takes four seconds to plummet. It's a vertical drop and I wondered how people kept from flying off the sides. My heart sank as I looked at this monstrosity. I quivered while measuring the vertical distance in my mind. My anxiety ceased when I grabbed Drake's hand.

We checked into the park and followed Tami, my brother and James. We went through a cave and when everyone was out of sight, Drake kissed me. It lasted about ten minutes. It was as if a magic spell had been cast and I couldn't stop tracing his lips with mine.

An older woman in her mid-thirties scrutinized our behavior and shook her head in utter disgust. I could hear judgments flying through the air like plates at an ancient Greek wedding, "I can't believe you are kissing like that!"

Like what? She must have been jaded, or perhaps, she never experienced young love. Maybe she missed out on the romance department. I'm not sure but she seemed quite bitter.

I stepped on all the imaginary broken dishware she had scattered on the wet pavement and shouted, "Opa!" My energetic partner grabbed my hand and said, "We need to catch up with everyone. Let's go!"

Leaving my Mediterranean celebration behind, we managed to catch up to our circle of friends. We went on our first ride, 'Bermuda Triangle'. This had three twisting, disorienting, downward tunnels that made you feel like you got lost on the radar, just like Amelia Earhart, hence the name. When we made it out, I dog paddled (because I cannot swim) over to Drake and splashed him. He splashed me back and I pulled him in for another kiss. As the waterfall stripped away his cologne, he was left with a natural scent that reminded me of eighth grade. I inhaled the memory of this intoxicating aroma. It was very intense. I hugged him feeling the wetness on his cheek against mine. He got out first, reached for my hand and pulled me up out of the water.

The next ride that everyone wanted to slide down was 'Drop Out'. "Are you kidding me?" I shouted.

We soon arrived at the long line of teens. I explained to everyone that I'll wait in line with them but then I'll escape through the chicken's exit. I glanced over at the sign with the pregnancy warning.

If anyone tries to force me on this ride, I'll just yell that I'm pregnant!

We all stood patiently, moving like cattle up a very high platform. I wasn't nervous at all because I had no intention of participating in such a ridiculous idea of fun. I had no desire to have a heart attack. At the last minute, Tami burst out, "Just do it and stop being a baby!"

"I have acrophobia!" I exclaimed with utter determination.

Drake looked at me and said, "Come on, Jeneen, you can do this and I'll be right behind you."

He gave me another sweet kiss and my knees almost buckled. "I'm in!" I said matter-of-factly.

I put myself in position by folding my arms in front of my chest as instructed. Staff running the attraction also forewarned me that my bikini bottom could fly off. "Okay... *now* I'm not going on," I squawked.

I almost started to go back to the chicken escape route but it was too late. The staff running the ride gave me a gentle push and down I fell, seven stories. What a rush! My bikini bottom was so far up my butt that it couldn't possibly fly off and get lost. It just hurt like hell.

Drake met me at the bottom. I paddled to get out of harm's way as others were coming down behind me. I soon felt his toned arms around my torso and he lifted me out of the water and up to his face. We were at eye level. Wow! His sky-blue eyes were so vibrant in the light. I took note of the little splashes of gold that looked like highlights in a watercolor portrait. He looked astonished, especially since I had made such a ruckus about dropping down that colossal waterfall. His face was wet and cold but the kisses were still wonderful. Somehow, I didn't seem to mind the drops of chlorine-flavored water on his lustrous lips. It was different.

PIECE FIFTEEN

C:\Jeneen\Heaven\Drake\MyCloudofTrust.doc

I WAS LOOKING forward to the back-to-school get together held at my classmate Penny Wilkenson's house. The freckles sprinkled over her arms and face complemented her bouncy platinum-blonde curls, deep sea-blue eyes and outgoing charm. She was our cheerleading team's voice and led the college prep class with enthusiasm. The well-rounded honor roll student's family home was a Conejo Valley castle with enough square footage for a dance floor. Justin, our DJ, (who looked like a cross between Tony Dow and Matthew Broderick) had his own huge collection of cassette tapes and records on his turntable. His speaker setup took over a large portion of the living room but we still had plenty of space for swaying to his hip selection of eighties beats.

This social event was an unexpected and pleasant surprise! It was an informal party for everyone at Cornerstone Christian School, located in the heart of Camarillo. It was a great and uplifting way to start off the school year. I really appreciated the special friendships I made at my private school. It was more similar to a church family. It was a time where I was really well-respected in school and extremely extroverted. My flamboyant personality caught the staff's interest; it also caught the attention of other students. Disappointingly, one girl in my Spanish class gave me the cold shoulder. In fact, she was obnoxiously rude to me for weeks whenever I would attempt to engage in conversation. Miraculously, the girl with the dark-brown curly hair finally warmed up to me. I finally broke through Molly Stifer's protective shell with my sense of humor. Soon, we became best buddies, speaking together in our newfound language — Spanish. Our teacher, Mrs. Sede, had two children of her own attending the school. She took us to an authentic Mexican restaurant on Olvera Street so we could practice our language skills. We walked through the different souvenir shops and kiosks. Mementos ranged from Mexican jumping beans to the Day of the Dead collectibles. The Avila Adobe museum, built in 1818, was the crux of historical Los Angeles. We exited into a marketplace filled with leather purses and assorted tchotchkes. This well-preserved landmark truly represented Los Angeles' Mexican heritage.

My popularity in school was at an all-time high. Our Junior Class only consisted of twenty-two students. I was well-respected by my classmates and faculty and I had a reputation for being studious and having a wide range of interests. I found it very unpleasant to be limited in my subjects and liked to challenge myself in order to expand my horizons.

As soon as I arrived home from school, I ran to the phone in my parents' bedroom and started dialing my favorite number, twisting the cord and fidgeting.

"Hello?" Mrs. McCallister said in a pleasant, harmonic tone. "Oh, hi Anna! May I please speak with Drake?"

"Okay, let me get him. Hold on just a minute," she replied, her Southern charm always present.

I held on for a couple minutes and stared out into our yard from the window. The view of tomato plants, lemon trees and parsley in pots reminded me, for the umpteenth time, of pasta dinners.

"Hello there, Jeneen!" he responded with that FM radio baritone voice you had to fall in love with.

"I'm wondering if you would like to accompany me to a back-to-school dance this Saturday?" I asked in my most upbeat voice, hoping for a quick response.

"Sure... What time should I pick you up?" he asked. "6 pm!"

"Okay... will do! How is school going for you?" he asked, genuinely interested.

"Great... I have a lot of homework and I'm studying until midnight most of the time but it's worth it. I love my English Literature, Algebra II and Spanish classes! How about you?" I exclaimed.

"I can't complain. Psychology is really interesting," he replied.

"That's great about psychology. I'm glad you like it. I wish I had that as an option. Well, I need to hit the books. I have three tests on Friday. See you at youth group on Wednesday?" I asked looking for reassurance.

"Yes, definitely."

D r a k e! I danced in my mind like a ballerina on stage. That is what I like about him.

When he said he was going to do something, he committed. His loyalty was a solid rock of stability.

"I love you," he said, making my heart melt like the last icicle of winter.

"I love you too!" I said, almost putting our conversation to an end. We had been on the phone for over an hour at this point.

"Okay Drake, you can hang up first because I don't want to!" I said, giggling like the lovestruck schoolgirl I was.

"Well, neither do I." he wined like a lovesick puppy, making it more difficult.

"Well, somebody has to take the initiative. You go first!" I said, making my move.

"No, you," he said, horsing around.

We kept this up for at least ten minutes until I finally gave up.

I suddenly heard the sound of *Fresh Prince* in the living room and my brother in hysterics at almost every scene.

I wish I could watch that and 'Family Ties' every night but I am sacrificing TV in order to focus on my studies. Studying was twice as difficult for me than the average pupil because of my situation at home. Being in a constant state of agitation made concentrating and remembering very difficult, but the obstacles didn't matter; I was determined to reach my goal of attending college.

It was finally Saturday and Drake was knocking on my cottage-style door. I circled around the dining room table collecting dirty plates to hand to my mother in the kitchen. I scurried to the front door, almost dropping my mother's inexpensive, flowered American Icon dishware. Remarkably, I managed to place them safely on the rustic countertop.

"Hi, Drake. I missed you so much!" I said cheerfully as he lifted me up and spun me around.

"Hi, Mrs. Mozzetelli. How are you?" he asked politely.

"Great! What time will you be back?" she inquired, concerned.

"Before curfew," Drake said, without hesitation and with a confident smile of reassurance to boot. Before we knew it, we were passing the Camarillo State Mental Hospital. The beautiful Mission Revival Style architecture and bell tower always caught my attention. The grounds were so inviting and I often wondered if that was part of a plan to lure one inside. Across from the hospital were strawberry fields — the irrigation system dutifully spraying the rows of my favorite fruit. Shortly, we arrived at Penny Wilkenson's home and I introduced him to all of my classmates Justin, Todd, Jamie, Penny, Paula and Brian, just to name a few. He already knew Tami so there was no need for an introduction.

We danced all night to Justin's DJ mix. I took my usual position on his feet so I could lean against him. I placed my head on his chest, nestling comfortably against him.

"Do you want something to drink? How about some punch?" he asked attentively.

"Yes, please," I responded politely.

He brought me back the colorful flavored beverage and asked if he could dance with Jamie. She had brown hair with frosted blonde tips. In the eighties, it looked really sophisticated and daring. Jamie and Penny were the most beautiful and friendly members of our student body and were always coordinating special events like this one.

"She's just standing there, all alone. Do you mind if I dance with her?" he asked, waiting for my consent.

"That's fine, Drake and really nice of you. I'll just mingle with my friends. I love you," I expressed, while kissing him gently on his soft lips.

I trusted Drake wholeheartedly and was confident that he loved me so intensely that I never doubted his loyalty.

This love is forever! was etched in my soul like a tattoo. I was surrounded by a mist of self-assurance, enveloped in a cloud of trust.

PIECE SIXTEEN

C:\Jeneen\Heaven\Drake\HiTops.doc

RAINDROPS PINGED AGAINST the window pane in my bedroom. The powerful smell of garlic and chicken permeated the air of our quaint one-story home. The aromas, I was certain, were clinging to me like a ghastly perfume. Suddenly, I was surprised by a loud knocking at the front door.

Who could that be? It cannot possibly be Drake… or could it? Oh shoot… I smell like I rolled around in my dinner!

To my astonishment, it was indeed my smoldering flame standing on my front porch, completely drenched. His hair was so wet it turned brown, giving him a different appearance. Mother Nature had given him a new look and I had to admit, I liked it.

"What are you doing here? This is such a nice surprise! Come on in and let's get you dry." I sang in a soprano voice as I grabbed a fluffy towel from the linen closet. He grabbed me and held me tight before I could give it to him. The damp moisture on his shirt, mixed with my Sicilian dinner fragrance, didn't slow him down for a second. I felt the towel slip from my grip as it fell to the green carpeting. The rain had left a refreshing scent on his chest and I was worried that he would be put off by the smell of food on me.

I waited for him to crinkle his nose but there was no sign of repulsion. *What a trooper!*

"Here's your towel, Drake!" I sang cheerfully before heading off, following the intense scent of minced garlic cloves. The pungent odor was disperse in the air like an anti-vampire bomb!

My father was making a hearty Italian soup with tiny pastas, tomatoes and chicken — perfect for this weather.

"Is Drake here, Jeneen?" my father asked.

"Yes, Dad. He decided to surprise me. Isn't that nice?" I answered cheerfully.

"Why don't you invite him to dinner? There is a vacant spot over there and you can set him up with a plate and silverware," he offered hospitably.

I smiled and gave Drake a quick brush on his lips with mine. I whirled around and made a beeline towards the kitchen.

Wow! What a rarity! I had better hurry up and set the table.

I stared at the flowery, golden-brown dishware once again as I distributed them on each placemat.

My father had the door open for ventilation because the kitchen had become quite warm. As I continued to set the table, I heard the tranquil sound of the rain beating against the pavement. The natural sounds of the storm could be the music for a spa. The relentless shower sprayed all of my mother's plants out in the front yard. Her spider plants, various cacti and geraniums were being well-nourished. Occasionally, we caught a glimpse of a flash of lightning adorning the twilight sky.

The bursts of flavor in the soup, the storm outside and the fire keeping us warm as we inhaled miniature Acini di Pepe, made us all crave seconds.

I beamed at Drake and he instantly returned the gesture. He stroked my hand and soon interlaced his fingers.

"Listen… I'm in a play at St. Julie's Church. It's going to be a stage version of the movie *Hi-Tops*. Do you want to come on Saturday?" Drake asked nonchalantly.

"Really? How did you possible fit a play in your schedule while maintaining straight A's and juggling a hectic social life? After all, I take up most of your time." I asked, wondering if he was some sort of superhuman.

He grinned at me and asked, "Would you mind if my mother picked you up before the performance? I have to get ready at the church beforehand. You know… rehearsals and such."

"Of course not, that would be wonderful!" I cheered, thinking it would be great to spend quality time with his mom, Anna.

The reassurance Drake gave me regarding how much his parents loved me really increased my self-worth. I always felt comfortable around his family. He would openly discuss their positive feelings about me when we were alone. His credibility and honesty had me convinced of their affections. If it weren't for his assurances, I would have been very anxious around them… but then I would be nervous in any family situation.

Drake squeezed my hand and changed the topic.

"What do you think of these tight black pants for the play?" he asked, seeking my opinion. Happy that he respected my fashion sense, I replied "They look fabulous!"

"I'm sorry but I have to leave shortly. I wanted to give you this and tell you about *Hi-Tops!*"

He slipped me a love note that was folded in tiny squares. It made the Rubik's Cube look like *child's play*. He kissed me on my forehead and playfully dragged me by the hand to the front stoop. I closed the front door behind us. He squatted at first, leaned his back against the stucco and then stretched out his legs. I joined him, pulling my knees towards my chest, wrapping my arms around them. The roof structure protected us from the downpour and in seconds, we were embracing each other for warmth. We kissed as if it were our first and last encounter. I wanted to freeze time because I didn't want this moment to end. I played with his hair and caressed him softly.

He was my emotional protector, my confidence builder and personal analytical genius, all wrapped into one. I wanted to nurture him too and protect him like an eagle coddling its young. Like the Rubik's Cube, we had many facets to our love. It was so complex but great relationships are worth the time invested.

As if hypnotized, I drifted for a moment when I heard the sound of a bicycle bell.

Who could be riding in this rain?

I continued in my dreamlike state noticing nimbostratus clouds floating across the mountainous terrain. It was my personal window to the universe. *Five, four, three, two, one — snap!*

I am instantly brought back to my younger years. I was only thirteen and Drake was fourteen during the period we shared the entire summer. I remembered us, side-by-side, as we rode our bikes to his house. As we passed the beautiful cookie-cutter houses in Newbury Park, I could see the curb appeal that excited the real estate agents. There were palm trees, geraniums, lantanas, daisies, roses and lilies filling the landscape. Like watching a video tape, I played back the images of myself propping my bike up with the kickstand. I walked towards my former *army captain.* Fortunately, his comrade Kirk was MIA. We stood with our fingers intertwined on the corner of Happy Trail Circle as we made our attempt to say our farewells. He took the initiative, bending forward and closing his eyes. I couldn't help catching the light sprinkle of freckles around his nose.

He said, "You have to close your eyes because that's what they do on the soap operas. Do you close your eyes?"

"Almost all the time," I replied.

The kiss was long and tender. For a first-time kisser, he sure knew what he was doing! Although inexperienced myself, I knew that no one could ever compete with him. I just knew it. I couldn't believe that I let him go before ninth grade. I wanted to experience other paths but it was evident that the right one was in front of me from the beginning. Perhaps I needed those other experiences so I could truly appreciate what Drake had to offer.

I blinked my eyes and found myself back on the porch, enveloped in Drake's sixteen-year-old arms. He held my hand again and made an about-face, walking towards his Mazda. I sprinted over towards the driver's door. He immediately rolled down the window.

"One more kiss?" I asked, knowing his answer. I touched him lightly on the lips with mine.

"I'll see you at St. Julie's," I whispered in his ear.

His car moved forward in slow motion and I caught him glancing at me in his rearview mirror. I stood in the driveway, waving at him until I could only see his car as a tiny speck, as he accelerated into the cold, wet night. I held my hands open towards the moon as it played peekaboo behind the veils of clouds. The dampness in the air felt like being surrounded by love.

I went straight to my room to finish my paper for my English Literature class, but before I did, I opened the folded love note that Drake handed to me. I collapsed on my waterbed, kicked my legs up, reached over to the boombox behind me and pressed play. The sound of Heart was echoing *I Didn't Want to Need You* in the background. My heart raced as I clung to every word of his love letter:

My Dearest Jeneen,

I'm in American History class, bored to tears because I'm already ahead of the lesson plan. I cannot stop thinking about us and how elated I feel when I'm in your presence. Even if I'm in a funk, you snap me out of it! Your soothing energy and your clever wit is the perfect remedy for any ailment.

Let's catch a movie this weekend! I miss you so much! Love you forever and a day,

Drake

After school the next afternoon, the phone rang and I ran as fast as my legs could move to answer it. Before the answering machine could switch on, I grabbed the receiver attached to a tangled mess of twisted cord.

"Did you miss me?" he asked curiously. It had been twenty-four hours since we had seen each other, after all.

"Of course, Drake," I replied with obvious shortness of breath as I twisted the long cord around my fingers.

I took the phone into my parents' bedroom so I could have some privacy.

"Jen Echman doesn't like my pants! She thinks my legs look too skinny," he gasped disappointedly.

"What? You look good in them to me and that's all that should matter! You look amazing and sexy! Don't listen to her! She apparently has no idea what looks good. You'll be fine," I lectured, reassuring him of the truth.

"Do you think I should wear them?" he asked, waiting for my stamp of approval. "Hell yeah… wear them! You look hot," I stated with confidence.

"I can't wait to see you tomorrow in your play. Are you nervous?" I asked. "No," he responded calmly.

"Thanks for surprising me the other night. You are the best boyfriend I have ever had! I'm not sure if anyone else could ever measure up," I stated.

"Yes, I do have a tendency to set the bar high and ruin it for the next guy who comes along," he said facetiously.

"I'm getting ready for Peleke (pronounced Plucky) and Kirk to come over to play some D & D. It's the guys' night on Friday," he said enthusiastically. I remember his mom suggesting at the beginning of our relationship to have some time apart because we were insep-arable. She wanted us to have a healthy and balanced relationship.

"What are you doing tonight?" he asked.

"I might end up having Tami come over for the evening to watch movies," I said excitedly.

Before I knew it, we had been talking for two hours. My left ear and neck muscles were sore and in dire need of a massage. It was most definitely worth suffering any kinks. I'm uncertain how the time passed so quickly... but it did!

"I love you!" he said.

"I love you too," I said before I hung up.

I am so fortunate to have someone like Drake. It is a mystical connection found only in the stars. The power of his love overflows my essence and fills me with confidence.

I had so much fun on my girls' night with Tami. We watched romance movies until 11 pm. *Pretty in Pink* and *Sixteen Candles* were the double-feature. I daydreamed about Drake. I couldn't wait to see him take his first steps towards stardom.

I only slept until 10 am the next morning. Although it was a Saturday, I bolted out of bed on the first alarm ring. I chose my wardrobe carefully for the day because that is what I would wear for the evening. I selected a white blouse (loose fitting) with a long blue skirt and white pumps with a worn-down heel. I decided to defer the process of making myself look glamorous for the evening since I had until 5 pm. I decided to finish up any loose ends from schoolwork. I had some verses to memorize for Bible study and formulas for Algebra II class.

Right on schedule, Mrs. McCallister was waiting out front, ready to take me to the church.

"Jeneen, Drake's mother is here. Are you ready to go?" my mother screamed, loud enough for the next-door neighbors to get a play-by-play of our lives.

"Hi Anna. How are you?" I gave her a hug.

"I'm doing well. How about yourself?" she responded in her upbeat southern fashion.

"I'm fabulous and looking forward to discovering one of Drake's many hidden talents!" I bubbled, sounding like a cheerleader.

We arrived at the church and walked to the recreation room. There were seats everywhere on what also served as a dance floor for its youth.

Reenie, Drake's sister, came up to her mom and hugged her tight. The strawberry blonde *tween* had skin of porcelain, rosy cheeks and a sprinkle of freckles like nutmeg.

Anna asked, "Where is Drake?"

"He's putting his costume and make-up on. I have to go, Mom!" Reenie replied, trying to keep her composure before going onstage.

"I didn't realize that Reenie was in this musical as well. What a nice surprise!" I said to Anna.

All of a sudden, the boisterous chatter came to a sudden halt. The lights in the auditorium went out abruptly. Darkness took its place demanding everyone's attention as the play began... Applause, whistles and cheers were the only sounds in this performing arts hall.

The spotlight focused on the sign that was placed on the center platform that read, *Hi-Tops*. In a blink of an eye, there was a group of teenagers scurrying back and forth across the stage. The familiar faces of Jen Ruperson and Jen Echman flash in front of me and although I had nothing but fond memories of Jen, I thought of her comment regarding Drake's skintight pants.

Oh well... I guess she is a direct person without a filter or a sense of style.

The next couple of scenes were solos including *The Fight Song* sung by Paul Marciano, one of the youth group leaders. His delivery was filled with energy.

There was another blackout and then lights flickered on again. Three angels appeared out of thin air — Grace, Lilly and Finnly. Grace dressed in a purple robe, Lilly in pink and Finnly (who was actually Drake!) in blue. The girls looked like Hershey Kisses and Drake looked like he was wearing a nightgown. I was laughing so loudly that I covered my face to hide the tears sliding down my cheeks as I bent over. I was shaking uncontrollably, trying to keep myself from snorting. Anna was in about the same state as I was. I couldn't bear to look over at her, fearing a complete meltdown. My wild reaction would altogether be a disturbance to the actors, especially when the audience fell silent. Plus, I wanted to enjoy the sets to come.

The next thing I knew, Gabriel was transforming each angel into a stereotype.

Lilly from the Valley, Grace a nerd and Drake became the punk rocker, Twinn Finn. We were all in hysterics, the comedy continuing into the next transition. This was the introduction to the song *Fads*. Teenagers, dressed in the latest eighties fashions, moved across the stage as if they were in some sort of fashion expo. Drake accidentally slipped but he immediately picked himself up — one could hardly notice. I caught it because I was focused primarily on him. It was the prelude to what the musical was really about — peer pressure.

Twinn Finn's character was played like Bobcat Goldthwait's in *Police Academy*. His jittery behavior was that of someone who had consumed a dangerous amount of coffee. Soon, he didn't need to say his lines before we all started laughing.

He had a lead role and I whispered to Anna, "When did Drake have time to memorize all of this?"

She smiled and said, "I don't know and I was thinking the same thing!"

Before we knew it, the play had ended. I sprang up quickly to find Drake. I was searching all over the recreation room and ran into Samantha. While expressing what a fantastic job she did, Drake tapped me on the shoulder. I turned around and hugged him.

"I cannot believe the incredibly outstanding performance you gave. You had such a big part. I was in stitches! How did you have time to balance schoolwork, a social life with me and this?" I asked once again, still in amazement.

He grinned and asked, "Did you like it?"

"Of course I did. You never cease to amaze me. Let's go celebrate after we've mingled with everyone for a while." He winked in my direction and I suddenly had luminous, colorful wings. Not more than a millisecond had passed, and I became the social butterfly.

PIECE SEVENTEEN

C:\Jeneen\Heaven\Drake\Homecoming1987.doc

HOMECOMING... A TIME for celebration of football season, the beginning of the school year and a chance to strut your stuff on the dance floor! It's also another excuse to have enchanted moonlit strolls on a sandy coast. Although never a fan of football, I love how creative the commercials that are associated with it are. I have never witnessed my brother, father or mother watch a single game by choice but it was on television at my Grandpa Raymond's home. It was unavoidable when we visited as he enjoyed watching it over the holidays. We could hear the crowd noises coming from an old television set, the *rabbit ears* antenna barely controlling the static. This pastime remained a noisy disturbance in the background for decades. Art and creative activities were my family's main focus.

"Jeneen, would you do me the honor of accompanying me to Newbury Park High's Homecoming?" Drake asked with anticipation.

"Yes, I would love to!" I screamed with excitement. Of course, I accepted his offer!

As I stepped out of the Mazda, Drake came around to escort me to the front door. I held him in my arms noticing the greenery on the porch. One could not help noticing the violets and daylilies surrounding us. Spider plants hung in baskets, water dripping from the bottom.

"So I'll see you this Saturday night? I'll pick you up at 5 pm, okay?" he said softly in my ear.

"I can hardly wait!" I said with exhilaration.

I kissed him softly, sweeping my lips against his. He smiled and spun me around like we were country dancing. The move caught me off guard and I fought to keep my balance on the concrete. His blue-gray eyes danced around under the porch light. Moths swarmed around us, drawn to the light bulb. The unexpected coyote howls across the street were no longer a threat. This time, I had Drake by my side. The wild creatures were now just part of the background. We squatted and then took our usual seats on the cold concrete. We held hands and cuddled for hours while we talked, gazing at someone on horseback across the street. The white fence glowed in what remained of the evening's light. My mother abruptly opened the door. The sounds of squeaky hinges announcing her sudden presence startled us.

"I thought I heard someone out here!" she said, proud of her discovery.

"Do you two want to watch a movie with me in the living room?" my mother asked.

"Sure, what are you watching?" "Full Metal Jacket!"

"Yes, let's watch it!" Drake and I said in unison.

We made our way to the couch and huddled under a warm crocheted blanket.

My mother sat on the opposite couch. We watched intense scenes of Sergeant Hartman (R. Lee Ermey) tormenting soldiers in basic training. I wasn't sure what was more horrifying to witness — the degradation or the war in Vietnam. I was relieved and thanking my lucky stars that I never would have to endure such brutality in a bootcamp. I would never volunteer myself because of the persuasive slogan "Be All That You Can Be!" I can *be all that I can be* doing something entirely different, however, God bless anyone protecting our country while fighting overseas.

We watched the movie and then it was midnight and Drake had to leave. I walked him to his car, my hands and arms around his waist. He pressed his lips against my cheek, wishing me a good night.

"I had a wonderful evening," he said with a pleasant expression on his face.

"Me too," I said feeling half excited and half exhausted.

The next day, I couldn't wait to call Tami and tell her about homecoming at Newbury Park High.

"Tami, will you help me find a dress? I saved up some money from working as a receptionist at Mary Health of the Sick nursing home. I want to look for a stunning cocktail dress at the Thousand Oaks Mall. Can your mom drive us over?" I asked with eagerness.

"I'm almost positive I can go but I need to ask my mom first," she said, matter-of-factly.

She placed me on hold and came back in less than five minutes and said, "Yes, I'll meet you at your house in an hour."

Tami and her mom drove up and parked at the curb near the mailbox. I could tell this was going to be an adventurous day. I could hardly wait to find something exquisite for the big night.

On the drive there, my window was rolled down and I could feel the cool breeze against my cheeks. I felt alive as I slowly inhaled the smells of the ocean air mixed with the scent of gardenias and marigolds. We pulled up to a space near the Robinsons-May's entrance. As we made our way past the Estée Lauder cosmetic section, women in white coats showered us with samples of perfume. Sprays of expensive scents entered my nostrils as I got whiff after whiff of the sweet floral essences. My stomach started growling as we swished by the Chanel counter. Price-wise, it was all out of our league so there was no chance we could stop and buy anything. As we raced our way down the cosmetic runway, I hoped that owning the products of these exclusive designers would become manifest in my future.

We decided to do lunch at an exclusive restaurant that only offered healthy choices. It was the number one affordable dining-out

experience for teens. There it stood, one hundred feet ahead of us…
the big M… McDonald's.

We skipped all the way to Windsor Fashions, working off our
economical meal. I could smell the newness of the clothing and appreciated that these items were not hand-me-downs or from a container
placed out by a curb. Today I will select something that fits properly
and is solely my possession without fleas or wilted lettuce ever having
touched its fabric. I walked towards the back of the store, trying to
find the clearance rack. I lifted up a silky, royal-blue sequined dress
that was sandwiched between two frilly dresses and asked the store
clerk where the dressing room was located. She pointed to the middle
of the store on the right hand side. I asked Tami to help me with the
zipper in the back and the sash in the front of the dress.

"What do you think of this dress, Tami? Do you think Drake will
like it?" I shouted with glee. I twirled around while the bottom material danced in the air as I examined myself in the mirror. I liked the
way it clung to my upper frame and then flared out at the waistline.

"Yes, you should get it! Do you want to try on more dresses?"
she asked before I made a hasty decision.

"No, this is the one. I know what I want and this is definitely
the perfect fit." "How much is it, Tami?" I asked with anticipation.

"It's only forty dollars," she said with enthusiasm as she looked
at the tag. "Splendid!" I said, sealing my decision.

That night, I couldn't sleep. All I could think of was the homecoming dance. I knew it was going to be spectacular and I couldn't
wait to see my friends from my former school, Newbury Park High. I
finally shut down as I imagined Drake wrapping his arms around me
and feeling his warmth. The kiss on my forehead was like a sleeping
pill without the unwanted side effects.

The light seeped through the bent blinds in my room, taking the
place of my alarm clock. I got moving right away because I had a lot
to do before tonight's festivities. Taking care of tasks throughout the
day made the time fly and before I knew it, it was late afternoon.

The doorbell rang and Drake decided to let himself in because everyone was too preoccupied to answer it. My parents greeted my handsome prince in the front hall. They snapped a picture of the sixteen-year-old boy in the rented penguin suit. I heard the camera clicking while I stood in front of the mirror in the bathroom. The camera was an extremely loud Polaroid. I could hear the picture being processed and dispensed into my parents' fingers. I could imagine the wavering blank canvas being painted in minutes by the vigorous chemical reactions.

"Jeneen, Drake is here. You better hurry," my mother shouted, charged up about taking pictures for her scrapbook.

I finished my make-up by applying dusty rose lipstick followed by gloss.

I ran into the living room where Drake was waiting with a corsage. The floral creation was filled with white roses, silver ribbon and glitter accents. I could see the trail of sparkle following us. His boutonniere matched my corsage. I glanced at his jawline and then his haircut style, spiked with a light gel — just the way I liked it. *Wow, he really looks good in tails!*

My father was so eager to take our pictures. The former photographer snapped pictures utilizing our green curtains as the backdrop. He positioned us in various poses, capturing a few candid shots. It was my father's time to display his talents which had been squelched by self-deception and the need to provide for his family.

I was laughing at Drake while I tickled him during a serious take. I raised my arm with the corsage hanging on my wrist. The clicking sounds of the camera echoed in our living room. Flash, click, flash, click, flash, click.

After the photo shoot was over, Drake glanced at his Timex.

"We better get going. We don't want to be late for our school dance. After you... m'lady," he said as he held out his right hand. He then intertwined his arm around mine and escorted me to his silver chariot.

"Have a great time!" my parents shouted as they waved goodbye.

He placed the key in the ignition and I heard Heart playing the song, *What About Love?*

"Did I tell you how beautiful you look tonight? Wow, that dress is amazing!" he said as he placed his hand on my knee. He leaned over and gave me a kiss that would have knocked me down if I had been standing. It was a good thing I was sitting in the passenger seat.

We arrived at the school and made our way to the gymnasium. I interacted with classmates I had not seen in some time. I reunited with Jen Echman, Suzie Q, Andrew Buckingham, Mike Ginseng and Todd Bakersfield. I hadn't seen them in a year. It was a nice reunion before we made our way to the dancehall. We waved to Samantha and Mike.

Once inside, there was scarcely any conversation because the music was so incredibly loud. The sound of Salt-N-Pepa's *Push It* was our introduction to an energetic night. I grabbed Drake's hand and led him as fast as I could to the dance floor. I loved dancing and we rocked to many fast, upbeat songs. The Beastie Boys' *Brass Monkey* drove me wild. During the ballads, I employed my normal technique of placing my feet on Prince Charming's patent leather shoes. I looked up and could see helium balloons heading for the ceiling as well as the unique archway around the basketball court. I heard the sound of the piano version of Chris de Burgh's *Lady in Red*, our last song for the night. We must have had a workout because we were both perspiring. Drake grabbed us a couple waters to stay hydrated. We must have danced to every song.

"It's time to go. Are you ready for the rest of our evening?" he said, a hidden surprise written on his expression.

"Where are you taking me?" I asked in a giddy fashion. "You'll see," he said, reading my body language.

We made our way to the car. Drake put the key in the ignition and Heart's *Magic Man* began to play. He took off his black jacket revealing his white pressed dress shirt and midnight blue cummerbund. He proceeded to put the car in drive. We drove down Reino Road heading for Potrero Road, passed by my house and headed for the shoreline. As usual, he parked on the right hand shoulder of PCH and walked around to the passenger door to help me out. It was a bit frigid and we could feel the chilly ocean breeze through our formal attire but that did not discourage us. My boy scout draped his coat over me. We made our way on the path that led to the stairs and climbed down, heading for the beach. I could feel the sand sliding under my silver pumps. I held on to the rail so I wouldn't slip and fall. When I got to the bottom of the stairs, I kicked off my shoes. Drake lifted me and carried me to the spot he had chosen for us. The seashore was lit by a beautiful moon. I fell into a trance as I watched the water curl against the shore. It was a sight to behold on this treasured evening. The whitecaps and the waves created a mesmerizing picture. Drake placed me on the sand and we intertwined in a passionate kiss that felt eternal. We talked for some time, hypnotized by the moon and the water. I could hear the ocean crashing as we held each other. The hair on Drake's arm stood on end as the gentle wind graced us with its presence. This night could not have been any more magical.

PIECE EIGHTEEN

C:\Jeneen\Heaven\Love\Drake\Christmas.doc

CHRISTMAS DAY IS a time to rejoice. It is when families and friends gather to inhale the smell of pine in the living room, gingerbread cookies in the oven, and if you are really traditional, chestnuts roasting on an open fire. I could almost see the eggnog displayed in decorative snowflake glasses with extra nutmeg sprinkled on top.

My father would receive homemade holiday breads, pastries, decadent See's Candies and cash from people on his many routes. Although our tree was artificial, I was somehow still able to smell the December festivities. I remained in good spirits because there wasn't anyone putting the *kibosh* on our caloric intake. The smorgasbord of sinfully delicious desserts put us into a frenzy.

The telephone rang, making the universal sound of teen romance. I picked up the receiver and heard Drake's calming voice on the other end. He was more beautiful and valuable to me than any gemstone could ever be.

"What are you doing?" he asked, his words caressing my ear.

"I'm going on a date with you," I said, confident of the end result. "Well then... how about I take you on a drive?"

I hung up the phone and headed for my bathroom. I sprayed some Primo perfume on my neck and wrists. The musky baby powder mist clung to my skin like Aqua Net to my hair. I thought I smelled sexy and that was enough to make me certain Drake would as well. The label on the bottle read: "If you like Giorgio, you'll love Primo!" Drake gave me this on my sweet sixteen birthday bash.

About thirty minutes later, I heard him tapping on my window. I intentionally left the window ajar because I wanted to serenade him. I was singing Madonna's *La Isla Bonita* and wanted him to know the song was intended for him. He nearly scared me half to death because I was lost in the song and my daydreams. I ran to the door and, gripping his hand, dragged him back to my room. A poster of Michael Jackson hung on one wall and a picture of Madonna on the other. The waterbed took up most of the space in my room but I didn't mind. The luxurious bed was a gift from Samantha's parents in my Freshman Year.

The memories of meeting her at lunchtime at Sequoia Junior High were as clear as day. We would ride our ten speed bikes to school together every day and I practically lived at her house in the eighth and ninth grades. The endless borrowing of her Archie comic book collection and the making of countless homemade dance videos patiently filmed by her dad, were enough to keep us occupied. I knew she would someday make her way to Hollywood as a director or a dance coordinator. She was just as motivated and ambitious as I.

I closed the door for some privacy and started kissing Drake on the neck and then I whispered, "Merry Christmas." We didn't need any mistletoe to remind us to activate our lips. I shoved his present into my blue, denim purse as I nibbled on his bottom lip to distract him. I didn't want him to see me hiding his present.

"Mom and Dad, Drake and I are going to take a drive to the beach!" I shouted to let them know where we were going.

"Have a good time!" they said. They were in the kitchen preparing for a dinner party. I looked forward to Nita attending our soirée tonight because we always played the dominoes game, Mexican Train. It was our little tradition.

As we headed for the blue waters, I couldn't wait to give him his gift.

We parked in an area that overlooked the coastline. The warm sun was glistening over the horizon. Its light danced on the water.

I gave him the carefully wrapped box with snowman paper and curls of decorative red and green ribbon. He tore open the folds to unveil a gold chain and a charm that read, 'Best Friend'. I showed him that it was actually two charms; one was for him and the other one was for me. I knew we were connected and I wanted a symbol of our eternal love and friendship.

I peeked by his side to find a small cubed container. Drake handed it over and I placed it in my lap. Before I was able to open the tiny treasure, he gave me another. He leaned over to kiss me. It was especially romantic because with the car window opened a little, I could hear the sound of the crashing waves. I was expressing my hunger for his love in every brush against his lips. I think we made it into some sort of art form. I can honestly say from my experiences that you could not put a price tag on those kisses.

"Why don't you open your gift," he said, curious to see my reaction.

The sound of his voice was soft, gentle and passionate. The melody caressed my soul and the butterflies in me fluttered with every note. The little box was wrapped with care. I opened the paper exposing a milky white box. Inside was a gold chain with six tiny gold balls in a double layer. The chain was petite and definitely my style. I wouldn't have cared if it had been something from a gumball machine at a five and dime store. The price meant nothing to me because he selected it. I knew his heart and that made this token priceless.

"Come here. Let me put it on you," he said lovingly.

I felt this symbol of his love drape around my neck and it surrounded me with an emotional fervency. It was a symbol of our genuine affection for each other.

I vowed never to take it off.

PIECE NINETEEN

C:\Jeneen\Heaven\Drake\MovieNight.doc

THE TELEPHONE SIGNALED *love alert* throughout our cottage-like home. I sprinted to my goal, grabbed the receiver and stretched the cord into the living room. As I untwisted several knots, I found a corner of the room that offered some privacy. Trying to take cover was useless. As long as I was connected to a cord, there could be no real privacy.

"Hi Drake… How was school today?" I asked inquisitively.

"Psychology was interesting. We learned about Pavlov's Theory," he replied.

"So tell me about this scientific theory?" I asked intrigued.

"Let's say every time I kiss you I ring a bell. I do this several times. After a while, when you hear 'ring-a-ling-a-ling', you salivate. Your involuntary response is to hunger for my sensual lips," he expressed, wanting to test this theory.

"When can we practice this?" I responded, only half joking.

I was not opposed to volunteering to be his guinea pig for the week. Contributing to an educational experiment, especially this one, was worth my time. My dedication to science was no surprise to him.

"What would you like to do tonight?" he asked, without hesitation. I twirled the cord with my fingers, fidgeting.

"How about a scary movie and junk food?" I replied, faster than a speeding bullet.

"Sounds like a plan. I'll be over in fifteen minutes," he said decisively.

"I love you Drake," I said and felt the familiar butterflies.

"I love you too, Jeneen," he whispered softly through the phone line.

I scrambled, searching for something fashionable to wear. We were only heading for his couch and a home movie but I wanted everything to be special. I meticulously singled out my white beaded dress. I scurried to the bathroom and misted myself with an intoxicating, musky aroma. Involuntarily, I choked and accepted the sacrifice of my respiratory system for *Mi Corazón*. I slowly braided my hair in the front and applied pink lipstick, creating the perfect pout. The talisman of love was draped around my pale neckline. I touched it feeling its mystical properties.

The doorbell rang, and moments later, my brother knocked on the bathroom door.

"Drake is here!" he sang.

I had heard the bell, the sound of the chime making me so jittery that I dropped everything. My eyeshadow case, hair brush and lipgloss fell to the floor. I ignored the mess. Was I salivating? I ran down the hall and jumped into his arms. I kissed him soft and long, not wanting to stop. There was so much feeling with those kisses that each brush of his lips indicated the burning passion he had for me.

You can always tell how someone feels about you by the way they kiss you.

Drake noticed the gold necklace. He realized that I wore it every time he saw me including the occasional surprise visits, especially when he tapped on my window in the middle of the night.

"Do you always wear the necklace I gave you?" he asked, astonished.

With a smile, I replied that I never wanted to take it off. He mimicked my facial expression and I watched his eyes sparkle and dance. "Maybe we should get going or we'll be late for our own home movie. We need to stop at the store to pick up our goodies. What do you want?" he asked.

"Chips Ahoy chocolate chip cookies," I replied.

"I don't have much of a sweet tooth. I like salty junk food," Drake informed me. We compromised and bought both.

On the drive to Albertsons, Drake listened to heavy metal music and then switched to pop for the next song. We alternated genres by switching stations or tapes. I considered my tastes in music to be eclectic with the exception of country, rap, punk and hardcore headbanger stuff. It worked for us. The heavy metal ruckus was deafening though. I pressed my lips against his arm thinking I could distract him and change the station to something I liked but I managed to tough it out.

He opened the door to his house. The smells of the south greeted us as we entered the foyer. We whisked by the upright piano located on the right. As we passed the kitchen, the aromas of Reenie's baking grew stronger, permeating the air. He led me into the family room and reached for a blanket because he knew I was always cold.

He said, "You're like a little old lady." I laughed at his dry humor.

The spread of junk food in the middle of the carpet looked dangerous. I momentarily heard the irritating voice of my mother as she lectured us about sugar and the reasons why we shouldn't have it. I remembered a time when, searching for a notepad in my parents' bedroom to scribble down a phone number, I stumbled onto a Snickers bar inside the top drawer of my mother's nightstand. That took care of the guilt and I snuggled up next to Drake without any remorse. We started to eat our sinful delights and Drake fixed his blue eyes on me.

"What?" I asked curiously.

"How on Earth do you eat all of that and stay so thin? You must have a bottomless pit or a tapeworm," he said.

Gram, his father, walked in and acknowledged us with his heartfelt smile. He stood tall just like Drake and his demeanor was warm and accepting. He was always in a good mood and the spirit of the family was welcoming. One of his hobbies was operating a ham radio, communicating with people all over the world. The rapid-fire sound of Morse code was especially intriguing to me, as in the eighties, this technology was fascinating.

The introduction to *Children of the Corn* started and fear popped into my RAM in the blink of an eye, threatening to overwhelm my CPU.

"Would you like something to drink?" Anna offered, breaking the tension.

"Yes, I would love some ice water with lemon in it! I replied as I inhaled another chunk of cookie.

The music alone was enough to frighten the daylights out of me. Scared half to death, I clenched onto Drake. We were underneath the blanket, making it our woolen fort. He kissed me sweetly. I peeked out to find my beverage on a newspaper coaster.

"Thank you, Anna." I cheered politely.

Drake stood up to rewind the VHS tape because we had missed much of the beginning.

Drake scolded me, "Watch the movie!"

I gulped down some water, taking a break.

I was not very good at following directions. I ended up getting the upper hand by kissing his neck. I bit softly with my lips, working my way up to his ear. The trail of kisses scrambled his thought processes until he surrendered. Soon I discovered it was my turn to rewind the VHS tape.

PIECE TWENTY

C:\Jeneen\Heaven\Drake\PositiveReinforcements.doc

"JENEEN... TELEPHONE! IT'S Drake," my brother sang in his enthusiastic tone.

My heart skipped a beat as I overflowed with joy. If I glanced at myself in a mirror, I would see myself lit up like a Christmas tree. Regardless of what time of year it was, when Drake called, it was Christmas to me.

"Hello, Drake!" I said in a confident, flirty voice. "Hello, Ms. Jeneen. What are you up to?" Drake asked.

"I'm getting ready for our date. Where would you like to go?" I asked zealously.

"It's your call," Drake insisted.

"Very well... How about a hike to the waterfalls across the street from my house at Sycamore Canyon Park?" I asked, knowing his answer.

"I'll be there in half hour," he said. "Great!" I cheered.

I slapped on my war paint and tied my hair in a ponytail. I carefully placed a barrette on the side to hide any flyaway strands and doused it with hair glue to seal in the style. I knew Drake would like this. He complimented me no matter how I looked. He truly thought I was beautiful inside and out. He always made me feel sexy and intelligent. I was secure in my self-image thanks to his continuous reinforcements. He was my confidence plug-in and I apparently had the upgraded version.

I started to make sandwiches for our picnic. I took several slices out of the iconic Wonder Bread bag and carefully placed them on the cutting board, when suddenly, the doorbell rang. My heart rate instantly shot through the roof.

Somehow, he was able to confiscate more beautiful red and pink roses from his parents' garden. He handed them to me as he wrapped me in an embrace that made me feel... complete. I immediately put the colorful arrangement into a vase and placed them on the dining room table. Soon, paper bags filled with sandwiches, chips, pretzels and drinks sat next to the flowers.

Drake sang, "What is all this? The food really looks great." "Let's go, Drake!" I said eagerly to get our date in motion.

We made our way across the street heading towards the park. Drake offered to carry the backpack filled with water and I gladly let him. It weighed a ton. Since we had all the time in the world, we stopped for a moment to pet the horses at the Moorpark College Equine and Management Program. We then walked up the big hill in front of us and towards the Satwiwa Native American Indian Culture Center.

The door was invitingly open so we walked inside and explored all the artifacts on display. I gave him a playful shove and said, "Let's look at the teepees out back!" As we walked through, I thought about having our picnic in one of them. It would have been adventurous but I did want some privacy with Drake so I allowed that creative idea to slip away.

Next, we took the narrow trail leading to the waterfalls. Eucalyptus trees filled our nostrils with a pungent scent. We stepped over the brown, reddish and orange leaves and the wildflowers that lay on our path ahead. I could see the spectacular view of Old Boney Mountain.

I grabbed a water from the backpack and as we stopped for a drink, Drake finally shared a story about Sally.

"You remember Sally, right?"

I nodded with a smile because I remembered her quite well.

"She was the class clown at Sequoia Junior High, correct?" I asked.

Drake responded, "Yes, that's the one all right. Well, you are never going to believe what she did in class. She grabbed her backpack after our teacher gave her permission to use the restroom. Our teacher then asked, 'Why are you taking your backpack with you?' Sally retorted, 'Where else am I going to put my tampons?' The whole class started laughing."

I giggled for what seemed like an eternity.

I tried to think of anyone comical in my class and the only ones who came to mind were Ed Laughlin and Todd Wilkenson. They created a Vietnam video for history class. Obviously, the war wasn't funny but it was hysterical watching these two guys playing soldier in their backyards. What really cracked us up was watching them crawling around firing toy M16s at the camera. My stomach was sore for a week from laughing so hard.

"Jeneen, what are you thinking about?" Drake asked, concerned.

"I am thinking about… you." Then jumped on his back, expecting him to carry me for at least a while. I was confident he could manage my one hundred and ten pounds.

We walked and talked while we descended into a canyon, entering the Boney Mountain State Wilderness. We crossed over a streambed and the trail ascended as we made a sharp right turn. We then took the narrow trail at the junction on the left. The sound of the waterfall gushing over the rocks grew louder and louder as we reached our destination. It was a beautiful sight. I told him the story about my cousin Franco and me climbing all the way up to the top and how we got stuck for hours.

I explained, "One of the Native Americans who lived at the museum came to rescue us. I truly thought we would be stranded there for days. We were lucky someone found us."

We found a spot near the waterfall and I spread out the blanket. If someone said that there was a lovelier place anywhere on Earth, I wouldn't have believed him. I reached into the backpack to get our food. I hardly had an appetite but I needed to keep my energy up to get myself back to my house. I managed half of a sandwich and some pretzels.

Drake complimented me and said I was the best girlfriend he ever had. I was pretty sure I was the *only* girlfriend he ever had, but it sure felt great that he said it. I reached over and gave him a hug and soon we kissed underneath the shade of eucalyptus and oak trees. I followed the stream of rippling water with the corner of my eye. Drake nibbled on my neck, playfully tickling my skin until it was covered in tiny goosebumps. I giggled, happy beyond belief.

PIECE TWENTY ONE

C:\Jeneen\Heaven\Love\Drake\ThePiano.doc

ONE LATE AFTERNOON, before twilight, Drake and I decided to study at his house.

Exam time was nearing and I needed to prepare.

We made a path to a section on his carpet by scooting aside articles of clothing. I watched camouflage pants fling like a slingshot across the room, landing near his bed.

Wow! Were those from junior high?

I felt like a bird looking for twigs and leaves to add to my nest. In this light, the scattered freckles on his face appeared more pronounced. I stroked his cheek with the side of my hand and caught his eyes as we locked in the moment. I checked my Algebra II homework and everything looked accurate. I slipped it back into my math folder which, in turn, I placed into my yellow Pee-Chee portfolio. I brushed his arm with my lips and kissed his hand.

"Come with me for a second. Let's take a break," Drake said. He stretched, stood straight and then gripped my hand firmly and pulled me up to stand.

He led me past the kitchen and back to the foyer. The upright piano had been there for as long as I've known him. For all I knew, his mother sat there with him when he was still in diapers. I imagined him in an animal print onesie, covered with monkeys and elephants — his tiny fingers stretching for the ebony and ivory keys. There it stood alone and silent until…

Drake slid his body across the bench making room for me. He held his hand out inviting me into his world. I stepped in, excited, knowing I was about to experience something special.

The dramatic introduction awakened my senses. I glanced over at the sheet music. The title was Bach: Cello Suite 1 in G Major, Prelude. As he pressed his fingertips along the once soundless keyboard, the music sprang to life. For a second, I contemplated bringing out my dormant cello.

The air was filled with the passion and beauty of Bach's spirit. It made me feel alive. The melody reflected off the walls and surrounded us. The bewitching power of the music was a metaphor for our love — intense, transcendent and eternal.

Drake possessed talent and his hard work and dedication were evident in his playing. I remembered my fifth-grade music teacher, Mr. Weeks saying, "Sacrifice… You will be good if you sacrifice your time and you practice!"

Drake was wearing a short sleeve shirt which showed off his biceps and triceps, and although on the lanky side, I liked them. I made small kisses all the way down his forearms. It's a good thing I didn't get to his fingers because I didn't want the music to stop. I admired his ability to continue to perform while I distracted him. *Walking while chewing gum was never my strong suit.*

"Je t'aime," he said to me while he was playing. "Te amo," I whispered softly to him.

There is nothing better than hearing it in French. Drake studied French and I studied Spanish. One time I had a dream that I recited numbers one through a thousand in Spanish.

The scene continued to play in my mind like the contents of a time capsule. Sadly, the illusion begins to fade. As it disintegrates, I am horrified to find myself back in my personal hell.

All I see now is white drywall. I am trapped and I cannot escape.

The walls are closing in on me and it becomes hard to breathe. I gasp for air, feeling suffocated, because I have finally come to grips with my reality. I am in *the Get Right Room*. The angry preacher from hell is still shouting at me. His voice is now in the forefront as the monster's never-ending badgering continues. I hear the girls in the school weeping as they accept Jesus as their Savior. My life, as of now, has been stolen.

Punching my fist on the wooden floor only brings excruciating pain. I am left isolated from the world, sitting inside a closet of torment.

PIECE TWENTY TWO

C:\Jeneen\Hell\Victory\HowIGotOutofGR.doc

I DON'T KNOW how much time has passed. I have no contact with the outside world. Finally, the door is cracked open and light beams from Dorm Three. My eyes are sore and bloodshot from crying. I find it difficult to open them fully against the light that has flooded in. The other barracks are like caves. Is this one, with extreme fluorescent lighting, meant to compensate for those shadowy torture chambers? I'm starting to feel like the protagonist of *Lisa, Bright and Dark.*

"Do you think you're ready to come out now?" Ms. Arizona yells in a militant fashion, expecting my answer to be, "Yes, ma'am."

"No!" I say without hesitation.

"Well in that case, since you like it so much in there, you are coming out!" she spews angrily with a smirk on her face.

I hold my hand out and respond in my normal polite manner, in spite of her behavior. "I don't believe we have formally met. My name is Jeneen." I feel it would be in my best interest to make friends with her, especially since this is now my new place of residence.

"Your mother did warn me that you are only nice when you want something," she replies.

Rage bubbles to the top as I imagine the defamation of character my mother must have conjured up. Is that how they accepted me into this reform school... her *word?*

"This is your *Buddy*, Alexandra. You are to stand behind her, no more than three feet, and do whatever she tells you. She will explain all the rules. You will be on *Buddy* for one month. If you cannot follow the rules, you will be on *Buddy* until you get it right," Ms. Arizona explains with authority.

"I don't want any pity parties from you from now on. You are not allowed to shed one tear!" she says in a well-rehearsed manner.

"Do I make myself clear?" she screams wickedly. "Yes," I reply.

"The answer is, 'Yes, ma'am,' and when talking to a male, it is 'Yes, sir.' Are we clear?" she questions with a militant attitude.

"Yes, ma'am," I say mechanically, in hopes she cannot hear my actual thoughts.

Alexandra is only twelve years old and I ponder why she was sent to this prison camp. She has platinum-blonde locks and has the appearance of a normal, average *tween*.

I inquire, "How did you end up in this place? You are so young."

She responds, "I'm a disgrace to my family and I've caused them nothing but pain."

This young girl sounds robotic and I feel like I'm talking to a "Stepford Christian child." Was I next? Would I soon be blaming myself for my family problems?

I follow Alexandra around Victory as if I were a dog on a leash. It is degrading, but then again, I've been placed in a school for the wayward, although I was a top student in my Junior Class. My memory of Tami is triggered. She mentioned the possibility of my being nominated for valedictorian. With a total of twenty students in my soon-to-be Senior Class, that goal was definitely within reach.

"This is where you will sleep. You'll be on the bottom bunk," she orders, opening the drawer located on the bottom.

"Here is your storage for all of your possessions," she voices sternly.

In Dorm Two, the bunks are a dark-brown, stained oak. The presentation is meant to look normal if parents were to visit. The hardcore truth for all the students here, whether they are *Helpers* or not, is that this is a sadistic environment.

"Your socks go here and everything has to be folded. You will get a demerit if it's not right. You have to cut your nails as well. You cannot have any white showing or you'll get a demerit," she adds commandingly.

I proceed to cut my nails with a nail clipper. I don't care about having them anymore; my outward appearance is no longer a concern. As I'm clipping my polished nails, Alexandra informs me of something else.

"Oh… we have to write our parents twice a week."

"We have to write our parents twice a week? You have got to be joking, right?" I gasp.

I just about came unglued. This was the cruelest twist of fate I have ever experienced in my sixteen years of existence.

"You can't talk like this. You need to watch your attitude!" she yells.

They locked me in this hellhole. Now I'm forced to communicate with them through letter writing? You have got to be fucking kidding me!

"What could I possibly write…

Dear Mom & Dad:

What the hell were you thinking placing me in a lockdown reform school? Perhaps you do not possess the ability to think or is logic just one of your missing parental skills.

By the way, why did you accuse me of lying about statutory rape when you lied to get me in here? Actually, you have to be a poor student, criminal, insubordinate to authority and get into a shitload of trouble to be a candidate for a reformatory… or did you miss that memo? You do realize what REFORM SCHOOL means, right? You may want to invest in a Webster's Dictionary.

*To make matters worse, you said I would be receiving ther-
apy. Well, there isn't a staff member here who is a qualified
therapist. By the way, I'll keep writing to you like this until...
you get me the hell out of here. How could you do this to
me? You just tossed me into the trash without any regard.*

*Get me out of here. Get me out of here. Get
me out of here. Get me out of here.*

I have no qualms about writing that every day for a year but
I have a sinking feeling, deep in my gut, that the staff scrutinizes
our mail.

"Alexandra, do they read our letters?" I ask, knowing the answer.
"Yes," she says solemnly.

Unfortunately, that fantasy letter was never going to happen.

"Can we write anyone else?" I ask, fearing her next response.
"No," she answers matter-of-factly.

My heart feels like it's being ripped out by carnivorous animals.
I could feel jaws clamping against my flesh and tearing the meat
from my bones.

I'll never be able to write to Drake and that was my only hope for
survival in this place. He was the only person I could vent everything
to so I could get rid of the poison. I have no freedom to express
how I feel to the boy that I love so much. It is a cruel injustice that
I have to hold any emotion inwardly for fear of being punished as
a consequence. I cannot tell the person I love what I'm feeling or
what I'm going through. There will be no reciprocation. None. My
life as I know it has been ended by Victory.

They prohibit me to express myself in writing at all. Writing in a
journal at Victory is not allowed; they will confiscate it. My voice is
no longer my own. The simple freedoms of my life have been taken.
The first amendment does not exist here.

*Please tell me this is merely a frightening dream, and any minute
now, I will awaken in my room.*

I follow Alexandra and make sure I am three feet behind her. I notice that whenever I speak there is always a repercussion.

"Don't look at the other girls. If you do, you'll be accused of being an *eesh*," Alexandra barks as all girls turn their necks in our direction.

I ask with a tone of confusion, "What the heck is an *eesh*?"

"Girls who like girls. By the way, you cannot say 'heck'," she states, fearing to even say it herself.

We get in line for lunch. All the girls are carefully glancing at me since they are forbidden to stare. I know I remind them of someplace foreign — home. I am fresh from the world outside and everyone wants a taste of their memories.

I keep my head down, avoiding eye contact. I start to feel as though I'm not good enough to hold my head high or look at anyone. I am being trained to separate myself from humanity. I take my role as an outcast in society.

As we walk closer to the food line, Alexandra informs me of something else. "You need to pick which portion you want. Do you want to be a *half* or a *whole*? If you choose *half*, you can't get seconds. If you chose *whole*, you can get seconds, but remember, you have to eat everything on your plate no matter what you decide."

I choose *whole* because the only thing I have to look forward to in this dungeon is the taste of food. My mother wasn't the best cook and we were always on a budget. I thought cafeteria food always looked appealing but never had that luxury because we couldn't afford it. I believe this meal will be yummy.

I follow Alexandra to the dining hall. There are about six tables filled with girls. The staff has its own, separate from ours. I smile at a girl who is not a *Helper* and ask her to pass the pepper.

Alexandra growls, "You cannot speak to any of the girls until you are off *Buddy*. You can only talk to a *Helper*." "Yeah, sure," I say.

"You can't say, 'yeah.' You have to say, 'yes.' You have to say, 'I will say yes' one hundred times. Start saying it now!" she says with authority.

I feel eyes piercing and judging me as if I committed a mortal sin.

I start reciting, "I will say yes, I will say yes, I will say yes, I will say yes," over and over again until I lose count, but Alexandra is counting as well. Thank heavens for that because chanting is a lot of work!

Is there anyone here who thinks this is normal? No one is doing anything to stop this. No one voices how she really feel regarding what is going on here, including myself. Everyone must be on the same neurotic page. Either they feel the same as I do inside and can't do anything about it or they truly feel that I just committed the most heinous crime of the century. Yeah... maybe that's it!

"Okay, girls... let's bow our heads and say a prayer before we eat," QC says sternly.

"Dear Father, please bless this food that we have before us. Thank you, Lord, for Ms. Ethel and the girls who put this food together. Lord, thank you for giving me this opportunity to help these girls who truly need you. In Your name, I pray. Amen," QC recites, his words well-rehearsed.

"Amen!" everyone sings in unison.

Dear God, can you hear me? It's me, Jeneen. Please get me the hell out of here. I want to be back home with Drake, where I belong. I miss him so much. Please God, you have to send someone to come and rescue me. I can't stay here anymore. The joke is over. It's just not funny. I promise, I'll be good. I'll do anything. Please... just get me out. Amen.

"You have to eat everything on your plate and you have to be finished when the time is up. You have twenty minutes at every grub session." Alexandra informs me of another rule.

Although I enjoy eating, I do not like having stipulations because it causes major anxiety regarding meals. If I don't care for something, I will just force myself to consume it. It won't be so bad as long as I don't develop an upset stomach.

I hear a girl crying at another table, "I can't eat anymore."

QC yells, "You will eat everything on your plate, young lady. If you don't comply, we will send you straight to *the Get Right Room* and it will sit for days and weeks until you eat it."

"I feel like I'm going to throw up," the girl screams, gagging.

I do not want to look at the girl for a couple reasons. First, I will be accused of being a lesbian. If the staff and *helpers* treat heterosexuals like garbage, I cannot imagine how bad it would be if I swung in the other direction. Second, I cannot look at her suffering. It makes me so sad and guilty because I can't stop it. I keep my head down.

"If you throw up, young lady, you will eat your own vomit!" QC spews sadistically.

Are you kidding me? This man just said a prayer to the Lord. Now he is threatening to force-feed a child her own puke? Does any of the staff think this is wrong? What is going on here? I thought child abuse is against the law. I thought this is illegal. Why isn't anyone saying anything? It's like another world in here and all of the laws in the United States of America do not apply.

It's a free-for-all. Apparently, all of the staff is fine with this because no one is contradicting QC's behavior and taking a stand. In fact, one staff member is reinforcing it!

Ms. Arizona chimes in, "I think we should make a shake out of her dinner and force-feed her with a funnel. What do you think, Brother QC?"

"I think that's a good idea," he replies.

Before we know it, we hear the poor girl retching and sobbing while they push the food down her throat. The sounds of her choking and her hysterical whimpers fly through the air like bullets from an M16. As the noise pierces my psyche, my internal sensors become aware of damage occurring on my hard drive. Subdirectories containing happy memories are being wiped and a hacker is replacing my *Clouds of Hope* files with swastikas.

Oh my God… I think she just threw up.

I go numb inside with a new nervous tension regarding our scheduled chow time.

It makes me sick that we all have to sit here and watch this torment with our hands tied behind our backs and our mouths gagged. If we try to break out of our metaphoric restraints, it's an absolute certainty that the same treatment will befall upon us. No one is rescuing this poor student.

I know I have to inhale everything on my plate. Apparently, deciding *halves* and *wholes* is a big deal around Victory. It is evident that the staff was making an example out of that helpless teen for the rest of us. It's now embedded into our minds that if we don't follow their rules, we will suffer. It is an unspoken fact.

An hour later, Alexandra leads me to chapel. I follow, keeping the same humiliating animal-in-training distance.

It is QC and he is ready to put on a show. He slams down the Bible.

"I see we have a new girl here. Stand up, Missy. What's your name?" he yells. I stand, shaking, and meekly utter "My name is Jeneen."

"Welcome to Victory Christian Academy. I heard that you came here for therapy. Well, we do have a therapist here if you need one. Julie, could you go and get our therapist for us? Thank you so much," he smirks charismatically.

Julie comes back with a dog that looks like a teddy bear — a Chow Chow. All of the girls start laughing. I turn red from embarrassment. Their eyes are on me like laser beams. I take a deep breath and sigh. QC mimics me by taking a deep breath in and slowly exhaling. He stares me down as if I were a criminal on trial. All of the girls giggle. I imagine it is their only form of entertainment. I am the star of the show this evening and perhaps all the girls need an escape from their putrid lives here.

"In case you are wondering, Jeneen... this is a reform school. You will be reformed here at Victory whether you want to or not and you will come to know the Lord Jesus. Isn't that right, girls?" he says, chuckling like the lead character in a psychological thriller.

"Amen!" the girls respond in a high-pitched, gospel fashion.

But I already know the Lord... I AM a Christian. Doesn't he see that I previously went to a Christian school? Did he not receive my transcripts? I wonder if he knows what my grades were in my Junior Year? Does he know me? I guess my parents forgot to mention that I was a good kid, I ponder silently.

QC has us turn to Luke 3:14 and I am daydreaming about being rescued. A feeling of sadness starts to overwhelm me but DANGER, ALERT flashes in my mind. It's a reminder of Ms. Arizona warning me about pity parties. I conjure up a way to let out my emotions.

"Let's pray, girls," QC yells.

We all turn around and get on our knees facing our chairs. I bury my face in my Bible and cover up with my arms. *Perfect... I can now cry in peace. They will just think I'm crying because I've come to know Jesus!*

I silently pray, *God, can you hear me? It's me again... Jeneen. Please help me. Please help me. Please help me. Please help me.*

I stare at my soaked, gray, King James Bible. I notice the shiny, silver font. The front cover is already starting to look worn out and faded.

PIECE TWENTY THREE

C:\Jeneen\Hell\Victory\TheStagnantPiano.doc

I TRAIL ALEXANDRA, keeping three feet behind, like an obedient little soldier. I wonder if I could borrow the faded, camouflage army trousers Drake saved. I need them now to fight in this war that I've been unjustly thrown into — except — I cannot wear pants. In fact, I am forbidden to utter the very word. Fire and smoke are everywhere; there are hidden snipers and I don't know when one will decide to take a shot at me. Frightening wails of air-raid sirens are screaming red alert.

I look around and spot a thick, wooden cross. It was something that I once looked upon as a gift. Now, it's a constant reminder of where I am — hell.

I am left behind. No one from the outside knows my location and if I were to collapse, would the Red Cross find me? There are no signals, no communication, no phones, no letters and no visits from outsiders (excluding the ones that threw me in here). My whereabouts are top secret. I do not have any comrades to give me comfort or to reassure me that I could survive this battle.

All I have is your voice, Drake. Can you hear me? I need your strength to carry me through this.

My knees are weak and my energy has been drained like blood

during an embalming. The emotional beating that served as my welcome has emptied me. I have no survival strategy.

Alexandra is giving me another tour around Victory. Far ahead of us, I see a vintage upright piano near the wooden podium. QC previously used it as an anvil, striking it with *his bible* and unleashing his demons to feed on us. I stare at the beaten-down platform it stands on and wonder how it remains erect.

Ms. Arizona is wearing a conservative, long, navy-blue dress with a white cloth bib. The fabric is stitched in the front covering her bosoms. Perhaps she uses it as a napkin in between meals or for cleanup after force-feeding *subordinates*. Her shoes remind me of Dorothy's from The Wizard of Oz and she is sitting majestically on the piano bench. It is interesting that her outward and inward appearances do not match. Her soul has been frozen and her association with QC makes it impossible to thaw out. I'm not sure how it turned solid but she is definitely damaged, taking out her frustrations on *troubled teens*. Perhaps she never felt love, the touch of someone's hand or tenderness before. She only has been exposed to a cult of destruction, barricaded in seclusion.

I guess if I were to spend my life locked up in this environment, maybe I would lose it as well. It would be very similar to putting a crab in a pot of cool water and slowly increasing the flame.

"How is your *Buddy*, Alexandra?" she asks with her usual smirk.

"Fine, ma'am," Alexandra responds.

"How are you, Jeneen?" she asks curiously.

What kind of answer could I possibly have? I'm doing just peachy right here in this prison camp. Oh, by the way, thank you for displaying such hospitality and love in the name of Jesus last night.

An idea comes at me like a freight train. Its light grows brighter and brighter as it snaps me out of depression. Color returns to my once zombie-like complexion. My processor starts to function again.

I can study the piano! If I can make music, if I am productive and creative while I'm in here marking time, maybe it will be bearable. I can already see an X marking July 20th, 1988.

I will learn how to play *Clair de Lune* for Drake as my act of love. It will be my gift to him as we communicate as one. One love. One melody. One spark. One passion. One spirit. One.

"Ms. Arizona," I sheepishly utter.

She pauses, her hands resting on the keys, and looks up at my overly optimistic facial expression.

"Yes, Jeneen," she sings almost angelically.

"Could you teach me how to play the piano?" I ask enthusiastically. "Sure I could!" she replies joyously, almost matching my tone.

"It will remind me of Drake because he is a pianist." I express without hesitation.

"Who is Drake?" Ms. Arizona asks inquisitively.

"He is my boyfriend," I answer truthfully, exposing the small, flickering amount of life I have left.

"The answer is no. You cannot play the piano because it reminds you of your boyfriend. There will be no discussion of him. You cannot utter his name, D-R-A-K-E to anyone. I do not want to hear a whisper of his name ever again. Do I make myself clear?" she yells wickedly.

"Yes, ma'am," I reply, numbly.

I am better off not voicing my thoughts and keeping my burning desire for him private. This could have been my coping mechanism, my way of dealing with my captivity.

Now it's gone. The flickering candle has been snuffed out and its wick is charred. I take the soot and make the mark of the cross on my forehead with my index finger. It's Wednesday.

I fucked up. I shouldn't have said anything. I naively thought I was still living in a free country, not a Christian dictatorship. Where am I? I wish I were in a minimum security prison — at least there, I would have more rights. I would be permitted to make phone calls, write letters to Drake and he could come visit me every week. Now, walls are closing in on me. My lungs have collapsed and I can no longer feel my breath. I cannot cope with the fact that I have been ripped from my world. I am forbidden to communicate with anyone. I have to hide Drake on my hard drive, burying him deeply in the subdirectories. These skillful computer programmers are trying to erase me as if I had never existed. Where is my pulse? Am I alive? I feel myself go into a robotic state, giving Victory metaphoric control of my soul.

If I react by crying, if I lose my temper, I will be locked up for days, weeks or months. *Jade was locked up for three weeks at a time.* The staff and girls, who are *certified Nazi soldiers*, will literally drag me to *the Get Right Room* again. Ms. Arizona would only accuse me of having a pity party or a bad attitude if I react. Besides, I don't want to give her the satisfaction. Like a strong, mechanical soldier, not a drop exits the corners of my brown eyes.

I mentally carry myself away from Victory. I am in front of a heavy punching bag hanging from a ceiling. I make a fist and connect. The bag breaks off the secured clamp. I restrain my tears while I listen for the sound of the piano. I do not hear anything. There is only the sound of the rage I have directed at my parents for throwing me to the wolves. I try to suppress the anger and it feels like regurgitation. I swallow and it burns my esophagus.

These people are stripping everything I have that's vibrant and destroying it.

My spark is dead. My soul is outside at the front of the school, mangled on the barbed wire fence.

The piano comes alive again but it is the eeriness of Ms. Arizona I hear. She sings, *Victory in Jesus* as she caresses the now morbid instrument.

Hello, God? Are you out there? H e l l o? I thought my parents were nuts. These people are worse! Are there more out there? Hello, God? Please send someone to get me THE FUCK out of here.

PIECE TWENTY FOUR

C:\Jeneen\Hell\ChristianCounseling.doc

I HAVE A vision of a tall, dark-haired, slender man in his forties. His appearance reminds me of Dick York from the old *Bewitched* TV series. He exudes the perfect combination of humility and intellectualism. This middle-aged gentleman can be, at times, witty and corny, but at all times, his temperament is even-keeled and upbeat. He stands up for what is just, no matter what the cost. I envision that he will be the man that Drake will grow to become. I don't see why not; he is already heading in that direction. In fact, Drake is the most mature seventeen-year-old boy I know. He already has his future mapped out, for God's sake. I hear shouts coming from the prison check-in.

"I want her out of this place and I want her out now! She doesn't belong here and I am willing to be her legal guardian until she graduates! My attorney is sitting out in the car and would like a few words with you!" he shouts at QC.

Drake's parents are appalled by the twelve-foot fence surrounding the premises and shake their heads in disgust. They tilt their heads simultaneously, block the sun with their hands and stare at the former FBI facility. They feel the warm breeze while they watch the children working in the front garden. My fellow inmates are pulling weeds, tilling the soil and working on other projects assigned to them. After all, it's Saturday — the day we do heavy labor for eight hours or perhaps more, depending on the project that was at hand. Some parents will be visiting their daughters tomorrow and everything needs to be in tip-top shape.

I hear someone coming towards my dorm. I continue to scrub the powdered-blue concrete with a dingy rag. I am using soap and hot water, without gloves, not giving a shit about the effect it will have on my once soft hands. The grime is hard to remove but I am determined to make these stubborn stains vanish. I aim all of my hostility and throw it at the dirty wall. I watch it hit the brick. It boomerangs and smacks me in the face. I feel the sting as if I had endured a hard slap.

The sound of footsteps increases in volume as someone walks towards my location. My heart goes into overdrive, its valves working to keep up with the increased demand my sudden burst of hope has placed on it.

A young woman starts to speak in a southern drawl that is both motherly and soothing.

It must be Anna!

I'm escorted through the dark maze towards the office. I can almost feel the culottes I wear being replaced by an off-the-shoulder evening dress. Its fabric sparkles in spite of the darkness. I look down at my feet and see the glass slippers. I wiggle my toes to confirm this is not a dream. My height increases as my posture becomes strong and straight, like a ballerina. Ms. Ethel hands me a pumpkin from the kitchen and I watch magic dust disperse into the air, creating a horse-drawn carriage before me.

I walk into the office where the new students are greeted and I scour the room for Gram and Anna.

My manufactured fairy tale ends abruptly. I drop the cleaning rag and it makes another filthy mark. I crash back to Earth with tremendous force. My breathing is out of control and I have chest pains.

There is a black swivel chair in front of me. It spins around, unveiling a staff member. Mrs. Wagsters possesses a pale complexion, dark hair and carries a submissive demeanor, but only when her husband is around.

"So what seems to be troubling you? Why do you think you are here?" Mrs. Wagster speaks like a concerned counselor.

I stare at the cherry-wood desk that she sits behind. On the desk are stacks of folders which I assume are our files. *I can only imagine what my parents put in my paperwork when asked, "Why does your daughter need our 'Christian' guidance?" I imagine their response on the application was, "Our daughter is disrespectful. She does not listen, she talks back and she told us a lie about her uncle."*

I begin to tell her the whole drawn-out story. Before I can express to her how I feel and the guilt I have over what happened with my uncle, she interrupts, "We need to pray right now and ask God to forgive you."

Is this woman nuts? Is she telling me that what happened when I was fifteen was my fault and not the adult's? Every counselor that I have visited tried to reassure me that it was not my fault. Yes, I've heard it many times but I couldn't quite grasp it in my heart. Now I have to pray to God with this woman and ask for forgiveness? I cannot voice how I really feel. Anger immediately rises to the surface as if heated by huge flames underneath me. I stare at the volcanic pit beneath my sneakers. *I have to go through the motions and just pretend that this is not happening. This is not happening… This is not happening… She is only a figment of my imagination and not my reality.*

"Dear Father, I pray for Jeneen and that you forgive her of any wrongdoing.

Help her find peace in her heart," Mrs. Wagster prays. "Okay, now it's your turn," Mrs. Wagster demands. *Dear Lord, please get me the fuck out of here.*

"Dear Lord, please forgive me for my evil doings. I'm so sorry that I ruined a marriage and destroyed my family. Again, I ask for your forgiveness. I pray this in your name. Amen." I recite this like the Pledge of Allegiance. If you say it repetitively over the years, eventually it loses its meaning.

God looks down on me with disappointment. Mrs. Wagster just thinks I'm a tramp. Now I feel nothing but shame. I am starting to feel like the untouchable that QC claimed I was.

I plod down the hall with a tremendous amount of guilt at what I had done. Alexandra is three feet ahead. I realize now that no one can save me. I'm already starting to believe that everything is my responsibility and the weight is heavy. *I wish I can have my nervous breakdown now but it is forbidden. Maybe a healthy release could make me feel human again. Ms. Arizona will just lock me up in the Get Right Room for having a pity party and I'll never get off Buddy. If I could just crawl into a corner and cry hysterically. I want to voice that I hate this life but I no longer have any control.* I must transform myself into a solid rock so no one can break me. I have to tune this noise out in order to save myself. An altered state of mind is my only way to cope with this treatment center.

It is now the evening after the *chapel of hell* and we are preparing for bed. I head towards my bunk bed and unravel the perfected hospital corners that I folded this morning. I feel the crisp sheets touching my skin.

I hear *Helpers* yelling, "Lights out, everyone… right now… It's time for bed!"

The torture chamber shuts down at Mach speed. The silence is daunting and reminds me that I am alone. I look at the floor. Laser beams crisscross every square inch of it in every direction. If I get off my bed to get something, an alarm will go off making a dreadful, high pitched, screeching sound. If I wake up a *Helper* to turn it off, I will have to write five hundred lines consisting of: *I will not wake my Helper in the middle of the night to use the restroom.*

My surroundings are similar to some futuristic movie. *Tron* comes to mind. I am horrified at the extreme measures QC takes to keep us confined. The laser light show on the floor just reinforces where I am once again… the *devil's underworld.*

I am trapped in a computer-generated arena where I am maneuvered by QC. Love does not exist here, except for what resides in my memory, but even that's being tampered with. The ultimate tool of religion is now my enemy. The love I have for Drake must remain hidden.

I wish I could have a cup of chamomile tea to settle my nerves like I did when I was at home. We are not permitted, however, to drink or eat in our dorms or off of scheduled time as demanded by the mastermind of programming, Brother QC. If we get off our beds to get a drink of water, we get a demerit. Most choose dehydration because of the hefty repercussions. The negative affirmations are ruthless and they will double, triple and quadruple in a weeks time.

I still cannot grasp that this is happening to me. I have been taken prisoner and I'm being held captive within QC's CPU. Inside these mazes of directories, my love for Drake does not compute. I wish I could take pictures of this place. Perhaps I could mail them to someone like Drake but I am in another dimension where freedom does not exist. There can be no proof of what is going on behind these gates of suffering. The only proof I will ever possess is my memory. In the movie *Tron,* the heroes had to hack into a computer called the Encom 511 in order to gain their freedom. Perhaps one day, I will be able to do the same with my memories and finally be free from this place.

PIECE TWENTY FIVE

C:\Jeneen\Hell\Victory\QC'sManifestations4Us.doc

"LADIES, COME ON in. It's time for another round of the *good word*," QC states, grinning like Jack Nicholson in *The Shining*. He invites us like it's a concert in the park. I search my surroundings for a blanket and a picnic basket but there is no sign of the good life… anywhere. His righteous demeanor makes it seem as if he has something uplifting to broadcast.

We walk into the chapel in single file. U.S. Army commanders would have been proud of our regimented behavior. The diabolic QC is methodically reprogramming us. I have been building a firewall to prevent his demented conditioning. I sense another attempt at control as he thoroughly examines us. The energy with which he scans us, scrutinizing our souls like an x-ray, is meant to strip away our dignity. This of course is part of his daily procedure as he tries to solidify his control.

Is this his way of making us feel we are unworthy to him and God? Heaven forbid we fail to meet his expectations.

"Let me remind you of who you are, ladies! You are a bunch of druggies, alcoholics, high school dropouts, juvenile delinquents, thieves, manipulators, derelicts, home-wreckers, sluts and streetwalkers. You know who you are!" he yells, passing judgment. He combs the room as if searching for an infestation. His gaze locks onto one student. Her head droops towards the dingy carpet.

"With all that said, some of you will be lucky if you can hold a job at Taco Bell. The rest of you will be fortunate to graduate from high school," he snarls, trying to sound concerned for our well-being.

I start feeling the tug-of-war of QC's contradictions. One side is pulling at my upper extremities while his teeth are gnawing on my lower.

Five, four, three, two, one… I'm in a different sermon on a different day. The humidity is thick and girls are fanning themselves with their Bibles.

"Ladies, it's better to be uneducated and believe in the Lord than an intellectual heathen!" he yells as he slams the Bible on the pulpit.

There was no need for an amplifier; this man's voice alone could fry us to a crisp. The boisterous preacher shouts like a deranged man, "Turn your Bibles to:

Genesis 2:17

But of the tree of the knowledge of good and evil, thou shalt not eat of it: for in the day thou eatest therof thou shalt surely die.

Jeremiah 4:22

For my people is foolish, they have not known me; they are sottish children, and they have none understanding: they are wise to do evil, but to do good they have no knowledge.

"Now you see, ladies… Knowledge is the root of all evil."

I find the distorted doorway back to my present. It took me a while because the scenery appears to blend together. I blink my eyes again, finding myself in a fold-up chair. I grip the metal to validate that this is my reality.

Yeah, I'm back all right... in a different sermon, in the same chapel. I take the fact that QC wants us to do more than work at Taco Bell and I involuntarily shove it into another compartment.

Hmmmmmm... doesn't that require an education or using on-the-job training as a form of knowledge? We can't do that, QC. You might accuse us of being heathens!

I'm too tired from working in the field with Brother Green to analyze this one. It requires way more effort than I'm capable of giving right now.

"You think your friends will be with you until the bitter end, but they will *fly the coop* when you are caught doing something illegal. That's right! Some of you will end up in prison because of your friends! They will only throw you under the bus," he yells as I feel myself being rolled over by the same means of transportation. *I'm stupefied by how he is trying to convince us that we are anything but trapped in the Bastille.*

The mind fuck continues...

"As for the men in your life, let's see... You will attract a man who is an alcoholic, a bum, an abuser who burps in your face," he lectures, as if he has a clue.

"You think your boyfriends are waiting for you when you return? Think again, ladies. They were just using you for sex. I know what boys are thinking. I was once one myself. They absolutely have no respect and they are probably with some other Jezebel right now," he predicts, as if he is a prophet. He is merely a dark sorcerer, trying to convince us that there is no spark of hope for love. On my hard drive, the file called *mycloudoftrust.doc* is renamed by QC. I regret the fact that I did not encrypt that part of myself. My core, which was once organized and whole, is now in fragments.

Wow, this is coming from Mr. Right himself — my mentor, QC, giving us such positive reinforcements on a day-to-day basis. Ironically, we could end up with someone just like how he described BECAUSE of his disturbing prophesies. QC only graduated from high school and it is evident he didn't receive a degree in psychology or even acquire basic behavioral skills. He had stupidly told us his qualifications in one of his tedious religious lectures.

I have a good guy in my life that possesses rare qualities that are hard to find; he is my gem.

My boyfriend treats women with respect. He always put me on a pedestal and I reciprocated. You, on the other hand, need some guidance, and I'm unsure where we should start. Your mother should have instilled proper manners a long time ago. It's astounding to me that he wooed his wife many moons ago with his lack of etiquette. 'Ripley's Believe it or Not' could not air this man's angry outbursts. Everyone would say, 'This is too far-fetched.'

What happened to you, QC? Quite frankly, I am too spent to dissect your erratic paranoia tonight.

"Ladies, get down on your knees and let's pray in silence. Think of what I said about your so-called friends and boyfriends," he shouts with tenderness from his soiled heart.

God, where the fuck are you? This man is screaming in chapel claiming to have a direct hookup to your mainframe. He stands in front of a cross and calls himself a preacher. He truly believes we deserve a future without any expectations, without a good man that holds us in high regard, a prosperous job or an education. He is stripping my layers as if I were an onion. I'm not certain there will be anything left of me when he is done. I have faith Drake will be waiting for me. He is different. There was something really special between us and I know he experienced it as well. On my return from this den of blood-thirsty beasts, I'll reboot my system. I'll search for his files, bringing them up in my RAM. I'll be able to resurrect all of my buried files.

I deserve to have everything I want out of life. I am sure of this.

As I pray, it slipped my mind for just a second that I was on QC's cutting board — my psyche being peeled apart, layer by layer. I have hundreds of files stored away. They are daily affirmations that I meticulously built and saved over the years. They are my protection against a catastrophic storm and my inspiration to move forward during excellent weather conditions. They are the first ones to go. QC releases his personal demons to run amok in my mind like the little ghosts chasing Pac-Man around the game screen. QC violates my memory by keying in 'del C:\Heaven\Jeneen\PositiveManifestations.doc'. His index finger hits the enter key. I scream silently.

PIECE TWENTY SIX

C:\Jeneen\Hell\Victory\DogLeash.doc

IT'S MORNING HERE at Victory Christian Academy. I'm standing in the meal line with the other cattle, waiting to assemble at the troughs. The herd moves at a slow pace because we need to inform our fellow *jailbird* who is serving us if we are a *half* or a *whole*.

There she stands in the meal line, Sissy Wilson. She is petite, has dark curly hair and freckles sprinkled around her nose. She is merely twelve years old. She has a rope attached to her wrist. I am horrified as I follow it to the other end, which leads to her *Buddy*. Her *Buddy* is conditioned to believe that Sissy deserves this treatment because she probably was not abiding by the rules. Sissy's *Buddy* was certainly fearful that her own status could be revoked. She could easily find herself connected to a strap or cord and being guided like the very *animal* she is pulling.

I'm unsure which is more disturbing to watch... the redness on Sissy's wrist or the degradation of it all. It is horrifying enough that I have to be three feet behind a twelve-year-old girl; I can't imagine how she must feel.

QC shouts in the hall, "If any of you girls stand four to five feet behind your *Buddy*, as opposed to three, you will be tied too with a dog leash!" He walks past the line of girls while whistling the hymn, *Victory in Jesus.*

I see the despair in Sissy's eyes and though she tries to camouflage it, her façade doesn't fool me one iota. I know QC is fracturing her spirit. He boasts of *breaking the will of children* all the time in chapel. He calls her a heathen and conveys to all the girls exactly how she will suffer in fire and brimstone for eternity. He berates her every day with Bible verses and has taken so many swings at her self-worth that I'm wondering how she is still standing.

I type in cd C:\... then key in C:\Hell\Witness\Sissy\GR.doc and hit my return key. I start counting backwards until I'm thrown into the past. I have a vision of Sissy being ruthlessly dragged to *the Get Right Room*. Ms. Arizona purses her lips in self-satisfied victory while she recruits other teenagers to participate. I notice Sissy's ghostly white skin and matted hair. She is being fed baby food for nutrition, according to QC. He flaunted that bit of information in chapel right in front of Jesus' symbol of salvation. No staff member reacted as though this action was out of the ordinary. Of course not; these disciples are empty terminals, mere extensions of QC's power. I wish I could save Sissy but my hands are tied — I'm on *Buddy*. Then again, what could I do off *Buddy*? Try to throw her over the fence and pray she doesn't get caught on the barbed wire? We'd get tackled before making the climb towards the path to freedom. After all, we are surrounded by surveillance cameras.

I jump forward in time and find myself back in the savage formation.

It sickens me how I have to watch this. I feel helpless to save anyone, including myself.

I stare at the sign near the kitchen, *Home is Where the Heart is*. That would be meaningful if my heart wasn't shattered into a million pieces. *This place disguises itself with meaningful signs and Godly verses.* If you look close and toss your blinders aside, there will be an unveiling of the real horror. If these walls could speak on parent visit day, one would only hear screams.

I went through the robotic motion of picking up my whole

plate. My stomach is in knots and I hope I can finish everything. I'm having severe anxiety over the threat of being forced to eat my own vomit.

I grab my plate and head for the table filled with girls. I observe their attempts at putting a mask of happiness on their cold skin. The false emotion sickens me.

We clean our plates and I finish in record time. I have programmed myself to eat like a survivor in the wild. I break my own records so I won't get demerits or get locked up in *the Get Right Room*.

We make our way to our assigned morning chores and then, it's chapel time. One by one, we trail in, our cloven hooves following the ones in front of us. I'm paranoid about the exact distance between Alexandra and me. Too far and I get put on a leash — too close and I might get accused of being a lesbian. I hear the beeping sound of an alarm going off in my operating system. *It's a no-win situation. I'm fucked either way.*

"Welcome, ladies... Have a seat," QC orders, saying it as if it were a polite request. Loud smacks of the Holy Bible striking the podium echo throughout the room.

"Turn your Bibles to Deuteronomy 22:5."

Deuteronomy 22:5

King James Version (KJV)

The woman shall not wear that which pertaineth unto a man, neither shall a man put on a woman's garment: for all that do so are abomination unto the LORD thy God.

"Girls, I have told you time and time again... This is why women should not wear pants." He continues abusing the Word, hitting it with all of his force against the battered pulpit. It's a good thing we are the maids of this outfit. We dust, scrub and scour everything. If no one was thorough, we would definitely see particles of dust flying everywhere, making their way into our lungs.

"You girls think you look cool in your jeans and tight hot pants but this gets you into trouble! This is why you are here, ladies. You are not following the Word." He uploads more garbage from his damaged mainframe. He increases five levels of volume, as if he weren't already loud enough. Veins protrude from his neck.

So this is why we can't say the word 'pants'? I was always curious about that rule.

I try to put this ludicrous, complex puzzle together, but my brain just responds with the message: FAIL — FAIL — FAIL.

I don't remember a preacher back home speaking like this and using scripture to torment his congregation. This is not right. Was I dropped off on an unidentified planet populated by insane reptilians... or... is this poor excuse for a human being blaming the human race for his own psychological problems?

"You women wonder why you are raped? It's how you dress, your demeanor and how you tempt a man. Turn your Bibles to Genesis, shall we?" His temper escalates, rearing its ugly head in this so-called place of God.

"Turn to Genesis 3:1-13. I would like a *Helper* to read this."

A girl almost six feet tall raises her hand, eager to inhale the Word. "Bernadelli, you can start reading now," QC says.

As she starts bringing the chapters to life with her voice, I wonder what my rape counselor would have to say about all of this.

Genesis 3:1-13

King James Version (KJV)

1 - Now the serpent was more subtle than any beast of the field which the LORD God had made. And he said unto the woman, Yea, hath God said, Ye shall not eat of every tree of the garden?

2 - And the woman said unto the serpent, We may eat of the fruit of the trees of the garden:

3 - But of the fruit of the tree which is in the midst of the garden, God hath said, Ye shall not eat of it, neither shall ye touch it, lest ye die.

4 - And the serpent said unto the woman, Ye shall not surely die:

5 - For God doth know that in the day ye eat thereof, then your eyes shall be opened, and ye shall be as gods, knowing good and evil.

6 - And when the woman saw that the tree was good for food, and that it was pleasant to the eyes, and a tree to be desired to make one wise, she took of the fruit thereof, and did eat, and gave also unto her husband with her; and he did eat.

7 - And the eyes of them both were opened, and they knew that they were naked; and they sewed fig leaves together, and made themselves aprons.

8 - And they heard the voice of the LORD God walking in the garden in the cool of the day: and Adam and his wife hid themselves from the presence of the LORD God amongst the trees of the garden.

10 - And the LORD God called unto Adam, and said unto him, Where art thou?

11 - And he said, I heard thy voice in the garden, and I was afraid, because I was naked; and I hid myself.

12 - And the man said, The woman whom thou gavest to be with me, she gave me of the tree, and I did eat.

13 - And the LORD God said unto the woman, What is this that thou hast done? And the woman said, The serpent beguiled me, and I did eat.

"It's Eve's fault that women suffer childbearing pain. She didn't listen to God, ladies, and tempted man. You don't listen and you continue seducing men with your provocative clothing and body language," he scolds, caressing his Bible while he violently forces his own interpretation on us. His insanity spreads over us like a highly toxic gas. I start to smell the chemicals and cough; my lungs burn. I am stuck breathing his toxic spew because I must sit strapped to this pew. I am enveloped by the thick cloud of QC blaming women for his miserable life.

Hmmmm... it sounds like he's giving women complete power. He is admitting that men cannot think for themselves. So, it's the fault of women when men make a bad choice and maliciously commit a heinous criminal act? It's our intoxicating presence that leads men astray? So... a man is always in control unless, some evil woman seduces them. The contradictions continue...

It is the year 1692. I am tied to a stake, displayed on holy ground. I am a victim of the Salem witch trials. The unjust Court of Oyer and Terminer levy false accusations. Ignoring due process, these ignorant religious extremists pass judgment. I feel the burning of my clothing touch my beaten and torn flesh.

Oyer and Terminer have passed the torch to QC and the pattern continues...

What else can this *demonic killer* pull out of King James to justify his sadism?

"Chapel is now dismissed," QC says, wiping his fogged-up

glasses. As we walk past, we can practically see the steam rising off him.

We make haste to set up all the school tables. We scatter like insects to our designated dividers. We each have a flag that sits up in a crevice on one side of our area. The red and white striped material is, unironically, lifted high in this unconstitutional organization. This symbol of optimism is used to call someone over for help or to use the restroom. Suddenly... I start to feel hopeful. The separating plywood of my divider can be temporary shelter to hide my sadness. I take a gander at Mrs. Wagster's desk off to the side of the room and notice the box of Kleenex. Jackpot! I raise my flag...

"My nose is running! May I grab a tissue?"

She permits me to grab the box of Kleenex. I return to my seat and stare at my P.A.C.E. lesson. This accelerated Christian program is wrapped up in a workbook that a fifth grader could complete. I let out a sigh of relief. I am so distraught that I'm unable to focus on anything. I am not emotionally grounded at all. My mind starts to drift and I replay over and over again... *My parents had the audacity to throw me in prison without doing the crime. I despise them! Where is my Drake?* I bury my face in my clammy hands. I grab tissue after tissue and suddenly have a revelation of how this company stays in business... It's this oppressive, evil camp and all the captive girls that have to endure its horrific tortures.

I start to read the first sentence of the lesson, searching for mis-spelled words. I circle them. I feel myself being carried off by the thought... *I wonder if today will be the day that Drake rescues me.*

PIECE TWENTY SEVEN

C:\Jeneen\Hell\Victory\MouthSealedShut.doc

FREELY RUNNING WATER — a source to replenish ourselves — was something I unfortunately took for granted. Now that I am living in the *evil gatekeeper's dwelling*, basic needs, including water, are only available at the whim of our keepers.

Alexandra and I whisk by *Lucifer's* right-hand man in the narrow hallway. I spot the water fountain ahead, across from the countertop where we grab our grub during meal time. I have cotton-mouth from all the mandatory physical labor. What I would give for the simple freedom of drinking whenever I was thirsty. At this boarding school, I have to get a green light before I can let one measly drop touch my tongue. *The dog doesn't even have to ask permission... not in this exquisite, high class prep school of suffering.* Here, I am commanded to be three feet behind my *Buddy*. If

I don't ask her first, she would just continue walking and then there would be serious repercussions — all for exercising a basic human right.

"Alexandra, may I get a drink of water?" I ask, desperate to ease my thirst. "Sure," she replies.

As I turn around, I am startled by Ms. Arizona's shadowy presence. She does not notice my fear because I have learned to keep my face expressionless. She inquires like an obedient hell's angel, "How are you doing and how is your relationship with the Lord now that you are at Victory?"

Well, ever since I've been hidden in the depths of Victory, my relationship with the Lord has been quite different. This god is now demonic and no matter what I do, this 'divine light' is going to punish me in the afterlife by sending me to the burning flames of the netherworld. I am now nothing but a tramp and instead of a scarlet 'A' stitched viciously on my front shirt, I carry the letter 'T'.

QC reinforces my self-worth twice a day in chapel by reciting his list: you are thieves, liars and harlots — just to name a few. He then uses the Bible to justify his accusations. Helpers carry his foul message everywhere and the cycle continues during every waking hour. The conditioning is starting to worm its way into my brain. The parasite is slowly eating its way to the core of my inner being. It is a bullseye shot by an arrow of destruction, targeting my thought control. I am starting to feel unworthy of any kind of acceptance from God, thanks to this master archer.

"It's great. I've been reading the Bible more and I'm finding cross-references from the Old Testament to the New. I searched the description of the crucifixion in Isaiah and it fascinates me because it is BC." I grab my Bible and open it to:

> **He is despised and rejected of men; a man of sorrows, and acquainted with grief: and we hid as it were our faces from him; he was despised, and we esteemed him not. Surely he hath borne our griefs, and carried our sorrows: yet we did esteem him stricken, smitten of God, and afflicted. (Isaiah 53:3, 4 KJV)**

"So, do you think you could get through this program without giving us any trouble?" Ms. Arizona asks, showing some concern.

"Yeah," I say, utilizing my teenage vernacular.

"That's 'yes, ma'am'. From now on, you will answer, 'Yes, ma'am', no, ma'am', yes, sir and no, sir' to all adults here. Do I make myself clear?" Satan's assistant scolds, her voice now ear-piercing.

"Yes, ma'am," I reply robotically.

"I can't believe I said, *yeah*. It's just a habit. *Oh, shoot*," I say immediately. "You can't say that either. You will write the entire Book of James," Alexandra rebukes.

I thought that was a good substitute? Well, can I say *darn?*" I ask, trying to part the *Red Sea* with my bare hands.

"No!" Alexandra shouts firmly.

"Oh, my gosh?" I ask, hoping for a better replacement.

"No, you cannot say that either," she states, sounding annoyed.

"Well, what can I say?" I inquire, without showing my true frustration. "Oh, my Word," she answers, excited to share her preferred euphemism.

Oh, my Word? Isn't that like saying, Oh, my Truth or Oh, my Bible? Wow, aren't these psychopaths taking the Bible in vain with that expression? Well, if you really want to identify with the cuckoo's nest, why not fly all the way? Why hold yourself back on my account? It's a pity I don't have a beak and cannot squawk my frustration or peck my way out of here! The only sounds I'm allowed to make are the ones they teach me.

Where am I? This cannot possibly be a finishing school for children of God. What kind of place is this? I cannot use any of the vocabulary common to people my age without incurring the wrath of the staff or the Helpers. It's just nuts! How do they expect a teenager to talk without saying 'Rad' or 'Dude'? Well, I won't be using any sort of slang while I'm in this particular funny farm. There is no point in trying to be yourself in this gruesome place.

"I need to get something from my drawer in our dorm. Quick, come follow me," Alexandra orders.

We walk past the chapel. I look into the home of my once forgiving God and imagine that the crucifix should be turned around so that Jesus can't see what happens in there. I see a six-foot blonde, slouched over, her nose pressed against one of the chapel's support columns. Her name is Alexi and she is reciting, *I will not be a game player and will follow all the rules,* over and over. Her *Buddy* squats on the floor next to her, watching and waiting for her slightest mistake.

She screams, "I told you to put your nose up against the pole! Did I tell you to stop? You have to recite over and over, 'I will not be a game player and will follow the rules.'"

I have seen Alexi before — she is pretty low-key and mellow. I wonder if she did drugs and if it has taken its toll on her. She appears out of sorts. It is a toss-up in my mind between the effects of drug use or her just having 'checked out' as a means of coping with Victory. Perhaps it's both? It suddenly occurs to me that drug users are not being treated medically in this outreach program. The girls here have no other recourse than to quit *cold turkey* and embrace the Bible for comfort while going through withdrawals. *We all know how soothing QC and his Bible can be, especially when he quotes scripture out of context. It's difficult enough getting through this poor excuse for rehabilitation... but then to add withdrawals into the mix? I never have been tempted to try them. The anti-drug PSA's have made an impact on me.*

"Okay, last time. This is drugs. This is your brain on drugs."

The visual of my brain sizzling in a frying pan wasn't appealing in the least. Besides, I needed all the brainpower I could get. I was serious about school and my future. If I ended up throwing my life away through substance abuse, it really would have been a living hell.

Ms. Arizona passes by and asks Alexi's *Buddy*, "What did she do now?" I notice the passive-aggressive dorm mother displaying a crooked smile.

Brother Green and Mrs. Wagster pass by without a care in the world. Ms. Arizona just angrily reinforces the punishment by reminding Alexi, "Do you want to get thrown into *the Get Right Room* as an alternative? You will face that column all day until you get it right!"

I ponder the possibility that it could be occupied. *What's the matter? Is the creepy, unlit dungeon full?*

I cringe at the fact that I remain, once again, helpless to rescue another hostage. My mouth is sealed shut though my private thoughts of anger are wide open. The staff would never do this at a mental institution, according to my personal experience. Is it possible I would have more rights and better self-esteem if I were locked up in a hospital instead?

I wonder why Alexi is getting such a harsh penalty. *Did she say 'oh, my gosh', 'shucky darn', 'golly gee', 'pants' or 'shoot'? Did she sing the 'Star Spangled Banner', 'Lucky Star,' 'Little Red Corvette'? Did she talk about a boy she liked back home, or worse, the theory of evolution?*

PIECE TWENTY EIGHT

C:\Jeneen\Hell\Victory\OnTheRoadAgain.doc

THE INSANE REQUIREMENT of keeping three feet between Alexandra and me becomes evermore degrading. As we make our way down the same corridor, we power-walk by another typical military lineup. Girls are wearing bland-colored culottes and oversized T-shirts without any printing that might remind us of the outside world. Cartoons, football teams, movie themes and musical artists are among the forbidden images on any clothing. As I follow the trail of anxious girls, I spot Ms. Ethel. She is a portly, elderly woman with curly gray hair. She is known as Victory Christian Academy's nurse and is passing out medication. She is not actually a nurse of any kind, but somehow, she is honored with the title. The line of teens fills the narrow space. The *medicine line* is similar to an inmate commissary. Parents deposited funds so we could purchase hygiene items, beauty and writing supplies. I have no desire to waste any time standing in an unnecessary line which would take time away from my assigned duties. I don't want my demerits to double, triple or quadruple if I fail to complete them within the twenty-four-hour period. I have to juggle assigned manual labor, memorizing verses and writing words that are meant to assist in my reprogramming. The daily data entry is causing irreparable damage.

I thought about the hair remover for my upper lip. I'm not going to bother with making a purchase. I refuse to use one penny that may or not be sitting in my account. I spit on the concept of the dirty money that was spent to have me tortured daily. I stare at the hairbrushes and colorful sponges being passed out to girls, reminding them of home. I do not wish to be reminded of the life that was stolen from me. I mentally spray my disgust all over the carpet and the makeshift storefront filled with pharmaceutical packages.

I couldn't care less about making myself look feminine again. What difference does it make? There are no dates with Drake in my immediate future. Besides, I'm spent. My energy and self-assurance have been sucked out of me by the most powerful vacuum I've ever experienced. I'm sluggish and I try breathing, but even the oxygen is gone.

"Do you need anything from Ms. Ethel?" Alexandra asks politely.

"No, thank you."

It's the end of a long week and everyone seems to be in better spirits. Everyone is focused on Friday night.

"As long as you have not received more than seven demerits, you can attend," Alexandra informs me.

"What's Friday night?" I ask.

"It's our special night. We can play games, eat junk food, watch an occasional Christian movie, perform skits and have Bible studies," she continues.

You mean it's a chance to forget you are an untouchable in a prison camp for a couple hours?

I continue to follow Alexandra. I see the same washroom up ahead that I was introduced to upon my arrival. I will always remember it as the first torture chamber I encountered in this *academy from hell.* She swings the door wide as I relive the moment of my arrival.

"Do you need to use the restroom? Go ahead and go," she offers.

I might as well. I was cramping badly earlier and I think I may have an upset stomach.

I can hear Noella shouting in the next stall, "I think the powdered milk is giving me diarrhea!"

Noella spoke her mind without a filter. I find this bit of normalcy refreshing.

Unfortunately, inside this vessel of punishment, there is a hefty price for such talk.

Noella is fifteen years old and very extroverted. One cannot help but notice her smile — a beam of hope in the middle of our distress. She allows the colors of her comedy to paint the dreary walls within our prison. She has short brown hair and you cannot help but like her warm heart. She is definitely approachable, except I'm unable to interact with her because I'm on *Buddy.* We cannot be friends. *God forbid, I might tempt her to backslide!*

Last night, I heard her voice, "Everyone says I don't have any common sense.

If it were that common, then everyone would have it, right?"

My guess is that she probably received a punishment of writing a million lines. I can almost hear a *Helper* telling her to write that she doesn't have common sense.

It is not out of the ordinary for *Helpers* to reinforce how incompetent we are or that we are responsible for our demerits. *"I will not make dumb mistakes and leave a hair- brush in the sink"* — one hundred times. *"I will not be a game-player"* — one hundred times. I witness numerous students writing endless rows of sentences every day because they are unable to meet deadlines. They missed them because they were forced to waste their time on insane side-tasks and hard labor and could not keep up with the twenty-four-hour time crunch. It is a vicious circle. Once you are caught in their silky web, you're lunch. Incomplete work assignments are one of their favorite rationales for locking us in *the Get Right Room.*

Morning chapel is over. The details of what to expect from tonight's special event were described by *Pastor Feel Good.* Peanut butter and banana sandwiches, potato chips, pretzels, candies, soda pop and other tasty comfort foods, will be given on this joyous occasion. Sadly, half of the Victory girls will not attend, it was announced, because they did not qualify. Our *camp commandant* couldn't wait to dangle a morsel of civilization in our faces only to snatch it away seconds later. QC wipes the moisture from his spectacles for the millionth time.

We are ordered to meet outside on Victory's exercise yard. Girls start to follow *Helpers* in a mock version of *Simon Says*. If they hop on one foot, then we hop on one foot. If they form circles with their right arm, then we make the identical motion.

We are now hopping on one leg but a girl switches legs because her muscles are starting to ache. In the middle of our workout, I can hear several *Helpers* shouting. Another girl of lesser rank but one-step above me, cannot keep up with the rest of us.

I look to my right and notice the frightened preteen. I cannot utter a word to protect her because they would use me as the ultimate example. I will be dragged across the concrete and thrown into isolation. The staff and all the girls would look down on me as if I were a ghoul.

"You are just a game-player! Do you hear me? Look at me when I'm talking to you. You WILL keep up with us!" Janet screams violently, like a sergeant in boot camp.

"Okay, everyone… Since Rebecca messed up, we need to do it all over again," Janet shouts.

Moans and groans come from the majority of the students.

"Stop whining. If you complain, you will do it twice!" she adds cruelly.

I start following *Helpers* in front of me. My leg is on fire but I don't give up because I don't want to be singled out like Rebecca.

"Keep going, ladies. Do it for the Lord!" Janet psychotically cheers with charisma.

I can see Rebecca sobbing from the corner of my eye.

"Stop crying! If you continue to act like a baby, everyone will have to do it again!"

I just want this to end. Where is Drake? It shouldn't take more than a week to research my location and drive to San Diego. I imagine he will bring his parents as backup. The hallucinations of Drake busting through the barricade continue. I see him fighting for our indestructible love as he stands up to QC and staff. He grabs me by the hand and we run through an obstacle course of black magic. His parents have the car door wide open, ready to make a quick escape.

I hear his parents shouting, "She doesn't belong in *Hades!*" *Come to think of it... no child belongs in this wretched place.*

"Okay, ladies... Everyone gather at the dirt road out front. For those who received a demerit, it is one lap per infraction," Janet shouts again with authority.

Are you kidding me? Who doesn't get demerit after demerit in this terrorizing pit of flames?

Every time I turn around, there is another set of unjust regulations that I can't make heads or tails of.

My *Buddy* waits for me to complete my laps like a master at a dog park. I was given six of their tediously insulting writing assignments this week along with verbal punishments. I barely qualified for Friday night's festivities. I start to move my legs slowly, transitioning into a run. I accomplish my six full loops around the front of the encaged *garden of evil.*

We prepare ourselves for the night of artificial happiness, gathering in our normal herd-like way. The sound of QC dismissing girls that did not qualify, sending them back to Dorm Three, is outright disturbing. Their punishment is *dorm silence.* They are forbidden to utter a sound. No accidents are permitted. They are allowed to read the Bible, complete unfinished negative affirmations or write to their so-called *guardians.* Our *God-loving minister* performs the segregation in front of everyone in order to maximize the embarrassment. The girls that did not make it must walk past the others that managed to survive the treacherous waters. I imagine they could feel our hyped-up excitement and energy level. I have empathy for them because *Helpers* spread demerits like venereal diseases.

Alexandra leads me to her small group of friends: Melissa, Karen and Believe.

They are all *Helpers* so I can speak to them. Their small talk mainly consists of what God did for them this week.

Interrupting their conversation, I blurt out, "I don't belong here. I didn't do anything. I was an honor roll student without any behavior problems. I didn't even party!"

Laughter fills the circle and a predictable response fires at me, "Sure, you don't belong here!" Karen giggles and shakes uncontrollably.

I assumed they could identify with me. My lack of judgment may have cost me. I gulp.

Moments later, Ms. Arizona approaches me, "So, I heard you say you don't belong here. Your parents wouldn't have placed you at Victory if you didn't *fit the bill.* I don't want to hear any more pity parties from you. I thought I made myself clear the first time," she said angrily while walking away — leaving all the students and staff focusing on me like I was target practice.

I start to sing *On the Road Again* by Willie Nelson. I notice the prominent look of fright my *Buddy* displays on her face. One would imagine I just took toxic waste and spilled it all over her khaki culottes. Alexandra stops me and exclaims, "You are not permitted to sing any songs unless they are Christian and approved by the staff. If you go against the grain, you will write five hundred times: 'I will not sing secular music because it's of the *world'*."

Does that include 'Happy Birthday'?

"Meanwhile, you will start saying out loud, "I will not sing secular music" — one hundred times," Alexandra grumbles.

"I will not sing secular music, I will not sing secular music, I will not sing..." I chant on demand. Alexandra counts with her slender fingers.

Who are these people? It's hard to soak in that everyone in here is a Christian. My church back home was nothing like this. This is maddening. I clearly fell through a black hole and now I am stuck in Bizarro World.

The flames underneath me increase by a couple degrees. Everyone wants to see me boil. They want me to break so I will surrender to conformity. *I condemn this transformation of my thoughts for this peculiar spiritual world order. They will not strip me to my core for their own personal gratification.*

God? Umm… where are you? Are you on sabbatical? Are you asleep? Wake up! I need you to send someone to rescue me NOW!

I send my prayer out to the universe, fueled by rage. *I will have God's attention!*

My voice will be heard!

…God?

PIECE TWENTY NINE

C:\Jeneen\Hell\Victory\ReligionBashing.doc

"LADIES, I NEED you to open your Bibles to:

Exodus 20:3, 4 KJV

Thou shalt have no other gods before me. Thou shalt not make unto thee any graven image, or any likeness of any thing that is in heaven above, or that is in the earth beneath, or that is in the water under the earth:

What are the Catholics doing? I'll tell you what they are doing… They have statues all over their church including: The Virgin Mary, St. Jerome, St. Augustine, St. Joseph… and the list goes on and on. Most of their time is spent worshiping virtuous humans. They habitually pray to these figurines, light candles and perform their traditional rituals! Those Catholics are putting gods before God. It clearly states not to do that in the Word!" The shrills and shrieks of QC's voice assail us once again. The thumping noise of the King James striking the pulpit, echoing turbulently through the house I once thought was God's, is altogether astounding.

I try to guess how many girls in here are Catholic. I was born and raised as one myself and I'm quite familiar with the schtick: stand up, sit down, kneel, go to confession, go to communion, light candles and exalt beings that once walked this planet. There was a point in my childhood where I had the whole program memorized, including the Act of Contrition. The 'Garland of Roses' were not foreign to me and at one point in first grade, I wanted to be a nun! Of course, that was before I understood what the cost was, on a personal level. My grandfather paid my tuition at a private Catholic school for two years. After dealing with a teacher named Ms. Perkins, I'd had enough. This bitter, domineering woman in her sixties couldn't nurture a cat, let alone a child. She deserved her harsh reputation — even the parents were put off by her authoritarian presence. I don't know if Ms. Perkins was a nun but my view of women married to God changed in second grade. We were threatened if we didn't comply unquestioningly; we would be spanked numerous times at the principle's office. The habit I imagined myself wearing was blown away by a storm of negative associations.

The most influential instructor I had at that school was Mrs. Grace. This charismatic teacher was the answer to all our prayers. She left an imprint that will last longer than the church itself. In my book, she was my guardian angel and was truly connected to God.

"Be kind to others with sincerity. Be generous and give to the less fortunate.

Make God smile every day and you will be happy." This was the lasting lesson of Mrs. Grace. The next day, I put what little I had saved from my allowance into the donation box. I noticed the walls of marble. As I stared at the exquisite artwork, I imagined it was a replica of the Vatican.

My family practiced this faith until my parents moved us to Newbury Park. Up until thirty-something years old, my mother did not know how to drive and First Christian Church of Newbury Park was in close proximity to our house. If there was a Jewish Synagogue around the corner, I'm certain we would have been there every Sabbath instead. In between Catholicism and our new non-denominational Christian church, my father dabbled in Christian Science. We were obviously a well-rounded family when it pertained to denominations. It is enough for me to thoroughly comprehend QC's criticisms and judgments. *It doesn't take a rocket scientist, however, to come to the conclusion that this man wasn't firing on all cylinders.*

"Let's talk about the Book of Mormon, shall we. Please open your Bible to:

Revelation 22: 18-19 King James Version

18 - For I testify unto every man that heareth the words of the prophecy of this book, If any man shall add unto these things, God shall add unto him the plagues that are written in this book:

19 - And if any man shall take away from the words of the book of this prophecy, God shall take away his part out of the book of life, and out of the holy city, and from the things which are written in this book.

"Joseph Smith received another testament of Jesus Christ from a heavenly messenger, Moroni. The Book of Mormon... are you kidding me? I've never heard of such *hogwash* in my life! They are obviously not listening to the Word of God," QC states with hatred and revulsion.

He slams the pages of the Holy Book, making a sound like gunfire. His level of explosive hostility is frightening. The first row of girls jumps from the impact of his delivery.

Why can't this malevolent human have a performance like this when our parents are present?

"The Jews are waiting for the Messiah's first arrival. Well, he's been here. Turn your Bibles to Isaiah please.

Isaiah 50:6 KJV

I gave my back to the smiters, and my cheeks to them that plucked off the hair: I hid not my face from shame and spitting," QC quotes with animosity as he tries to justify his point.

"Please don't get me started on all the New Age *mumbo jumbo*, people speaking in tongues or the sixties… filled with bald heads and tambourines sending peace, love and flower power. Hare Krishna!" he chuckles at his own demented sense of humor. A number of the girls robotically laugh and chant an 'amen!'

"Well, I'm not here to spread God's love and sugarcoat the Truth," he hollers, leaving us in utter disappointment.

Really? You could have fooled me. I always thought you were a 'feel-good Christian' filled with agape love — here to offer us a good example for our behavior modification and serve as a building block of our self-regard.

My internal sarcasm is now cranked up to its highest setting.

"I follow Paul's way of preaching. I don't throw flowers around or tell you how much God loves you. I want you to know all of the information in the Word. I want you to know about God's wrath. This congregation notices that I often preach about hell. Well, how are you going to get saved unless I warn you?" He continued his illogical speech, convincing himself more than us, that he is doing us all a favor.

I'm so turned around. This so-called deliverer of a higher message clearly spoke of the seven deadly sins, wrath being one of them. All I hear is a belligerent clergyman having a temper tantrum, making God into an evil force. God's pure light carries a toxic poison? I don't think so. This tyrant pulls God's rage out of the Bible using it as ammunition in his private holy war, yet it is a forbidden emotion for us to possess? Well, that's pretty egotistical and hypocritical, don't you think? Man is more than capable of hate and wrath without God's help and I have proof of that right in front of my face. After all, men did write the Bible.

PIECE THIRTY

C:\Jeneen\Hell\Victory\Dreaming.doc

THE SHARP RINGING sounds traveling through the air are another indication that I am no longer in the comfort of my own bed. I am not in my wonderfully decorated room. I am not going to fix myself to impress my darling in paratrooper cargo pants.

The klaxon is alerting the hostages that our former lives have been ruthlessly confiscated. My heart beats rapidly and a sense of loss touches every fiber of my being. It diminishes somewhat when I remember Drake and how the warmth of his embrace made the hairs on my arm stand up. I feel peace now… but only for a second.

"Down on your knees," a *Helper* shouts, demanding we pray to the demonic god of QC's imagination. It is not an option, but then again, nothing inside this reformatory is. It's 8 am on a Sunday. The Smith and Wesson is cold as it presses against my forehead. The smell of gunpowder permeates the room as *Helpers* enforce their demand for prayer. The silence is unnerving.

God? I hate this place. Please forgive me for what I have done. I promise, I'll be good. Just get me out of here. I cannot take this wicked iron-handed treatment anymore. Amen.

I hastily pull my long, brown wavy hair back into a ponytail. I clip an eggshell white bow near my scrunchy. They are the only two possessions linking me to my past life. If I reminisce too much, the wave of melancholy will hit me so hard, I'll weep.

Students frantically scramble to get ready for the circus that will soon unfold in God's place of business. After the *heartfelt* sermon, it's parent/daughter visit day.

It's where young prisoners are reunited with the real criminals — the loving parents that trapped us in this chilling gulag. My mother will not be allowed to descend into the pit of serpents until my three-month anniversary. It seems so far in the distant future. Time moves very slowly in prison.

Quite frankly, I don't want to see my poor excuses for parents. I'd rather have some normal visitors — ones who might notice the twelve-foot fence topped with barbed wire. The razor-sharp wires are a nice touch for a girl's school. You know… for curb appeal. One cannot help but notice the surveillance cameras, set up high and lurking in every corner. It doesn't take Sherlock Holmes to figure out what's going on here. Anyone with a shred of intelligence could piece together that this place should be condemned.

I hope QC shows his true colors today. I hope the *Destructive Disciple* slips up and reverts to his normal ungodly ranting and cross-examinations. If sane adults could view his twice-a-day per-formances, my shackles would be removed, however, I'm sure he's rehearsed at putting on a good show for the parents.

"Open your Bibles to Revelations please," QC shouts in a char-ismatic tone, all part of the theatrics. He proceeds to rant and rave about hell. His cheeks are flushed and he is drenched in sweat. He wipes his face with a white cloth and just for a second… the imprint of the Antichrist is revealed. Only we girls know it is there.

The false *man of god* points his fingers at couples living in sin. He combs over the scriptures pertaining to *fornication* and spreads the Word all over the flock. I imagine that by now, the parents are probably thinking… "We'll tolerate his moral superiority as long as our little girl transforms as promised and we receive our outrageously priced robot."

I certainly don't see anyone disagreeing with the craziness QC is selling. Unfortunately, everyone in this compound is part of the 'Stepford Wives' community.

I cannot help but notice the infant in the pew in front of mine. I have clear view of him sucking on his blue pacifier, apparently content. He is precious. My desire is to have a child with Drake in the future... after college, perhaps.

I picture holding our baby, full of the joy that my parents seemed to be missing. Rocking and cradling my future child is a pleasant thought. Fortunately, this child is free to leave the premises. He giggles and I smile.

"Don't look at the baby. You are not allowed to look at any of the guests. Keep your head down at all times," Alexandra whispers with trained authority.

I thought having a transparent leash *tied* to Alexandra for one month (if I'm compliant and don't screw up) was an absurdity. I can't look at the visitors because I do not matter? I am now officially undeserving to glance at a newborn. Am I not good enough to have a product of myself? We are all just treated like misfits, unworthy of God's grace. Our parents, the outside world and anything moving must shun us as well. Criminals in actual prisons have more basic civil rights than we do. We are fed a steady diet of repugnance, self loathing and fear.

I am becoming more and more of an untouchable each day that passes. I focus my attention on the splintered wooden cross. I have put all my hope into waiting for a miracle that never came. It's been one solid week and Drake never came with his parents. I am going to rot in here. My fairy tale is swiftly growing faint. I grab at what's left and hang on for dear life. He will be waiting for me when I get out; there isn't a shadow of a doubt. His love is so intense that I can feel it more than the loaded weapon these lunatics hold against my head.

We all head in a single file back to the dorms, like soundless droids. It's downright silence in the *barracks*. We are bound to our berths unless we get permission from a *Helper*. If we ask a *Helper* for anything during *quiet time*, we receive a demerit. The greater the offense, the harsher the punishment. *Five hundred lines is a well-deserved consequence for needing to pee, don't you think?* They consist of: "I will not disturb my *Helper* to go to the bathroom during *quiet time*."

Smiles everyone, you are on Freddy Krueger's private island. It's a pity our former legal guardians are not privy to this. I guess QC left that out of his itinerary for family day.

I just hope I do not have to use the facilities during these grueling four hours tied to my mattress. I'll just hold it in. I'll read the Old Testament to distract myself.

Let's start with the beginning, Genesis...

I read the genealogy of so and so begat so and so... I start to feel drowsy.

I'll just go to sleep so I don't have to think about going to the loo.

I'm with Drake and he is holding me. The feeling of refuge envelops my body. I bury myself in his chest as I weep uncontrollably. His touch provides the shelter I have been yearning for. I tell him, in detail, what took place in the despicable torture chamber for the wayward.

"Stay here at my house with my parents. Look at me." he says as he places both hands on my shoulders and turns me so that we are face-to-face. Drake looks into my eyes, pouring his abundant radiance into my soul. "Your parents can no longer haunt you. Do you trust me?"

I look back into his eyes, communicating my belief in his supernatural strength.

I feel his lips touching mine and our energy is as one. He spins me around and lifts me up.

"I missed you so much. Don't ever leave me again." he facetiously comments and then smiles.

The dream is very intense and my pillow is drenched from perspiration.

Regretfully, I awake to the sight of blue brick walls staring back at me. It was so cruel for my subconscious mind to take me where I most want to be, only to drop me back into the bottomless pit. Reality and grief are rapidly sinking in. My sorrow transforms into fury. All I can do now to cope is to forcibly hit that solid blue wall until my hands bleed. The blood of my anguish is smeared alongside my dreams of freedom.

PIECE THIRTY ONE

C:\Jeneen\Hell\Victory\HardLabor.doc

I HAVE MY *Buddy* in sight, three feet in front of me. The beige material of her culottes is swishing back and forth. I take note of the plain white T-shirt. I imagine my attire is about the same. Who knows what I'm wearing today? These are just garments. Any sense of style or interest in the latest trends have been flushed down the Victory toilet.

Alexandra abruptly heads towards an oversized tan man in his mid-fifties. Brother Green is another *inspiring pastor in this underground madhouse.* I can almost see the flag wavering in the gentle breeze. I am outside… sort of.

The summer weather is inviting for picnics, beach activities, barbecues or a walk in the woods. The quail singing a tune in the trees would seem glorious if I were not caged up like an animal. Instead of enjoying the beautiful sunshine, I obsess over my captivity. I am consumed, mentally and physically, by my entrapment.

Brother Green orders Alexandra to help out with a group of girls digging ditches. "Take your *Buddy* too," he demands.

We grab a couple of hoes and start loosening up the earth. As I begin to use the physical exertion to release my tension, I get distracted by my thoughts…

What are we accomplishing? I am working diligently without an agenda, part of an unknown plan. What will I receive for all my hard labor? I don't want a salary; I want my right to act, speak and think without hindrance. I need to have the freedom to bare my soul. If I have restraints placed on me, I cannot move forward in my healing process. Worse, I am just a fraud because I am not my true self. I will never reach my full potential.

An hour has passed and we're all sweating profusely. We feel our aching muscles and could use a rest. A couple girls stretch their backs in unison.

Alexandra yells, "Don't stop. Do it for the Lord! The next person who stretches will get a demerit."

A few seconds later, Angelica succumbs.

"That is it, you all get demerits," she yells with a vengeance QC would be proud of. *It's a sign of accomplishment when you can crush someone's dignity, like a heart in your hand.* I watch mine fall from her fingers onto the ground. Miraculously, my body is still moving.

I am accustomed to hard work. I already had a strong work ethic while I was living life as a normal teenager. This is ridiculous! I am being forced to work at gunpoint. God forbid I speak of the brutality to anyone, including my fellow inmates. Instead of a water break, I receive a whip to my psyche. Another arbitrary punishment, doled out by a child. Where are OSHA, the union and child labor laws? Sweatshops workers would usually get paid less than their daily expenses. We do not have that privilege — WE ARE MERELY SLAVES.

My internal monologue continues…

We are to be punished for having normal human limitations… and that is for the Almighty? So let me get this straight… God is displeased with us for being exactly as he designed us? I lift my long-handled digging tool so high that when it comes down, I split the dirt in pieces. I start breaking up the hardened gravel in the same manner that Victory is destroying me.

I pick up the metal blade again and again. For each blow to the ground, I pull up another traumatizing memory of how my parents threw me away like a piece of garbage. As I grunt from the effort of digging into the hard ground, I mull over how… *my parents, those betrayers, are paying someone to treat me like an untamed beast. I must be such a disgrace in their oh-so moral eyes for them to send me to this subterranean dungeon.*

Each blow to the ground is another strike against someone for telling me that *I am not good enough to look at a baby, I am a home-wrecker and a Jezebel. These absurdities continue daily. I feel like I needed thick layers of clothing to cover my shame. Just because it is written in the Bible, I have come to realize, doesn't make this abuse necessary or acceptable. If it were, everyone would be dead — judged and sentenced to death by stoning, as demanded by the holy being him-self… man.*

I recall saying a prayer while in Bible class at Cornerstone Christian. I specifically asked Him to use me as a vessel. *Son of a bitch… I didn't mean in this way!*

I continue swinging the hoe, repeatedly breaking the soil. It's as if I were searching for the meaning of my captivity, buried somewhere in front of me. My rage is beginning to turn me into a workhorse. I'm taking swings at my bitterness. My aggression is noticed by some of the girls. I can almost hear them saying, "I wonder why she held back this long?" What if my current state of mind is reality and everything else I remember is just… bullshit?

Alexandra grants us permission to stop. We come to a grinding halt and quickly race to put our landscaping tools away. Brother Green inspects our work with a fine-tooth comb. He appears pleased. We still have no idea what the purpose was of our hard labor.

I follow the leader. Alexandra leads me to the rows of showers located near Dorm Three. I notice a tall, slender girl sitting on a stool in the lavatory near the shower area. She reminds me so much of my childhood best friend, Jennifer Paris. Her sense of humor has frequently been the only relief from the constant tension in here. I extend a hand in greeting to this comedic *Helper*. I am left with my hand in midair.

I am immediately scolded. "We cannot shake hands or hug any of the students. You will write one hundred times, 'I will not touch any of the girls'," Alexandra scolds with authority.

This is insane. When I attended a private Christian school back home, I was able to pray with my friends and embrace them.

The girl on the stool smiles and introduces herself as Believe Jackson. It is so maddening to see someone showing positive emotion when I know it's not real. How could this be? Believe was locked in *the Get Right Room* for eight solid weeks! But that's the whole point... Victory is controlling our emotions too. Again, we are conditioned to put on a facade of joy despite our suffering. The name Believe is so fitting for this lockdown. We need to have some sort of faith that authorities would come and rescue us.

Out of the blue, I realize that I am overdue to start my period. I need a tampon just in case I unexpectedly start.

Uh oh... I'm sure I cannot insert anything into my vagina, even a tampon. God forbid, I even say the word tampon. I might get hit with a thousand lines for that unholy thought. I do not want to take a chance on that. Hmmm... What can I say that will take the place of the words tampon or Kotex?

The paranoia of making a mistake continues.

"Believe, can I have a sanitary napkin?" I ask in hopes of escaping a punishment. *These people need to have a manual of their preposterous rules or would that take the fun out of being a sadist? Perhaps written evidence of child abuse wouldn't sit right with the parents?*

"What's that?" Believe naively replies.

My twelve-year-old *Buddy*, Alexandra, explains to the upbeat sixteen-year-old.

Believe starts laughing and her light-hearted demeanor shows through.

"Oh, why didn't you just say Kotex?" she questions, as if unaware of the ludicrous restrictions placed upon everything we say.

Believe thought it was comical, and a little quirky, that I would not say the words tampon or Kotex. She thought it was quite odd to choose an uncommon synonym, but what the hell do you expect in this *concentration camp? Little Hitlers* are lurking around every corner! Alexandra also mentioned that there are intercoms set in each dorm so that our conversations can be listened to. Victory is an Orwellian nightmare come alive.

I flashed back to Margaret Lopez, a pregnant Hispanic fifteen-year-old. She was in the kitchen having a glass of milk along with a snack during an unscheduled mealtime.

Although I never inquired, Alexandra informs me, "She's pregnant. That's why she is able to get something to drink and eat off-schedule." The scene shifts to one of many *witch-trial* chapel sessions. QC looks at Margaret and makes a special announcement, "Now girls, she can't stay at Victory because she is pregnant."

Wow, what a break! It's better to be knocked-up because that's an 'E' ticket out of this agony.

I blink my eyes and I'm back staring at Believe and Alexandra. I haven't spotted yet. *Could I be pregnant?* The probability was virtually nil because I was on the pill and Drake always used a condom. We were extra careful. *There is just one sliver of hope, aside from Immaculate Conception, to get me out of here… I could get struck by lightning.*

I ask permission to use the bathroom before we take a shower. Alexandra replies, "Yes."

I check my panties and I am period free… and late.

There is a chance that, despite our precautions, I could be carrying a piece of our love inside of me. I smile in the privacy of my stall.

After washing my hands, Alexandra reminds me, "All girls are timed in the shower. If we have the water running for just a split-second after the whistle blows, we will get a punishment. We have five minutes to shampoo, condition, shave, and wash."

Being Italian, shaving is an all day affair. How am I able to do it in three minutes and shampoo and condition in two?

I notice the curtains giving us the luxury of some privacy. I look inside my personal partition and start organizing my plan to beat the buzzer. I scour around to find the other drain the eight girls are sharing.

"Okay, you can start the shower," Believe yells as she blows the whistle she wears around her neck.

What is this, the hygiene olympics?

I chuckle in my silent dwelling, listening to my own sarcasm. I lather my legs and thighs with soap and start shaving briskly. I am not going to attempt to shave my pubic hair. Cutting myself there because I'm in a hurry would be bad news... besides, who am I going to impress? Next, I start mowing my armpits, making efforts to avoid nicking my skin. I do not want to bleed all over the place.

I look down and see blood coming from a different stall and heading for my drain. "Ow, I cut myself. Believe, can I have a Band-aid please?" Bernadelli cries out.

One of the girls notices a stream of yellow heading in their direction. I hear screaming and wonder, *what could possibly be happening now?*

"Someone just peed in the shower! It was Elizabeth," Bernadelli horrifyingly shouts.

"Elizabeth, you get a demerit," Believe cries, enforcing policy. I hear the whistle sound.

"Shut off the water," Believe yells.

"Sounds of water striking the shower floor come from the stall next to mine. "Cindy, you get a demerit. You kept the water on after time," Believe robotically announces, only following protocol from QC and staff.

Cindy whiningly replies, "I'm just wringing out the excess water from my hair…"

As I dry myself off with a generic white cotton bath towel, the moisture from the steam soaks into my olive skin.

My rushed shower visits are my only *almost-alone* time. I can think of Drake while I'm cleansing the soil of Victory off my body. I watch the filthy water as it runs down the drain. It carries a mixture of blood and urine. In contrast to my surroundings, I think of Drake's soft plush lips pressing against mine. I can still feel the love and the warmth of his arms. I feel protected from the dangers of these barbarous disciplinarians.

Drake, please get me out of here.

I shout my thoughts in silent optimism. I am convinced the message will somehow alert him to come and release me before I suffer irreparable damage.

PIECE THIRTY TWO

C:\Jeneen\Hell\Victory\SearchRaid.doc

It is **6** am but as there are no windows in this dorm, there's not a glimpse of outdoor light to give us any indication that it's morning. The *Helper*s begin firing orders at us like high velocity bullets. They're flying around my dorm and I feel like I'm in Vietnam. Several rounds hit my body, waking me out of deep REM sleep.

"Everyone on your knees, NOW!" another *Helper* yells.

I am wounded by the negative associations of prayer and scare tactics. It's the same humiliating routine every day. It is no longer my choice to get on my knees and pray. God wants us to have free will but everything in here is forced doctrine. I have no choices and everything is mapped out for me, including when I can perform my necessary bodily functions. I am no longer a human being who can think or do anything by myself. Worse, I'm praying to a god who, I'm told repeatedly, hates me.

Girls scurry like insects after *prayer time* to get ready for the day. We are timed, as usual, so everyone is in a rush because we have to prepare our drawers for inspection. Our daily searches are performed by *Helpers*. The investigation is to make sure all of our personal belongings are folded and in the right order. I would never dare keep a secret journal. The truth about Victory and my feelings will remain hidden. If the writings were found, QC would only exploit them to humiliate me in front of my peers in chapel. I would be labeled as a heathen and a phony. I have witnessed this unjust crucifixion of students too many times. They constantly make examples of the girls here. The message of how we are forbidden to speak or write the truth is made clear... and often. If we do anything that is against QC's teachings or commands, we are commingling with the devil.

As for my parents — I could write the truth... but they wouldn't believe me.

Worse, QC would read my private thoughts in front of all the other girls before destroying the letter. I would be the laughingstock of this maniacal outfit. It really doesn't matter — either way it's a no-win situation. I feel defenseless and unprotected by my parents and these so-called *Christians*.

In this *school for positive reconstruction*, there are no pictures of my boyfriend and no physical proof of the love we once had. There isn't a prom, homecoming or eighth-grade dance snapshot, no photographs taped onto the distressed wooden post of my bunk — not even one of my brother because QC thinks it will cause the girls to be lustful. I am uncertain if I want that freedom anyway. It would only represent what has been lost. Newspapers, books (unless Christian and approved), magazines or TV do not exist. I recall QC taking scripture from the Bible to justify his decisions regarding media access. Secular music was the biggest gateway to the *wicked land!*

"Turn your Bibles to Ephesians 2:2," QC angrily shouts.

Wherein in time past ye walked according to the course of this world, according to the prince of the power of the air, the spirit that now worketh in the children of disobedience.

"The prince of the power of the air is Lucifer, ladies," QC installs.

All books are Christian based upon approval by the staff but, it is really the Bible or nothing at all.

I am merely a crab in a pot and I am on simmer. It's just enough for me to feel intense discomfort but not enough to kill me. QC is now making me feel like a lowlife, not only to God, but to society. I am a criminal. My head and shoulders are permanently pointing downward.

Ms. Ethel is preparing something in the kitchen and the mix of spicy scents is causing our stomachs to growl. She notices my slumped-over posture.

"Jeneen, why do you walk with your shoulders inward and your head down? You need to have your head high and shoulders back." The sweet elderly woman gives me a demonstration of the confidence with which she believes I should carry myself.

I am waiting in the line for my breakfast, keeping up so I do not fall behind Alexandra. I can smell the tantalizing aromas of French toast, eggs and bacon. I feel sorry for any girl who is a vegetarian. She will be force-fed, along with anyone else who does not eat what they're given.

Where has Ms. Ethel been during the hell-raising chapel sermons? Did she put on her Pollyanna glasses so she wouldn't see the thirteen-year-old girl standing with her nose against a column for hours? Did she miss the sheep and the goats demonstration where QC plays God? Did she have dirt smeared over her glasses so she couldn't see the force-feeding? Did she turn down her hearing aid to avoid the sound of a girl crying from threats of having to eat her own vomit? Did she miss the handcuffs on Jade and the thick gray duct tape over her mouth? Did she have blinders on when I passed her, trailing behind my Buddy, tied to an invisible leash, degraded and humiliated? She is merely just another robot that QC has programmed to ignore our abuse.

Meanwhile… French toast and eggs! Food is the only thing I have to look forward to in this place. It is the only means to fill my empty void.

I will be with my Drake again and that is what will keep me alive. No one can take away my positive attitude.

After our meal, I sit quietly staring out into space awaiting my discharge. Since I am not allowed to speak to the other girls, what else could I do?

"You are all dismissed," Alexandra orders.

We scramble back to our dorms to complete our normal assigned chores. Like a dog, I continue to follow the required distance behind the *Helper* towards the kitchen. Believe is in charge of the cookery this time and I ponder whether she's on shower duty. I am ordered to clean the food pantry. I remember when I offered my time at my church to help with cleaning. I was so well-respected by Christians outside of my family… and now…

First, I sweep the dirt out completely and then I double-check to make sure my work was thorough enough for the *Nazis.* I then get on my hands and knees and start scrubbing the floor with soap and water. Believe comes in to inspect my work.

"That's not clean, do it again," she says with authority.

I repeat the same process in the same way because there is nothing I can do differently this time. I gave it my best shot on the first try because I'm a perfectionist.

Believe comes into the pantry while I'm cleaning and says approvingly, "Now, this is much better!"

Alexandra informs me, "Let's go! We need to get ready for chapel!"

You mean, we have to prepare ourselves for another browbeating lecture?

As we march in like soldiers, I can feel QC staring us down, scanning again for the slightest defect, with a smirk on his face. He is now the official quality control inspector for God. His god, however, is demonic and looks down on every girl in this reform school, whether or not they have come to know Jesus. He hides behind his glasses so we cannot look into his eyes and see his black soul.

Amy Grant is brought up on the stand. Anger immediately rises to the surface as QC spits like an uncontrollable serpent. The beating of the Word against the podium begins.

"She claims to be a Christian but she runs on the beach naked!" QC yells, becoming more livid by the minute.

"She claims to be a follower of Christ but she's just a wolf in sheep's clothing," he shouts bitterly, as if he knows her soul.

If she didn't have any clothes on, how did that apply? Besides, QC is a wolf in wolf's clothing. It is that transparent to me.

QC and his *Christian* ridicule were our only sources of entertainment. It was mainly about us on a day-to-day basis but sometimes he would discuss others from the *outside world* to break up the monotony. He tells us his story of being out in *the world.*"

"I took a stroll along the beach and watched a couple holding hands. All of a sudden, this woman puts her hand right on her boyfriend's behind as if claiming her rights to him!" The alarming slam of the Bible startles two girls in the front row. They jump.

Maybe she was afraid QC had 'certain tendencies' and wanted to protect her boyfriend?

Sarcasm is my friend.

Smack goes the Bible for the millionth time. "Women today have no respect and... "

Maybe he's bitter because his gluteus maximus doesn't get touched by his wife. Is he envious of a tender display of affection? Now, I am really curious about where all of QC's eruptions, blasting lava all over God's temple, originate. Well, I have about a year to psychoanalyze his behavior. The irony of how WE are all in here for behavior problems doesn't escape me.

We are dismissed to our dorms. As soon as we enter, we realize we have been ransacked. It looks like a tornado has gone through all of our personal belongings. Our drawers, which we so diligently keep up to code, are disasters. Girls' socks and undergarments are in disarray. Our personal belongings are now intermingled. It would take an eternity to find our toiletries, letters (monitored and only from our parents), clothes and pictures. *I don't care about my pic-*

tures because they are only stills of the villains who sent me here. My mother actually had the audacity to send me a picture of her and my father smiling in a Jacuzzi, on their vacation! They're staring at me, flaunting their freedom, while I sit here on the carpet looking at the aftermath of an *F-5*.

Mrs. Wagster storms into our dorm with an announcement: "Someone is keeping a diary of the events that take place here at Victory. They are planning on writing a book. We had to look for it. Now, you clean up this mess! All of you, right now!" she screams like a drill sergeant.

We are all in a state of shock. I am determined not to shed a tear. I am uncomfortably numb.

In my opinion, this is just something to pass the time. *The busier I keep, the faster it will seem to go.*

My rage has reached its maximum.

This is a disaster all right but there is nothing natural about it. The tragedy is Victory *Christian* Academy, a destructive vortex of detestation and wrath, caused only by... MAN.

PIECE THIRTY THREE

C:\Jeneen\Hell\Victory\CareySun\2ndTimeAround.doc

IT'S MID-AUGUST AND it's difficult to fathom that I've been in this cesspool for almost a full month. I fight to stay awake during this particular Bible-study lecture. The oven-like temperature is making me drowsy. Girls are waving notebook paper fans against their perspiring bodies to combat the unbearable heat. Every so often, a cool breeze graces us with its presence because QC was kind enough to crack open the door. I have a view of the outdoors to the right of the weathered cross.

I stare at my faded gray King James and debate whether the withered front cover is the outcome of my misery or if it's because I'm an over-zealous Bible thumper. I know the answer, of course. I use the Word to hide the tears pouring down my cheekbones. I use *the Book of Inspiration* like a shield to cover my face so none of my *enemies* can see when I'm having a pity party. *They would just assume I was being emotional about Jesus! Apparently, you can cry your heart out about the Messiah but God forbid you show your reaction to this everlasting suffering.*

I'm avidly taking notes and inserting them in between verses. I'm paying close attention to these unorthodox lectures.

I am starting to feel like the rebellious child they see me as. The concept that *I am the root to all my family problems* has slowly crept its way into my mind. After all of these forced *come-to-Jesus meetings,* I have concluded that I am a poor excuse for a Christian. I ask God to forgive me every day because constantly, I am told by QC and Brother Green, that I am, in essence, a *fuck-up.* We are continuously told that we are heathens, juvenile delinquents, home-wreckers and liars. One may initially convince oneself that these are false accusations, but with non-stop repetition, it takes a heavy toll. Our minds are being slowly poisoned. I fought a good fight but my defenses weren't strong enough.

Defeated by my hot-tempered opponent, I find myself out cold on the floor in the fiery ring.

After all the browbeatings and the isolation from the outside world, I now believe that what happened with my uncle was my fault. I take one hundred percent blame because QC has deceived me into changing my thought process; I was a temptress and I provoked it. I am now an untouchable, not only to society, but to the *Eye in the Sky.* It is implanted in my mind that for me, heaven's gates are locked with a deadbolt and the shadowy figure's arms await me instead. My God is disgusted with me. The fact that I was saved before entering Victory is insignificant. QC continuously rips me open and every time I try to heal myself, he rips out the stitches.

Brother Green is on the pulpit, spreading hate like a forest fire. The fuel he is using today is the *seven deadly sins.* Such a *pity that mockery in the name of the Chosen One wasn't an item up for bid.*

"Open your Bibles to Revelations," Brother Green shouts. He commences his scholarly lesson hoping to frighten us into salvation rather than allowing us to make our own decision. Brother Green is a tall man that is extremely round. Ironically, he looks like a big teddy bear, especially with his tan. He looks quite fatherly, especially when he wears his glasses. Do not be deceived by his outward appearance. Inwardly, he is nothing like a nurturing father...

When Brother Green preaches on gluttony, he deliberately stares down at an overweight teen. Rebecca has straight, strawberry-blonde hair. He scans her in an up and down motion, following the same judgmental procedure as QC.

It's already horrifying enough to know she gets called out during our exercise program. Now, it's in front of The Man who rose from the dead and who tried to teach us about accepting others without scrutiny. I glance at the cross. I am witnessing a schoolmate being persecuted with an open Bible. It is being used, once again, as the ultimate tool of hatred in this place of worship.

The treacherous barbarian persists with his ferocious bashing.

"I repeat… gluttony is one of the seven deadly sins, Rebecca," he comments in a raised voice in order for the rest of us to hear. He remains fixated on Rebecca, staring her down while flaunting his own fat *righteousness.*

First of all, no one laughs because it's altogether mean. Second, we intuitively know we could be next on the chopping block. I feel so useless and empathize with Rebecca's defeated soul. The tortuous humiliation carries on through the study. I wish I could raise my hand and contradict these teachings but I will be severely punished. My out-of-the-box thinking has no place in this forum of persecution.

"You are all going to get a Bible lesson that you will never receive in Bible college! I am giving you so much information that you will never have the excuse of not knowing the Truth," he informs scornfully, still ignoring his own obesity.

I'll say an amen to that! No private college in their right mind would ever persecute an overweight girl in front of a congregation in order to humiliate her until she repents. You moron!

(Revelation 1:7, 8 KJV)

Behold, he cometh with clouds; and every eye shall see him, and they also which pierced him: and all kindreds of the earth shall wail because of him. Even so, Amen. I am

Alpha and Omega, the beginning and the ending, saith
the Lord, which is, and which was, and which is to come,
the Almighty.

"Are you ready for Jesus to come back again? What will you be doing when Jesus comes back? Will you be full of wrath, greed, sloth, pride, lust, envy or gluttony? Will you be in the back seat of the car with your boyfriend? Will you be doing drugs? Will you be partying and listening to secular music? You see, sin is like a piece of chocolate. It looks good on the outside but when you bite into it, it's full of maggots," Brother Green warns us as if he were personally saving us from Gehenna.

As Brother Green rattles off another sin, I circle _wrath_. I immediately think of QC and his disciples. _All I have witnessed since being thrown into Abaddon is the persecution of teenaged girls by angry preachers overflowing with 'wrath'. Now, it is a big 'no-no' in one of our lectures? I guess it's only a sin if we do it._

We are interrupted by the sound of a girl crying hysterically. Her hands are up in mid-air as she is led, like a criminal, to chapel by her _Buddy._ She is clearly indicating that she doesn't want to be touched. It's also quite obvious that she hates it here and is quite infuriated. It is an emotion that I still possess but cannot convey without losing rank (if I could reach any lower) or visiting _the Get Right Room._ We all stood in silence, identifying with her. She has wavy, light-brown hair and looks about thirteen years old.

Brother Green makes the unidentified girl's introduction: "Welcome, Carey Sun. I see you are back for another round."

Oh, my God. This unfortunate little girl has returned? She is the same age I was when I experienced my first kiss with Drake. Her childhood is ruined. She endured this castigation for one year and her parents dragged her back in again? What did they do, kidnap her in the middle of the night? It must have been something like that because I would have jumped out of the car while it was still in motion. There is no way *possible I could go through Victory a second time. Once I arrive home, I will never get in the car with my parents again!*

Brother Green continues the introduction, "Nice kid but she was backsliding in the *world* and that's why her parents brought her back. You see girls, she ended up hanging around a bad crowd and her so-called friends swayed her to listen to the *prince of the power of the air…* and that's what she did. Now she is not a *happy camper.*"

How about this… Carey Sun began to think for herself. She was enraged that her parents placed her in this hellhole. The knowledge that I have been abandoned here makes it clear that my parents did not accept me for who I was and wanted to change me. The majority of us do not have criminal records or behavior problems and were not placed here by a court. I speculate that all these girls were forced here by their parents because they couldn't mold them into their ways of thinking.

I hate this place. It's filling me with violent emotions instead of joy for life. I have invisible tape around my mouth and cannot speak. I used to love the Bible but now it's only about how I'm going to suffer in the afterlife because I am unworthy of salvation. I am already living with demons who belittle an overweight teen, blame youngsters for coming back in for a second round, duct tape a little girl's mouth because she doesn't comply with their ways, impose dorm silence and isolation from each other. These 'Christian role models' have placed landmines through my subconscious. I know what they are doing to me and yet I now blame myself for a biblical sin I carry in the depths of my sacred self. If Jesus came back, I would be left behind. The conditioning of chapel twice a day is finally breaking my spirit.

PIECE THIRTY FOUR

C:\Jeneen\Hell\Victory\Abomination.doc

I DON'T KNOW how much longer I can sit in this folding chair. Brothers QC and Green are implacable as they conduct their modern-day witch trial. I am torn between two thoughts: Is Victory some kind of penance for what I did to my aunt or is it just meant to drive me insane? So far, it's just Oyer and Terminer resurrected from 1690's Massachusetts. It is evident that our judgmental reverend blames us for his personal issues. I watch history repeat itself, but this time, the scars and burns are all internal. Nobody has been sentenced to hanging… at least, not yet. I glance over at the black piano to my right. The ivory keys are covered in grime and the sound of Ms. Arizona's playing is driving me a little mad. It all combines to form a unified destructive force that is slowly extinguishing my passion for life. It is mind-boggling but my inner light has been reduced to a mere flicker. All the girls await the predictable disparagements from the self-righteous judge and jury. *'Am I next?'* is the question on everyone's mind in this present-day Salem.

"Ladies, I want to talk about the music you listen to. You've got Prince who is a short, skinny little faggot that you all idolize. You listen to your rock bands, heavy metal and pop and the heathen messages they give you. You are just caving in to the ways of the *world*. It's no wonder you are in a reform school. Whatever happened to the bebop music we listened to in the fifties? It was upbeat and positive. Who wants to listen to "Janie's Got a Gun"? You need to listen to Christian music only. Take heed — there are Christian rock bands that can also lead you down a winding, sinful journey. Amy Grant, for instance, compromises her ways and does not have any convictions. She is too *worldly.* You need to be careful of the music you choose. You don't want to go back to your old ways. This is why Carey is back here for a second helping of our academy. She went back to her *rebellious behavior,* steered by the devil," QC yells as he slams his biblical knowledge down our throats for the umpteenth time.

"Rumor has it, Amy Grant was walking along the beach naked!" QC condemns her, leering over his stage of holiness.

Amy Grant? He's concerned about Amy Grant? Has QC ever seen Madonna's video 'La Isla Bonita' set in a church, with candles and images of Jesus all around her? She lights the candles and then seductively crawls on the floor, exploring her body, caressing her bosom and crotch while she sings. QC's panties are in a bunch over Amy Grant? I'll be damned!

As for Aerosmith, I have good associations to 'Janie's Got A Gun'. It's my memory of Junior Prom with Drake. I hear only laughter when I listen to it, however, if I listen to 'Victory in Jesus', 'You Are my Hiding Place' and 'Amazing Grace', I will only think of the pain that has been inflicted upon me. Christian music will never be the same and will only trigger horrific memories. 'Janie's Got a Gun' is child's play in comparison.

Another revelation occurs to me… Why have none of the former *Janies* come back with a gun. Maybe that's why QC is barricaded in here with surveillance cameras and an electrified barbed wire fence. By the way, why is he allowed to discuss secular music, naming worldly songs and calling people faggots near a cross? If I utter the words: gosh, darn, radical, John Denver, John Ritter, Fresh Prince, oh shoot or pants, I'm a pagan and have to write The Book of James countless times.

This is the hypocrisy of the dictator, writ large.

"You girls in here who are lesbians… do I have a message for you!

You know who you are, ladies… or should I call you heathens? I am sick of the gays and lesbians wanting rights and trying to fit into our society. You girls who hang around them are condoning their evil ways. You are just as guilty in the eyes of the Lord!" he says with a vengeance like a blazing furnace.

"Stand up, Heidi. You look like a boy with your *butch* haircut. Helpers, I need you to go in the back and grab a PINK bow and a ruffled dress for her to wear from now on. I am sick of you *spineless jelly fish* in here that love the gays and think it's okay! This is an abomination in the eyes of the Lord. Now, you will be able to distinguish the sheep from the goats!"

QC repeatedly slams his *holy book* against the pulpit. If the platform could speak, it would say: "What kind of clergyman is this? I don't like seeing the Bible used as a form of torment on little girls. This guy is completely out of hand. I've never seen anything like this. I want my old job in the conference room at the Hilton back!"

QC continues his daunting lecture, "Don't take my word for it; let's look at what God has to say. Open your Bibles to:

(Leviticus 18:22 KJV)

Thou shalt not lie with mankind, as with womankind: it is abomination.

(1 Kings 14:24 KJV)

And there were also sodomites in the land: and they did according to all the abominations of the nations which the Lord cast out before the children of Israel.

(Genesis 19:24KJV)

Then the Lord rained upon Sodom and upon Gomorrah brimstone and fire from the Lord out of heaven;

Ladies, there are no excuses. Homosexuality is an abomination unto God," QC shouts as he slam-dunks his twisted version of the *truth*. He stares us down as his eyes scan across the room.

I hear a loud commotion coming from the back of the hall. It's a girl talking back to her *Buddy*! I wonder what happened.

"Come on in and bring your *Buddy*, Rachel, with you. Don't worry, girls, God allows all His children into his Kingdom, including blacks!"

Wow! I haven't heard a racist comment like that since Archie Bunker on "All in the Family".

I can't believe nobody's reported this place!

"My *Buddy* says she wants to go to hell. She says she doesn't believe in God anymore and wants to die."

Most of us cringe at this because we share an unspoken fear that *we will suffer eternally, no matter how many times we accept Christ.*

Maybe she was raised in a different faith — Buddhist, Jewish, Wiccan, Muslim… It doesn't mean *diddly-squat*. Freedom of creed is prohibited here.

Maybe she just snapped because she has had enough?

I wonder what the ACLU would think of this? How dare he make racial slurs? I have a circle of friends who are of different cultural backgrounds and ethnicities. His words are, once again, downright disturbing. I have friends and family who are gay. Are you going to damn them all to the everlasting perdition just like you've done with me?

Flashbacks of Christian terminology I once embraced at my home church, come to me. Five, four, three, two, one… I am at Angeles Crest Christian Camp. Through First Christian Church, I earned a scholarship for the retreat for memorizing verses from the Word and vacuuming up the carpet. I wanted Drake to attend with me so we could be equally intertwined with Christ. I wanted him to accept our Savior into his heart in front of our youth group. I remember how emotional we became praying together. This was part of our special bond with each other. We were blended together, in spirit as *one*. Now, this separation from nonbelievers and believers is really starting to weigh heavily on me. And then I realize something… Only man-made religion can tell someone they are not equal to others. Only *man* seeks to tear his fellow humans into shreds for purposes of controlling them. To tell someone you are not *yoked equally* is a slap in the face. True divinity does not separate us because we are *one*.

My views are starting to change on a more philosophical/metaphysical level.

Hello, ACLU? Can you hear me? Where the fuck are you? Wake up! I need you to do a Nazi check tonight at Victory 'Christian' Academy. I regret to say, some of the girls in this hellhole are wearing pink triangles and they need your help.

My despair deepens, zapping more of my energy. Depression hits me and spreads like a fungus, enveloping me completely. I feel myself go more numb with each day that passes.

PIECE THIRTY FIVE

C:\Jeneen\Hell\Victory\GoatPile.doc

"Everyone on your knees... NOW!" a *Helper* shouts, beginning another typical day at Victory. Being forced to pray like this takes all the meaning out of it. It makes a once deeply personal act into a sour and bitter experience.

"Okay girls, you have fifteen minutes to get ready," a different *Helper* shouts with a voice that penetrates Dorms One and Two. I frantically put in my contact lenses. I don't bother applying warpaint or really fixing my hair. I just pull it back and secure it with a rubber band. I notice unwanted facial hair growing above my lip. I ignore it, sticking to my plan of managing priorities. *Who am I possibly going to impress today anyway?*

I rush so fast to make it on time that I leave my hairbrush on the sink by accident.

"Jeneen, you left a hairbrush on the sink. That carelessness is grounds for a demerit. You will write — '*I will not be stupid and leave a hairbrush by the sink*' one hundred times," Shelly says sternly.

We are ordered to write the name of the *Helper* who gave out the punishment in the upper right hand corner of our paper. I was so nervous about making a mistake that I accidentally misspelled her name.

She starts yelling at me in front of all my peers, "My name isn't spelled Shelby… It's Shelly. You are not stupid," she screams at the top of her lungs.

"You are a phony and a fake," she continues her tirade. She gives me another writing assignment — *'I will not be a phony'* one hundred times.

"Dorm One, Dorm Two, Dorm Three… line up," Shelly yells. We all move like cattle. One by one, we form a circle. "Everyone hold hands," Alexandra insists.

It's the only time we are permitted to touch.

I'm always afraid to make contact with someone's hand because I might be accuse me of being an 'eesh' and will be branded and tormented for the rest of my stay.

Sissy squeezes my hand, secretly, letting me know she cares about me. It's a brief but powerful reminder of our humanity. It's easier for her to take a risk because she's on the bottom of the pecking order. She's been locked in the *Get Right Room* for most of her stay. *What does she have to lose? She's at rock bottom.*

We begin to sing with a complete lack of enthusiasm:

It's a happy day and I thank God for the weather It's a happy day and I'm living it for my Lord.

It's a happy day and I thank God we're together, Living each day by the promises in God's word.

The words stand in such stark contrast to the sadness and despair of the girls in this tight-knit circle. The brainwashed *Helpers* are perplexed by our detachment and start to lose patience. "What is wrong with you girls? Can't you sing like you're happy?"

Are you fucking kidding me right now? Are you actually ordering us to NOT be miserable?

It's a pity twelve-year-olds can't grasp irony.

We all begin to smile robotically, fearing another arbitrary punishment. Alexandra reminds us that we have to memorize ten Bible verses to recite every day before breakfast. If we do not have them in our *database,* we will receive a writing assignment and a demerit for each verse we do not know.

This is an easy one for me. I memorized Poe's *The Raven* for literature class at Cornerstone Christian and I already have passages memorized from Bible study class. I feel sorry for the girls who I know will struggle with this task.

In single file, we are herded to the food line. I grab my food and it appears appetizing. I look forward to all of the meals, in spite of the stopwatch and force-feedings.

I stare across the table and am reminded, once again, of the emotional solitude. Conversation with a *Helper* is limited. There isn't any friendship or laughter echoing in this demonic facility. I stay inside of my own head and think of my dear, sweet Drake.

"Do not scrape the plate," Alexandra scolds another prisoner. "Time is up," another *Helper* chirps.

"If anyone has anything left on her plate, you get a demerit," Alexandra reminds us.

No need to reiterate common knowledge, Alexandra. We all witnessed the poor girl that was force-fed, remember?

Next, we head for Dorm Two and are permitted thirty minutes of *free time.*

When your time is delegated, is it really *FREE? Freedom* is when you can have a conversation about a song or write a letter to whomever you want or pick up the phone to call a friend. *Free* is being able to walk with your head held high. Girls use this *leisure time* to write their punishment sentences or memorize the verses that we were assigned this morning.

The half hour passes quickly. "Dorm Three, Dorm Two, Dorm One," Alexandra shouts. Time for chapel again. The two short, intersecting boards with the man hanging on them are no longer familiar to me as a symbol of forgiveness. They now stand for fear, abuse and hatred.

"Come on in here, girls... or at least some of you are," QC yells, staring down a girl with short hair.

One by one, we make our way to our assigned seats.

"Open your Bibles to:

Matthew 25:31-46

The Sheep and the Goats

31 - "When the Son of Man comes in his glory, and all the angels with him, he will sit on his glorious throne.

32 - All the nations will be gathered before him, and he will separate the people one from another as a shepherd separates the sheep from the goats.

33 - He will put the sheep on his right and the goats on his left.

34 - "Then the King will say to those on his right, 'Come, you who are blessed by my Father; take your inheritance, the kingdom prepared for you since the creation of the world.

35 - For I was hungry and you gave me something to eat, I was thirsty and you gave me something to drink, I was a stranger and you invited me in,

36 - I needed clothes and you clothed me, I was sick and you looked after me, I was in prison and you came to visit me.'

37 - "Then the righteous will answer him, 'Lord, when did

we see you hungry and feed you, or thirsty and give you something to drink?

38 - When did we see you a stranger and invite you in, or needing clothes and clothe you?

39 - When did we see you sick or in prison and go to visit you?'

40 - "The King will reply, 'Truly I tell you, whatever you did for one of the least of these brothers and sisters of mine, you did for me.'

41 - "Then he will say to those on his left, 'Depart from me, you who are cursed, into the eternal fire prepared for the devil and his angels.

42 - For I was hungry and you gave me nothing to eat, I was thirsty and you gave me nothing to drink,

43 - I was a stranger and you did not invite me in, I needed clothes and you did not clothe me, I was sick and in prison and you did not look after me.'

44 - "They also will answer, 'Lord, when did we see you hungry or thirsty or a stranger or needing clothes or sick or in prison, and did not help you?

45 - "He will reply, 'Truly I tell you, whatever you did not do for one of the least of these, you did not do for me.'

46 - "Then they will go away to eternal punishment, but the righteous to eternal life."

"We need to start separating the sheep from the goats so you girls know the difference. You shouldn't associate yourself with a goat. What are you going to do when you are out in the *real world*? *Birds of a feather flock together!* I'm tired of seeing a bunch of *marshmallows* around here. Have some backbone! You heathens know who you are. Sissy, I need you to come to the front and sit on the floor. Okay, ladies… that is the *goat pile.*"

He finds Jade and orders her into the *heathen* section. She walks over to the non-Christian group. Next he selects a *Helper* for the *sheep pile*, determining her salvation. On and on, he continues until his scan reaches me. His unnerving smirk crawls under my skin. QC stares at me for a while, trying to read me like a psychic. The length of time seems eternal and it reminds me of my father trying to determine if I have what it takes to be a runway model. QC miraculously concludes that I should be in the *sheep pile*. I can hear girls sobbing because they were wrongfully labeled.

What kind of clergyman is this? Am I the only one who thinks this is unacceptable? I want to stand up and lead the girls against this monster but I am not strong enough mentally. This lowlife is breaking me down and stripping away all my dignity. I truly feel like a non-Christian. He is driving me away from religion, not towards it. Goats or sheep, it doesn't matter. We're all garbage in his eyes. If this man truly represents God, then there's something seriously wrong with this universe.

Emotionally, I'm becoming completely numb. The loss of identity and total lack of power is like being sedated. I can't think straight and I feel nothing.

PIECE THIRTY SIX

C:\Jeneen\Hell\Victory\OffBuddy\Isolation.doc

TODAY IS THE day I will be taken off *Buddy*! I will soon be free of
the *choke collar* I've been wearing for a month. Just because I'm
free of my twelve-year-old *keeper* doesn't mean I don't still have to
watch my P's and Q's. Allow me to reiterate — I am forbidden to
discuss movies (even Disney!), music, friends, boyfriends, parents
(in a negative way), other girls' brothers, abuse that is taking place
inside Victory, sketches (including cartoons), writing in a diary, the
news or anything else that has not been specifically approved. It isn't
normal, not even for a Christian girl like myself. I still cannot fathom
this new reality. The only conversations I could have are discussions
from the *Sacred Guide* or the work of the *Anointed One*.

I pack my belongings and move out of Alexandra's dorm and
into Dorm One. I unpack my toiletries, socks, granny panties and
dingy culottes. I meticulously arrange them, in the correct military
order, in the drawer under my bunk. A young Middle Eastern girl
approaches me. Regina has dark, short hair, coke-bottle glasses and
appears to have perfectly bronzed skin. If I wore glasses instead of
contacts, mine would be as thick as hers.

"Hi, my name is Regina. What's your name?" she asks in a
jovial manner.

I am so relieved someone made an effort to communicate with me, in spite of her apprehensiveness.

I immediately respond, "My name is Jeneen. I have a fabulous idea. We can study our Bible passages until we memorize them all so we won't get any demerits. Do you want to practice and quiz each other on our assignment?" I ask with optimism, certain of her response.

"Yes, that would be wonderful," she replies, sounding relieved to have someone coaching her.

We start on the list, testing each other back and forth during our free time, until we memorize everything verbatim. It is difficult to miss *Helpers* watching us and listening to every conversation. They can't punish us because we only exchange ideas about our *heavenly Father* and the *Truth* — clearly our only option.

I am happy to have a connection with someone who likes me. I am finally starting to feel hopeful, until… a *Helper* pulls us aside and informs Regina and me, "You two are spending too much time together. We are putting you both on *separation.* This means that you cannot speak to each other ever again. You two have to keep six feet apart at all times. You also cannot write each other letters or notes (*not that we could ordinarily*). If you break the rule, it's five hundred lines and counts as five demerits. Is that understood?" The venom spewing from this *Helper's* mouth clearly comes directly from our dorm mother — Ms. Arizona.

These people are nuts. We didn't do anything wrong. Now I can't study the Bible with a friend? Victory is denying me the opportunity to make any new friends because I'll be put on separation again and again. It's difficult enough to avoid walking by one person in such close quarters. What if I'm in the bathroom and I'm unaware she's in the stall next to me? If a Helper sees us, we'll both get a demerit. No matter what I do, it's just considered wrong. I'll just keep silent, read my Bible and deflect any interactions with anyone. I'm by myself in here with a demonic god who hates me, a preacher who believes we are subhuman, a staff that revels in torture and power-mad children. What's the difference between being on Buddy or off? I'm still an untouchable and unworthy of having friends. When can I fucking die?

PIECE THIRTY SEVEN

C:\Jeneen\Hell\Victory\CareySunEscapesVictory.doc

THE UNMISTAKEABLE SOUND of an approaching helicopter grabs my attention.

I'm overwhelmed by a sudden flood of childhood memories. I am immediately reminded of the time my Nana Vera was babysitting my little brother and me. My parents were at a free theater show in Hollywood.

Violent rattling and tremors caused by the downdrafts of numerous helicopters shook our home. Giovanni and I, thinking it might be an earthquake, immediately took cover underneath the dining room table.

Shortly, I heard a knock on the door.

"Giovanni, stay underneath the table and do not move!" I yelled in a panic. "Who is it?" I answered terrified, due to the fear my mother programmed into my head regarding the danger of criminals.

I looked through the peephole and discovered it was an officer of the law.

Keeping the chain on the door, I slowly opened it.

"Are you home alone?" the man in uniform asked, concerned for my well-being.

"Yes, but my grandma is next door and she's watching my brother and me." I answered firmly, trying to control my jitters.

"Whatever you do, stay low to the ground. There might be gunfire!" he said quickly, warning us without a detailed explanation.

Later that evening, when my mom and dad came home, we were informed that there was a robbery at a nearby convenience store. The intruder had climbed over our chain-link fence searching for a hiding spot in our backyard. He was found two houses down. Shortly after this fiasco, there were bars on every window of our duplex.

What would a helicopter be doing here at Victory? A spark of hope ignites my optimism. Could this be a rescue? Immediately, the sounds of young girls screaming and crying fill the halls.

Wow, what a show these girls are putting on. Of course, QC has brainwashed the majority to believe we are nothing without him, so of course they can't cope with anything out of the ordinary.

Perhaps, they're just celebrating Victory being shut down! I can almost hear the sound of fireworks in the distance while the national anthem is playing. Apparently, my prayers of getting out of this lockdown have finally been answered.

Thank you, God!

I stop what I am doing because QC is calling everyone to the altar.

"Sit down on the floor, girls. I have something important to tell you," QC says in deep despair. I can clearly see that QC is crying. He appears restless and cannot help fidgeting while making this announcement.

"Girls, Carey Sun passed away." My fellow inmates start to weep. "How?" several girls ask at the same time.

"A stack of lumber fell on her. It was an accident... It was an accident! She was helping us build the church and the good Lord took her. I held her lifeless body in my arms and she was just an empty shell," he says as he continues to sob while blowing his nose on an eggshell hanky.

Yes, a stack of wood fell on her and she wasn't wearing a hard hat in a construction site.

Carey's work was forced child-slavery and she shouldn't have been in such a potentially dangerous environment in the first place. Damn this place and these people all to hell! Someone is bound to pick up a newspaper and read about Victory but certainly not my parents. I've never even seen my father holding a newspaper, let alone reading one. I'm almost certain, however, that other families would come through. I am now convinced that someone is going to come for us.

"Don't get any funny ideas, girls. Her parents are not going to press charges against me. They actually told me, 'She's better off in heaven than on the streets.' So don't think for a minute you are getting out of here," QC rants heartlessly. The stench of evil surrounds this man.

Karen raises her hand and then stands after receiving QC's *permission* and cries, "Carey used to tell me that she wanted to slip and slide with her socks on, through the streets of gold!"

QC continues, "That's right, girls. She's in heaven and in a better place. It's better than here!"

I could not agree more with QC. Any option is better than this excuse for an outreach program. I'm in shock that QC didn't take this opportunity to tarnish Carey's name further. After all, she came back to Victory with a bad attitude. According to QC, that is a big heathen quality. Is the guilt of this girl's death clawing at his conscience? What really happened to Carey? None of my fellow captives are permitted to say anything negative, even if it's the truth. I will NEVER know what really happened.

"Her lifeless body just lay there in my arms," he whimpers in hysterics. "Let's pray, girls:

Dear Lord, please know that I loved Carey with all my heart. I know she is in a better place with you, Father. The girls here miss her so much and I know that she is in your kingdom. She was saved here at Victory. We were able to bring her to you Lord, so it guaranteed her salvation. Please keep her safe, Father. In your name, I pray," QC says as he continues sobbing.

I could not collect any compassion for Carey or react to QC's comments about us not getting out.

What is wrong with me? I have turned into an emotionless droid. Ms. Arizona's instructions about 'no pity parties' have been permanently uploaded. Where are my tears for Carey? I couldn't talk to her because she was on Buddy. There was just an unspoken connection when I passed by her in the halls. If I can just muster up one emotion, it would prove that I'm still human.

As we march back to our dorms, everyone is in a state of shock. Any light of hope inside of us has been extinguished. There are no discussions regarding details, no speculations, no witnesses to this tragedy, nothing except how we all miss her. Most girls are scattered around their bunks praying.

It's a shame that I was forbidden to get to know Carey just because she was in 'isolated training', our lowest tier. She was forbidden to converse with any of the girls unless they were Helpers. I felt her pain when she came back the second time around. How could her parents do this to her again? Now she has exited this insane life. She has escaped the depredations of QC and his lunatic teachings. I secretly wish I was with her but I'm holding on to an earthbound angel... Drake. He is the only thing that keeps me grounded.

The next morning, we are back to our normal repetitive life. We carry out our tiresome routine of praying at 6 am, drawer check, nail inspection, reciting the same Bible verses and singing the same hymns. I am completely unfocused and the lyrics and passages have no meaning.

Besides, who wants to sing, *It's a Happy Day* and *I Thank God for the Weather*? It's not joyful for me here. It's heart-wrenching to come to grips with the fact that everyone on the outside is happy, safe and moving forward, yet I remain still and lifeless. I'm not going to thank God for the weather until he gets me out of here.

I sit and eat my breakfast in silence, inhaling my food in order to beat the clock and avoid more demerits. I start to feel queasy from all of the stress. Speed-eating has taken its toll. *I hope I don't vomit today.*

I wait in silence for the other girls to finish. I've come to the conclusion that I should not speak to anyone unless I am backed into a corner and absolutely have to. I patiently wait to be excused from the table by the *Helpers.*

"Five more minutes," a *Helper* reminds the girls. We march back to our dorms to continue our chores before chapel.

I have to clean the bathrooms today, scrubbing all of the toilets and the sinks. I admire my handiwork. Suddenly, the alarm of yelling *Helpers* signal my next move, "Gather up in line for chapel."

We march past QC as he leans up against his podium, scanning us up and down. I'm uncertain if he is looking over our anatomy or looking for damaged product. Either way, I feel naked being out in the open and vulnerable. His smile is intimidating because there aren't any positive thoughts about us behind it.

"Okay, ladies… We are going on a field trip today," he says with his devious grin.

We all look around in amazement.

Are we going out past the gate? Quite frankly, I don't want to because it would be similar to winning the lottery without being able to cash in the ticket.

"We are going to Carey's funeral. Her parents invited all of us. Now, don't get any funny ideas about running away. I told everyone that will be attending *what kind of girls you are* and everyone will be watching you. Everyone has been informed that you are thieves, liars, druggies, manipulators and that you can't be trusted. You will not talk to anyone there. You will not spread lies about this church. They will know you are not telling the truth anyway. If you try anything, you will be back on *Buddy* and will have to start all over again," QC yells as he wipes his glasses.

QC orders us to follow the staff, single file, onto a bus that is parked out front.

We all follow in a robotic fashion. It seems we can't even attend our friend's funeral with dignity.

We have been conditioned by QC to believe that society deems us as untouchables. I start to panic, anxiety flowing through my veins like poison. Now, we are forced to be around outsiders that feel the same way about us. *Is there a way to grieve over a death without a fucking speech about what kind of dirty little girls we are?*

I climb up and make my way to the back, deciding to sit next to a window.

The journey teases me with a taste of what the wind feels like outside of captivity. I look behind, wishing that this would be the last time I ever saw that hellish place. Victory is a portal to a flaming pit far away from God and soon I must go back. When I return to this flaming home of God's fallen angel, the fire will grow until, finally, I burn.

For now, I am on a prison bus on the way to the funeral of a comrade who died because of Victory's negligence.

PIECE THIRTY EIGHT

C:\Jeneen\Hell\Victory\FirstVisit.doc

IT IS HARD for me to fathom that I have endured three agonizing months in what amounts to solitary confinement. I am surrounded by approximately fifty teens but I can't really speak to anyone. I have been abandoned by my parents in this *educational institution*. Although I'm not in Victory's *Get Right Room,* I might as well be. I have only myself for companionship and I will soon become my own worst enemy.

It's a pity that my first forced visitation is with the people I least want to see — the ones that fed me to these wolves in the first place. Visitation in an actual prison is like a Las Vegas buffet compared to the meager rations here. If I had basic human rights, it would be Drake visiting me, hands down. I would have dropped a coin into a payphone and invited him to witness, first-hand, my transformation or I'd call a good attorney... probably both. One slight problem... we do not have a public phone... Not here at Victory... Who would've thought, in a million years, I could possibly be envious of the privileges afforded at a nearby penitentiary?

What will I say to the people that consider themselves caring parents? I can't ask them to get me out of this hellhole or tell them of the horrid things that take place here. They will just think I'm lying and then inform the loving, God-fearing pastor. It would only make my life more of a living nightmare than it already is.

My mind races, going through memory files. I see a young girl crying after she was told to stand up in chapel, about to be *crucified* by QC.

Karen wrote to her parents and explained what the staff does to us in here. Unfortunately, she did not know that all outgoing mail was monitored. It would have been nice if someone had warned her but now it was too late. "Young lady, you are a heathen. You are a manipulator. That's why your parents didn't want you anymore. The devil has your soul because you are filled with lies!" QC ranted, twisting our reality to fit his.

Once again, a young child pays the price for trying to do the right thing by telling the truth.

It is Sunday morning and we are sleeping in until 8 am. The now meaningless ritual of getting on my knees to pray to a God who believes *I'm scum of the earth,* is an ingrained habit. Before I lower my head towards the carpet, I focus on the texture of the powder-blue brick walls. I take a moment to think to myself that my period is now very late and that might just be my ticket out of this place.

God, please let my parents realize how cruel they were to lock me up. I want out of here.

Please let them see what they did to me. I just want to go home today. Amen.

I pick out a dress, unconcerned with the pattern or color. I ensure that all of my things are in order for the upcoming drawer check.

"Okay, girls, pull out your drawers so we can check them," Alexandra barks with authority.

Everything is in order and nothing is out of place. Fortunately, I was already a *type 'A'* personality at home. Neat freak or not, it didn't matter. *Helpers* would always find something wrong. Somehow, I passed with flying colors today.

"Okay, girls, lift your hands so we can run a nail check," Alexandra says commandingly. Nails had to be cut at all times. There could not be any white showing at all, otherwise you would get a demerit. I was in the clear because I trimmed mine so short, it made my skin bleed.

"Okay, girls, it's time to line up in single file. Dorm One, Dorm Two, Dorm Three," Shelly shouts as loud as she can. We live a military-like existence and we no longer can march to the beat of our own drum. QC now beats the drum and we move to the sound of his terrifying rhythm.

We travel behind the girl in front of us until we make our way into chapel. There they are, all of the villains that confined us to this prison camp. Most are smiling and waiting for their newly reprogrammed *Stepford Christian Child.*

My betrayers are sitting on folding chairs in the back. Their church-going attire is just a disguise to make them appear human. They have open arms for me but I do not want to embrace them. If I were free to, I would avoid them altogether. I have no other recourse than to hug them. I'll have to start my rehabilitation all over again if I do not. A cold chill rolls across my body. I could feel that my parents do not love me. It is not only pointless but also quite cruel to try and force me, against my will, to love the parents who thought nothing of me. No matter what, I was not good enough for them and they proved it by sending me here. The outstanding scholastics, ambition, motivation, hard work and self-discipline I possessed had no bearing on their decision to send me to a lockdown reform school. So, I got angry and disrespectful occasionally… What teenager doesn't push back against their parents? It was just easier for them to throw away the corrupted product and get something new. Something they could control better. Something with a remote…

My mother smiles, showing everyone her award winning mother-of-the-year skills but I know the truth. They're pretending to love me and I have to pretend right back.

Parents should protect their children and they did nothing of the sort. They did not trust or believe me about our family secrets. Then they made it worse by making me into the perpetrator... by sending me to prison. Where was my uncle? Why was I the one behind bars? Rage is rising to the surface and I want to take one of the chairs and throw it through a window but there are no windows around me... they only exist in my mind. Each shattered piece of glass would represent a part of my shattered soul. You want 'sugar and spice and everything nice' for a daughter and these 'Christians' are trying to create her just for you. How much money are you paying to keep me hidden in this private academy so that you don't have to face the truth? Let the show begin...

My mother wraps her arms around me and says, "I love you."

It is ten times worse than nails scraping a chalkboard every time she utters those words. It's meaningless. Anyone can give birth to a child but not everyone deserves the title of Mother. Is my father just a puppet on a string or is he just as guilty? I can't deal with this and I try to be someplace else, mentally, while this is happening.

I escape into a fantasy... Drake is holding me in his arms. The warmth of his energy sweeps over every inch of my body. He pulls me close to his chest. I caress his toned, muscular arms and I feel secure. I am numb at first but I then slowly relax. Once I soak in his love, I lose it and release all of the pent-up rage and pain. He understands what I've gone through and rocks me back and forth. Finally, I am safe, protected and cherished. I can breathe again. I inhale slowly as I allow the daydream to end and make my way back to reality.

"Turn your Bibles to Mathew 5:10," QC calls.

Matthew 5:10

New International Version (NIV)

10 - Blessed are those who are persecuted because of righteousness, for theirs is the kingdom of heaven.

How fitting!

I take notes in my Bible, as usual, to occupy myself and pass the time. I wonder if my mother will mention Drake or sneakily hand me a note from him.

QC keeps his sermon tame. Our parents won't ever get to see how he divides the sheep from the goats or his version of the Salem witch trials. He curbs his everyday tongue lashing but throws in his messages of fear of hell to get everyone to accept Jesus Christ into their hearts.

It is finally over and my parents and I decide to talk in the hallway.

It disturbs me that my mother brings up Giovanni. It only signifies that he is free, carrying on with his life and I... am not.

I desperately want my mother to bring up Drake... or do I? I don't want to risk losing my composure and spending the next two weeks in *the Get Right Room*. On the other hand, it would be so nice to have a letter from him, regardless of what is at stake. I would endure *the Get Right Room* for one month if I could have one letter from him telling me how much he loves me.

My mother inquires, "Why are you getting so many demerits, Jeneen?" *Let's see... Prior to being in this lockdown, I was in a private Christian school where I excelled scholastically, and was a model of excellent conduct. All of a sudden, I'm getting reprimanded for bad behavior. Is it possible that things are not what they seem here at Victory? Let's troubleshoot this together, Mother!* The idea that my mother was an analytical type who would see the truth in a logical way entered my mind and exited at lightning speed. That speck of hope is out of the question. *Emotionally, she is just an abused, five-year-old child herself.* My mother then proceeds to whisper in my ear. It is obvious that she was well-informed of the rules regarding discussions of Drake. She speaks softly and so very wickedly... "Drake has a girlfriend. I saw him with her when I was cleaning their house. He is much happier. Oh, by the way, her name is *J e s s i c a!*"

The ringing of her name buzzes in my ear, penetrating me like a million knives stabbing me in the heart. My mother made it personal. It might have been easier to handle if she was some sort of unidentified Jane Doe, but now… it's part of my reality.

Is this it? Is this where I melt down and go back to Buddy? My system just shut down automatically, without warning. I am completely disconnected and my equipment is now off. It's my only option since I do not have any other resources to protect my soul.

My father says something to me but I am obviously trying to slip out of this world.

"Yes, sir?" I ask in a zombie-like tone. I want them to see what QC has turned me into so they could get me out of here, but I sense they like it *a little too much.*

My mother is in a state of shock that I did not react in what would be a normal response to her bitter cruelty. My father sees the change. Brother Green interjects, "So, what do you think about your daughter now?"

"Oh, it's a one hundred and eighty degree turnaround!" my dad says with amazement.

I'm transformed because I have learned to bury my emotions so deep that no one could ever get to them. I metamorphosed into a child robot because you hired QC to rewire my hard-drive. My father doesn't understand that I don't care when he says 'I love you'. I am so damaged that I can no longer feel anything. I can't even manage hate for my jailers. I am empty and utterly defeated.

I look behind me and see my only companion — my shadow self. She is peering darkly at me and I feel the heavy weight of attachment dragging me backwards.

God? My mother is just saying this to be cruel. If he has a girlfriend, he's just lonely. He needs someone to fill in the gap while I'm away. When I return, we'll be together again as if time had not passed. We will just pick up where we left off. Our love is so strong that nothing can destroy it — not even this. Believing this is the only way that I can survive the pain and suffering. Please help me get through this.

I was better off not having *any* visitors. I make the decision to change my portion of food to half instead of whole. I'll do this first thing in the morning. I no longer have an appetite for food or anything else for that matter. I am feeling nauseated from grief. The bitter taste of loss is heartrending. Now I have to tamp down my sadness so I don't make myself sick. I do not want to be force-fed and then my own vomit before finally being locked up in *the Get Right Room.*

Soon, the night hovers over me like a dark cloud while I lay in a fetal position on my bunk. I think about the sheet covering my face, wishing I could suffocate myself with it. The only thing that stops me from trying is a spark of hope of getting out of here and reuniting with Drake. In spite of that optimism, I pull the material over my head and mull over the consequences of burning in the flames of fire for eternity. I thought about Drake's words, "It will only get better." I know deep down in my heart that I will have a life after doing my time. I pull back the pressed fabric and become aware of the hot droplets on my cheeks. I aggressively brush them away as if they are annoying insects.

PIECE THIRTY NINE

C:\Jeneen\Hell\Victory\LackofAppetite.doc

I AWAKE TO the shotgun sounds of *Helpers* hollering for us to open our eyes. We robotically get on our knees, in unison, on the dingy carpet. The cotton material of my long white nightgown aggravates me by reminding me of where I am. Disturbing thoughts swarm my mind like angry bees. There is no doubt, whatsoever, that I am not happy *in the moment*. The tranquil sounds of prayer have little chance of exiting my throat.

Instead of my usual morning prayers, I plead with God:

Please don't let me throw up today. My appetite has dwindled because my mother just informed me that Drake has found another girlfriend. I have been removed from the world as I knew it. Everyone is moving forward on the outside but I continue to rot and suffer in this hellish boot camp. I am in fear of being forced to eat my own spew. My stomach is incapable of handling food and I have no recourse but to change my status from a whole portion to half. Please help me get through this. Amen.

God? Where are you?

I frantically get ready for the day because time is running short. We all race in formation, called by the *Helpers* waiting by our bunks. One by one, we have our daily inspections, first hands and then drawers. The sound of nit-picky supervisors micromanaging us gets under my skin, but what else is new? It's just another day in an unchanging cycle.

We move like sheep to the circle. The chain of our interlaced fingers is the only thing that binds us together. We repeat our mundane Bible verses as the thorough checks continue.

"Jeneen, recite John 3:17," Bernadelli demands. I start chanting: *For God sent not his Son into the world to condemn the world; but that the world through Him might be saved.* Since I'm good at memorizing, I recite it verbatim. Jade stumbles over hers, just a little. I can hear *Helpers* saying, "You get a demerit!" Others get checked and I can hear written punishments being given out left and right. I wish I can help other students on what little free time I have but I'll just get put on separation.

It's now time to sing, *It's a Happy Day and I Thank God for the Weather* followed by *Victory in Jesus*. Now, I despise these Christian songs as if they were a fungus, spreading with each melody we sing. I used to enjoy singing in my youth group but that was when there were pleasant associations. Now everything just screams out barbed-wire electrical fences, damnation and persecution in the name of God.

My heart is going a million miles per hour because I'm about to ask Alexandra if I can change my meals to a half portion.

"Alexandra, I would like to ask you a question. Can I change my portion of food?" I sheepishly ask, fearing the answer. *Am I making a bad decision? What if I get hungry from all the work I do burning off calories? I will just change it back when I get better. I still have one pinch of pixie dust left to continue my fairy tale with. I should gain my appetite back eventually.*

"You can only change your portion one time. After that, you can no longer request whole portions," she says as she looks at me sternly.

My heart feels like it's on a rollercoaster. I realize I have no recourse other than to make a choice that will not jeopardize me. As I make my decision, I feel it burn in my throat. I'll have to choose halves because I do not want to risk being forced by the staff to eat my own puke. I know something will happen eventually because my despair is making me ill. It's a difficult thing because I also need fuel for the hard labor with Brother Green outside in the field.

I make my way to a silent table and catch a glimpse of Chrissy Nestleton.

Chrissy has long, beautiful, light-brown hair with gold highlights. She gives me an angelic smile. It astonishes me how she can hold strong and help others. I return her expression as my unspoken way of communicating.

I wish I could convey my struggles to Chrissy. I need someone to lean on and help mend my broken heart. I long to have someone I can trust to bare my soul to but the only one who can really hear me is God. I'm just hoping His hands aren't currently tied up. *Do you think you can move a mountain today? Please fix my digestive system.*

I start off a little slower this morning. I put the eggs gradually into my mouth, the English muffin and then the sausage. I finish every last bit of what's on my plate, despite my anxiety over Drake and Jessica.

The sharp pain hits me like a bolt of lightning. Out of nowhere, I start to cramp. I feel like I'm being stabbed in the abdomen. The pain is unbearably excruciating. It is by far the worst I have ever experienced.

"You are now dismissed!" Shelly says as she releases us from our first meal of the day.

I make my way to the bathroom. The seat is cold and I dread inspecting my panties. I see that I am not carrying Drake's child after all and the delay was merely due to the anxiety of being in this place. My only means of escape has, ironically, been denied to me by my own diligence. I stare at the toilet paper roll for quite some time searching for some sort of comfort. Secretly, I think I wanted to be a mother. I know I have much love to give because I actually felt it with Drake. Now... that's gone too.

My mother is completely disconnected and couldn't care less about my loss. In fact, she is the one responsible for destroying my life. QC doesn't care about my state of mind, because to him, I'm just an untouchable who deserves this lot in life. I have to bury these memories and feelings in a hidden file, deep within my hard drive. Now, I'm pretending my happiness with Drake never existed. I put that moment in time on hold, keeping it frozen, in hopes of thawing it out one day in the future. *We didn't break up. I will just remain in this purgatory until someone releases me from my bondage. Then, Drake and I can resume tending the seeds that we planted for our future together.*

Regardless of the devastating news, I have no other recourse then to shut it out of my mind. I am fighting a war for my own survival. I need to be functional. I will need all of my inner strength to fight this bloody battle to save myself.

PIECE FORTY

C:\Jeneen\Hell\Victory\Thanksgiving.doc

THANKSGIVING... CELEBRATED ON the fourth Thursday in November, is a time to observe the blessings of the harvest and the preceding year. The holiday is a reminder to be grateful for that which we sometimes take for granted: our families, jobs, friends and the nurturing food we have on our tables. Victory is abuzz because our parents are invited, on this heartwarming occasion, so we can see them twice this month as opposed to the usual once a month visit. Since my unfit progenitors are the only ones permitted to visit me, I am nonchalant about the whole experience. Perhaps, that is putting it lightly. I really don't want to see them and give my mother another chance to get under my skin, however, it is my only form of outside entertainment. I can't stop them from coming anyway. I wonder if this is how the president feels when he's obligated to host foreign dictators just to keep the peace. Besides, I am lonely in this place. I have no friends. All of the smiles here are empty and *zombie-like*, including my own, but I don't really feel like there's anything to celebrate. *Is it getting closer to my year yet? Eight more months to go...*

Holiday preparations are well underway and I see the festive decorations in the dining hall area. Leaves and pumpkins are everywhere and I catch an occasional whiff of pumpkin pie and cinnamon. It should smell like home but it's just rancid and disgusting.

We will have the day off from our regular routines and duties. There will be no screaming at girls in front of parents who are paying top dollar. Everything is on the down-low because some parents come to visit their offspring. No comic book hero ever protected his secret identity as well as Victory does.

I have some free time today because it has been incorporated into our schedule. It is mandatory that I write one hundred times: *I will not leave my contact lens case on the sink, I will not ask a stupid question* and *I am not a phony, so stop acting like one.* Then a whopping five hundred times I am ordered to write: *I will not be anywhere near the person I am on separation with.*

It is a damn good thing I didn't try to develop multiple friendships. Jesus! Well, there goes my Friday night. Since I have a total of eight writing punishments, I'll have to miss tomorrow night's 'sweets and charades' evening. It doesn't matter anyway. I would be just as miserable having a reward night. I'll be more productive during Bible study in Dorm Three… and it might just make the time go by faster. In a way, it's harder to have fun for two hours and then have to go back to the abuse. At least this way, there's no let-down. I think this is for the best…

I write my parents one of the mandatory twice-weekly letters. It's just twisted how this *Christian* organization regularly forces us to lie to our parents. The truth… Well, sometimes it's hard to swallow. It can be downright hurtful but is also the best remedy to fix what is broken. Again, what do I know? I'm just a teenage girl.

Dear Mom and Dad,

Please open up your Bibles to:

Parenting:

Colossians 3:21

English Standard Version (ESV)

21 - Fathers, do not provoke your children, lest they become discouraged.

Psalms 127:3

5 - Behold, children are a heritage from the LORD, the
fruit of the womb a reward. Like arrows in the hand of
a warrior are the children of one's youth. Blessed is the
man who fills his quiver with them! He shall not be put
to shame when he speaks with his enemies in the gate.

Matthew 18:12

14 - What do you think? If a man has a hundred sheep, and
one of them has gone astray, does he not leave the ninety-nine
on the mountains and go in search of the one that went astray?

And if he finds it, truly, I say to you, he rejoices over
it more than over the ninety-nine that never went
astray. So it is not the will of my Father who is in
heaven that one of these little ones should perish.

I hope everyone is well. Happy Thanksgiving!

Jeneen

I write a passage coinciding with my week. There is no real discussion about anything. There will be approximately ninety-six to one hundred letters, packaged up nicely, filled with scripture and *heartfelt bullshit*, however, anything important, anything real, anything about what I'm really experiencing, will never reach anyone outside of these walls.

How on Earth does Victory patch broken families? All they do is sweep the real problems under the rug and force the girls to pretend to be what they're not. Once we get home and away from the fear and intimidation, the problems that sent us here will still be there, waiting to resurface. Victory merely creates time bombs. It is inevitable. I'm fearing what my violent destruction will look like. I can almost see the distinctive mushroom cloud hovering over my Newbury Park home. I suddenly think about the girls who are regularly tortured far more than the rest of us — Jade and Sissy.

"Okay, girls! We are going to form one group that has parents visiting and one that does not. Jeneen, your parents couldn't make it. Your mom's leg hurts. I think she is going in for knee surgery," Ms. Arizona informs us.

My mother's leg hurts? So what happened to my father? Why can't he make it? Does he have lower extremity problems as well? It's okay. I don't need my dysfunctional parents here so we can pretend to be a loving family. I don't need my mother here to try and hurt me by mentioning Drake and Jessica.

Again, I can't help thinking about convicts in maximum security prisons. They can request or refuse visitors. They can send and receive mail and phone calls. They can study and earn degrees in whatever interests them. They have vending machines! They have... basic human rights.

I watch all the families reunite with their daughters at the separate tables and I hear the laughter of kindred spirits.

I am left with the other girls whose families couldn't make it either. We sit quietly and eat our *Thanksgiving* meal. We are forbidden to speak. I think to myself... *Missing this is definitely for the best.*

PIECE FORTY ONE

C:\Jeneen\Hell\Victory\Exercise.doc

"LET ME TELL you why we have exercise, ladies. Apparently, someone complained that we didn't provide an athletic routine here at Victory. One former student said I'm allowing *you girls* to get fat! Can you believe that? I am sick and tired of you *game-players* complaining to your parents about this program! You tell them that we use you as slaves by making you work. You wonder why we have all these crazy rules… It's because of you," QC yells, attempting to convince us that it's our own fault.

First of all, 'these girls' that he is referring to must have left the program. No 'prisoner' in her right mind would complain about Victory due to the serious consequences. Also, those particular letters would never make their way into the hands of the postal service. How about the Victory trash basket? I bet there's a dumpster filled with letters from teens hoping that their messages would reach their families, as well as social services. The crazy rules are a walk in the park compared to what I have witnessed and experienced thus far. I'm highly doubtful that the stupid rules are what someone would complain about! How about the child abuse?

Exercise is a joke. I would love to work out in my free time but we do not have those privileges. Everything is scheduled here — there is no real free time. QC doesn't want us to be idle.

"If you have idle time, you will more than likely get into sin," QC says, enlightening us with his wisdom.

I'm not afraid of hard work. In my former life as the 'rebellious Jezebel', I had a full-time job in the summer and part-time on weekends during the school year. I also volunteered to help at my local church.

"All of you think you have rights. You don't have any rights in this place! You lost your rights when your parents dropped you off!" QC screams, confirming the obvious, and causing two girls in front of me to jump.

"You and your social services. How many of you *backsliders* called social services on your parents?

Turn your Bibles to:

Proverbs 13:24

He that spareth his rod hateth his son: but he that loveth him chasteneth him betimes. (Proverbs 13:24 KJV)

Now, turn your Bibles to Proverbs 23:13." QC slams the Bible on the pulpit, waking up another student in the front row.

Withhold not correction from the child: for if thou beatest him with the rod, he shall not die. (Proverbs 23:13 KJV)

"For all of you brats who called social services on your parents… guess what? It's different here at Victory. No one would find you credible anyway! You are all just troubled teens in a correctional program! Your parents have signed you over to me.

I believe in spankings and corporal punishment but I take pride in the fact that I do not spank any of you girls like they do at the Roloff Schools. Lester is my mentor. He has been for many years," QC screams with passion.

Wow, that explains everything. QC is a product of Lester Roloff, and one day, QC will pass the torch.

"There is also a sister reform school in Louisiana called, New

Bethany. Brother Mack Ford is running it. He doesn't tolerate any of your nonsense and whippings are allowed!"

You mean to tell me, there are other schools like this, but worse? How is it that so many people can get away with child abuse and hide behind the name of God?

Five, four, three, two, one… Palm trees surround me. I am standing in front of a house. The Spanish-style window treatments and stucco give it a glamorous outward appearance. Life inside could be far less attractive.

I clench my fist as I peer inside the dining room at the terrified little boy on the black and orange studio couch. Burning tears are streaming down his face while his father, holding a badly worn violin bow, yells, "Stop crying or I'll give you something to cry about!" He found the bow on one of his collection routes. The only sounds it produces now are cries of pain.

I look to my right and, by the window in the living room, is a terrified little girl in her Mickey Mouse pajamas. Her mother just finished an hour-long tirade against her and her brother. Their father had just returned from his day of picking up a ton of garbage in the brutally hot West Valley. I look up over an archway and notice artwork made up of beer can pull-tabs. There must have been so many that the obvious choice was to create this masterpiece. It must have been a family project. I look at the girl again but she has her head covered in an attempt to hide from her parent's violence.

It's me, of course. I'm the small child cowering in fear. My father didn't only hit my brother, he was abusive towards my mother as well. I don't remember if he hit me. I know I *flew away*, disassociating myself from the trauma. I could tell he resented all of us, feeling that his dreams were smashed because he had to settle down and take care of his family. He did not hesitate to frequently remind his tribe of this fact. "If I didn't have children, I would still be a photographer and my shoulders wouldn't hurt!" he complained ruthlessly, as if I were his therapist and could handle what he dumped on me. I want to embrace the little girl and comfort her. I wrap her body with a crocheted blanket her grandmother made as a gift and swaddle her to provide protection.

The sounds of our eternally angry preacher fly me back to Victory. As I descend, QC gradually softens his voice a notch or two, transitioning into prayer mode.

"Let's pray, ladies. Father, thank you for giving me your words of wisdom to transform these girls and head them down your path. I praise you for the tools you have given me to polish them into the best Christian mothers. In your name I pray." QC wraps up his knowledge in a nice little package so we can take it home with us.

We head out the door and follow *Helpers* to the exercise area outside. It's unbearably warm and it's a good thing we are wearing culottes. We line up in rows, keeping an arm's length between us.

There are three *Teen Sergeants* in front of me performing jumping jacks. We have to follow them like mirror images. If anyone breaks formation, we are pulled aside or we have to do it all again.

"Rebecca, you need to keep up with us. You are not allowed to stop. You get a demerit and you have to start all over again. Get on your feet now! Do you hear me?" Maria yells loudly so that we can all clearly hear the sounds of humiliation.

"Yes, I hear you. My leg hurts and I'm having trouble breathing," Rebecca cries.

"I don't care. Get back up and watch your attitude. You do this all the time, Rebecca. Are you a game-player? You are nothing but a phony and a game-player." Maria shouts again.

The *Helpers* switch to a one-legged jumping exercise called *hot foot*. We cannot stop until they tell us to. I am wondering how much my body will follow my mind. My breathing is in overdrive and if someone paid attention to me, they could hear me gasping for air. If I use my pent up rage as fuel, I can keep moving. My anger will be the key ingredient in helping me survive this *evangelical dumping ground.*

The *Helpers switch to modified push-ups.* We follow like robots.

"Rebecca!... What did I tell you? You have to keep up. Do it for the Lord! If you do not follow, I will make everyone repeat the cycle. Do you want that? Do you? Everyone will resent you!" Maria shouts.

The use of 'Do it for the Lord' makes me sick to my stomach. It is so wrong to invoke God to justify punishment. I have only negative associations now when someone mentions anything about the Lord, God, agape, Jesus and Christ in this camp for the walking dead. I wonder what kind of effect it will have on me when I finally leave. At this moment in time, those words send a message of hate piercing through my heart. These feelings will most likely haunt me for the rest of my life.

It makes me so sad that the staff in this compound is turning 'Pure Love' into something that is corrupt. Religion now means control to me and not free will. Imagine if it didn't exist... I wouldn't be here today, spirit broken, filled with fear and self-hate, dehydrated in the hot sun and doing goddamn push-ups on the gravel, making my knees bleed.

PIECE FORTY TWO

C:\Jeneen\Hell\Victory\LaborVersusEducation.doc

THE GOLDEN HAMSTER wheel of chapel turns on its axle. Run or walk, it doesn't matter; I'm not going anywhere.

Our fearless leader, the former alcoholic, has come to know Jesus. Fortunately for him, someone groomed him into a *righteous Christian. Hallelujah!* The *humble* man told us of his triumph many times, placing his sins on the altar before us. Many girls would throw their past on that very platform, naively trusting the *empathetic* pastor. His calling is from *God* and his mission is reforming troubled teen girls. How *noble* of him. He can't be just some nut-job with a Bible! This school is his chance to repay the good Lord for forgiving him for slamming down too many bottles of vodka.

My experiences in life have given me the insight of the telltale signs of a drunk. I lived with two, let's not forget. The vicious words that fall uncontrollably from their lips strike at random. Logic and control are stripped away and all that's left is an angry five-year-old. Apparently, the hotheaded man standing by the podium is currently sober, and yet…

"Ladies, you are always going against the grain, trying to do things your own way. You are a bunch of lawbreakers! You broke trust with your parents. You lied, stole, ditched classes, partied, smoked weed, drank and cussed at your parents. Some of you went as far as to hit your parents! You are a bunch of juvenile delinquents! Yes, ladies, some girl in here stole her parents' credit cards and went on a shopping spree! You know who you are, Katrina," QC practically spits across the pulpit. Why do some preachers think that yelling and screaming make what they have to say more meaningful?

Everyone looks at Katrina because it's the only form of entertainment. She smiles nervously. Now, she is on QC's list.

Most girls are laughing; I am unamused.

Wow, that list does not apply to me. Oh, wait a minute... I talked back to my parents when they didn't believe me after I told them about my uncle. Oh wait, there's more... I pushed my mom away when she tried putting holy oil on me, thinking I was possessed. I also called her a bitch. At the time, and without my thesaurus, it was the best thing I could come up with. Oh, so that's why I'm in here. I was always wondering...

"Some of you were prostitutes before coming here and we picked you up off the street. We have picked up runaways and drug users and we brought you here to protect you," QC states as if he were some sort of hero.

QC continues, "For those who are not saved, you need to ask the Lord into your hearts.

Turn your Bibles to John 3:16."

(John 3:16 KJV)

For God so loved the world, that he gave his only begotten Son, that whosoever believeth in him should not perish, but have everlasting life.

I watch several girls sheepishly come up to the front to pray and accept Jesus Christ into their hearts. I hear them sobbing. *QC got to them... but not in a good way. I am not going up because I accepted Christ into my heart before I came into this hellhole. The only difference now is that I'm questioning my salvation because QC makes us feel unworthy of God's love.*

"Ladies, let's pray.

Dear Jesus:

Thank you so much for giving me the opportunity to help these girls see the light and change their lives for the better. I ask you to forgive and cleanse them of past sins in order to start anew. In your name, I pray. Amen." QC sings with an angelic and convincingly sincere tone.

Brother Green comes into chapel and makes an announcement that he is looking for volunteers to work with him. Normally, he just orders girls at random to help him but this time he is giving us the privilege to choose for ourselves. I automatically raise my hand. I do not want to attend school; I'm too unfocused and distraught. I'd rather submit myself to hard labor. I'm so relieved to have this option instead. It entails a fair amount of strenuous work but I don't care. Besides, I have a lot of rage I need to let out. I have an opportunity to release my tension out in the field. I don't give a flying fuck if it kills my back. Brother Green also likes my work and in some twisted, demented way, it makes me feel good.

"Jeneen, Bernadelli, Karen and Stephanie, you can come with me out back after you change into your work clothes," he says matter-of-factly.

We all march over to the laundry room to grab old culottes and shirts. We are permitted to go outside the gate for some projects but only when he is out there with us. Besides, it's not like we have the key to get out when he isn't around. There are rows and rows of digging ahead of me. I am prepared to work hard and be productive. Going out of the gate is not freedom; Brother Green watches us like a hawk. I wouldn't run anyway, because if I were caught, the punishment would be catastrophic. I wouldn't be able to work with Brother Green again. I would spend months in *the Get Right Room* and I would likely get a longer sentence in this prison camp. It's not worth the risk.

It makes me feel good that someone actually somewhat trusts me. Since we are considered thieves, liars, criminals and deceivers, this is considered an honor at Victory.

I start lifting the gardening tool and slamming it into the soil. This is my chance to keep as occupied as possible. The time will go by faster. I try to stay focused on my task but being outside the gate and feeling the cool breeze triggers another memory of my former life. I imagine the breeze growing stronger until it lifts me up and carries me off. I drift on the wind, farther and farther away, until I am no longer trapped. I inhale the air of freedom and immediately call out to Drake…

PIECE FORTY THREE

C:\Jeneen\Heaven\Drake\Mr. L\TheRaven.doc

THE WHIRLWIND BRINGS me safely to a familiar room. I touch the arms of my seat to make certain I'm firmly grounded. I'm in a basement and find myself having to adjust my eyes to the bright fluorescent lighting. I am presently in my former school, Camarillo Cornerstone Christian. I notice a ghostlike figure from my past. He is a middle-aged instructor, pacing back and forth and cradling a book in his hands. He is dissecting Edgar Alan Poe's literary work while encouraging us to do the same.

He is reading us Poe's 1845 masterpiece:

Once upon a midnight dreary, while I pondered, weak and weary,
Over many a quaint and curious volume of forgotten lore,

While I nodded, nearly napping, suddenly there came a tapping, As of some one gently rapping, rapping at my chamber door. 'Tis some visitor,' I muttered, 'tapping at my chamber door-Only this, and nothing more.'

Although Mr. L was a bit strict and ran a tight ship, he was a wise and motivational teacher. I made sure I was alert for all of his lectures, clinging to his every word. I sat in the front row primarily because of my vision but also because I was his top student.

One of my most challenging projects of the semester was to memorize poetry for my Literature class. I selected *The Raven* by Edgar Alan Poe. Memorizing the entire poem would earn me an

A+ in Mr. L's class. I rationalized that if I can retain the lyrics to a song, why not a poem? In fact, why not make it into a rap song? That would certainly allow me to show some of my own creativity. If Run DMC was capable, why couldn't I?

I decided to call Drake to share my plan of action as soon as I came home. "Dominos Pizza!" he answered the phone, jokingly.

"Hi, Drake. How was school?" I asked curiously, hoping to hear more Sally stories. The female class clown of Newbury Park took comedy to another level. Who wouldn't want to hear about her latest shenanigans?

"It was school," he said in a humdrum tone.

One of the many traits I loved about Drake was his dry sense of humor; you often didn't know if he was joking. It routinely turned into a complex challenge. A smile would make it obvious but he kept his hidden and tucked away for special occasions. His deadpan expression kept me guessing and on my toes at all times.

"I'm wondering if you would like to study with me at the library this weekend?" I asked, eager to tackle my *Raven project* while sneaking in some smooches.

"I'm sure we can arrange that. It's getting close to midterms so I could use some extra study time," he said in his whispering, baritone voice.

The next day, I launched out of bed like a missile. My life was full of excitement, contentment and romance.

I ransacked my closet searching for an ensemble that would make Drake's jaw drop. I decided to wear my favorite white mini dress, although a cigarette burn on the bottom seam from its previous owner made it imperfect. I was a bit apprehensive about wearing it but found its intricate beading and originality superseded any flaws. I was hoping Drake would overlook it as well.

I heard a rapping on my window. Could it be Poe's *Raven*? "Who is it?" I asked, knowing of course, that it was Drake. "Domino's pizza!" he announced.

Doesn't he get sick of being my delivery boy? I better get a pizza out of this rendezvous!

There he stood, without pizza, but carrying a rose.

"A rose for a rose. Wow, you look absolutely amazing!" he said, while gazing into my eyes.

Before I could return the compliment, he leaned downward to meet my lips with his. I was lost in a dreamlike state, wanting more.

He grabbed my hand and I quickly shouted, "Bye, Mom and Dad. Drake and I are going to study at the Thousand Oaks Library."

After escorting me to the passenger side, I noticed he was wearing my favorite blue shirt. I yanked on the material, pulling his chest towards mine, until I felt our lips touch.

Once the key turned, I heard a loud screeching vocalist and guitar noises that were foreign to my ears. I could see Drake banging his head to the intense rhythm.

He lowered the volume. I remained uncertain if it was for my sake or his but I don't think he was worried about his hearing.

He glanced over my lap and noticed the obvious but, gentleman that he was, never said a word about the burn. I'm sure he was aware of its other qualities.

Drake found a parking spot near a shady pepper tree. The architecture of the building made it look more like an art museum than a regional library. We settled for a table near a window with a clear view of the oak trees. It was absolutely breathtaking and I thought to myself… *How on Earth am I going to concentrate?*

I opened my literature book to *The Raven* and started the first two lines. I became a human beatboxer, tapping the floor with my foot, and creating puffing sounds into my hands. I was catching everyone's attention, including the librarian. I kissed Drake on the cheek and then it escalated into something more heated.

The librarian cleared her throat.

I continued, two lines at a time, to add more and more of the poem to my memory. Treating it like a rap song made it very easy for me to memorize quickly.

Unconcerned of the librarian's whereabouts, I found my way to Drake's ear and started nibbling. I expected to hear another *harrumph* from the librarian but none came. I continued, alternating between memorizing and nibbling, until we were done several hours later.

"Do you want to catch a movie tonight?" Drake asked.

"Yes, that would be great. What's playing in the theater? I have no idea because I seldom watch TV so I haven't seen any recent trailers."

"How about a date-night movie? *For Keeps* looks interesting. Molly Ringwald is in it." I accepted.

After arriving at the Jan's Mall Theater, we nestled into our reclining seats with our spread of junk food. I snuggled next to him and, as the trailers for other movies came on the big screen, I raised our interlocked hands and kissed his.

During the movie, I heard the sounds of Drake hysterically laughing when Darcy's (Molly Ringwald's) boyfriend's dad said, "Grow up! You had a gerbil last year. You forgot to feed it. It died!"

I tried sneaking in another kiss but Drake laughed as he teasingly demanded, "Watch the movie!"

The movie was about two teens having to make a serious decision to keep their baby or give it up. It made me think about my future with Drake. I thought about having a child with him but it wouldn't be until after college. The film reinforced these feelings.

I always felt Drake would make a loving father because I knew how nurturing he was with me.

Afterward, we headed for youth group at First Christian Church in Newbury Park. We had our couple's group session on relationships. Miguel and Florence were leading this particular biblical learning session and I really enjoyed our study time. We discussed the healthy way to resolve conflicts, matching scripture to the topic. Funny, we hardly ever fought. Was it because of the sheer bliss of teenage love… or was it because I was just more submissive at that time in my life?

I looked around the building and recalled a couple times when I volunteered to help out with the church. I would attend services and youth group twice a week. The sound of Christian songs at that time made me think of a kind God. It was all part of the memory of my first love with Drake. Our strong Christian foundation firmly supported our relationship.

Two weeks have passed and my nose has been plastered to the many pages of *The Raven* while I paced my room memorizing lines.

The time has arrived to share my big accomplishment. My heart is pumping like crazy as I sit in my chair waiting for my turn to present my project to the class.

Mr. L asked, "Does anyone want to volunteer to go first?"

I immediately raised my hand. I was always plagued by stage fright. I despised giving oral reports or a speech in front of the class. All eyes looking at me horrified me to the point that my hands would shake and my voice would crack. I forced myself to face my fear. It was easier to step out of my comfort zone because I had my Drake's spirit by my side. I just sort of took him with me to give me confidence. He said I was smart and I believed him.

"Very well, Jeneen, go ahead," Mr L said, intrigued to hear my choice of poetry.

I jumped to the front and became the first (and only) non-Jewish, female member of the Beastie Boys. The whole class started laughing but I didn't mind because I knew I had their undivided attention. I was sailing but the introduction came to an unpleasant, screeching halt.

Mr. L interrupted, "That is not how you read poetry!"

He started the first line with a classic rhythmic flow and I nearly had a cardiac arrest.

"Mr. L, I didn't memorize it like that! I memorized it as if it were a rap song. Can't I just do it the way I learned it?" I pleaded, carrying the look of fear on my face… my *GPA!*

"Very well, continue," he said sharply.

Oh, thank God! Good thing I prayed before this performance.

I carried on with my rap version of *The Raven* from beginning to end, with my fellow classmates in stitches. The cheers of encouragement gave me enthusiasm and helped with my stage fright. I felt empowered because I recited it perfectly while entertaining other students. I received an A+.

My brother once confided to me that Mr. L would use me as an example during other English classes, including his. It made me feel special that Mr. L was praising me but then I found out he compared me to Giovanni. Giovanni informed me that Mr. L said, "You should be like your sister who does her homework all the time." Mr. L was a no-nonsense English teacher and I liked him because he pushed me towards my full potential. I felt sad, though, for my brother being negatively compared to me. By the same token, Mr. L made me feel intelligent. Mixed feelings…

PIECE FORTY FOUR

C:\Jeneen\Heaven\PositiveReinforcement\Mrs.T.doc

KNOWING I WAS truly loved by someone energized me and gave me confidence. I could feel the intensity of it when Drake held me in his arms. You can feel the difference between a casual, friendly hug and the embrace of love. It's almost a psychic link, a feeling of deep connection. Every time I held Drake, his essence transmitted data to my hard drive. I stored away more and more files filled with beautiful images and emotions. I shot out of bed every day, excited about life. Who needs coffee when you're a fifteen-year-old in love?

I also darted out from under my sheets for another reason — to avoid waking up to the sharp, piercing sound of my mother's startling voice. My alarm clock was subdued in comparison to my mother's earsplitting screams. The 1400 square foot home kept us in close enough quarters that these lunatic drills every morning were highly unnecessary. Rather than get out of bed to knock gently on my door, my mother opted for yelling, at the top of her lungs, from the master bedroom. Too bad our house wasn't big enough to have an intercom system… at least you can adjust the volume on those. This proverbial *early worm* needed at least two hours to prepare herself for the day. Plus, I wanted extra time to review schoolwork and prepare for tests.

After sprinting to my parents' room to make sure my mother

didn't sound off (that was for emergency backup ONLY), I made my way towards the shower. I turned the knob towards hot and then a little push towards cold, making the temperature nice and warm… perfect! After getting out and drying off, I took three pumps of hair gel into my palm and vigorously rubbed both together. I applied the popular goop all through my damp locks. I scrunched my hair while blowdrying it until it resembled a rat's nest. I took painstaking measures, making certain the front strands were sticking up just right, and then spraying a generous amount of Aqua Net all over the whole thing. I coughed and I coughed again as I single-handedly destroyed the ozone layer above California.

I was nearing my sweet-sixteen birthday and I had a feeling my mother was planning a surprise party. I have had four birthdays that included friends. The other celebrations were family only. My twelfth birthday became my first sleepover. My fourteenth birthday was a party bash with my friends Samantha, Jennifer and Lisa. My fifteenth birthday party took place in New York and was hosted by my aunt Sylvina. I had an inkling this one was going to be big!

My mother yelled, "It's time to go to school!"

I was ready, right on schedule and looking forward to my Algebra II class with Mrs. T.

I liked Mrs. T because she offered extra credit as an option to jump our grade one level up. I definitely took full advantage of the opportunity. It took me some one-on-one coaching to comprehend the formulas, but once explained, I caught on.

One day after class, I asked if I could get her help with an assignment. Mrs. T stayed with me for the duration of her lunch break. Before I knew it, she was private tutoring me three times a week on her free time, without accepting any extra money. She had a huge heart and really wanted every pupil to succeed, even if it meant sacrificing her spare time.

She made me feel intelligent and played an important part in boosting my self-esteem. She was very nurturing and a strong role model; I put her in the *mother that I wish I had* category.

As I transposed numbers from the left to the right side of the quadratic equation, Mrs. T overlooked to make sure I solved the formula properly. It was easier for me to solve mathematical puzzles when displayed on a chalkboard. Mrs. T knew I was a visual and tactile learner. She also had a keen understanding of my drive and motivation and I believe that was why she went above and beyond the call of duty.

When I saw my report card for the first quarter, I received a B in her class. She wrote on my comments, "Jeneen will be a success at whatever she puts her hands to." I was so proud of my accomplishment and couldn't wait to share it with my family. If I were able to do for others what Mrs. T did for me, there wouldn't be a shadow of a doubt regarding my success.

I will always cherish her encouragement, like a keepsake preserved in a treasure chest.

PIECE FORTY FIVE

C:\Jeneen\Hell\TheIllusionofmyDreamhouse.doc

"Jeneen... Good news! Aunt Sylvina and Uncle Bud are coming to visit. They want to see how you're doing and they miss you," my mother screamed, her voice echoing throughout the house. One would assume from the way she shrieked that there was a dire emergency and I needed to evacuate the premises. Ironically, this time there was...

I immediately looked at the photograph sitting right near my calendar. It looked like a normal family photo of my aunt, uncle and me. We were in New York, on our way to Connecticut. That phony picture of a functional family was an absolute lie. The memories of my time living with them continued to flood me with anxiety and I began to panic. Shame and guilt washed over me like death and I felt like I was strangling. *Perhaps I deserved it?*

My aunt and uncle are coming to visit me? I thought it was over and everything had just evaporated into thin air. I've been so consumed with living a happy life with a boy my age that I completely forgot about the skeletons in my closet. I thought I buried that memory in the backyard along with my parakeets.

I was worried about the visit because my uncle was endlessly trying to get in touch with me over the past several months. I completely ignored any communication in the hope that it would be enough for him to get the message. I could never tell anyone my well-kept secret because I truly felt it was all my fault. Also, I knew intuitively that no one would believe me.

Since I came back to California, my uncle would write me letters but I continuously ripped them up and threw them in the trash. I was determined to cover up the ugly the ugly truth. He called me numerous times but I just did not respond. I also monitored the recordings on the answering machine and deleted any evidence that indicated our relationship was anything more than a guardianship, which was every phone call.

My aunt and uncle occupied my bedroom while I stayed on the hideaway bed in the living room. They were just in town for the weekend.

I'll never forget the lecture my aunt and uncle gave me just before they left to return to New York. When my parents were out of earshot, they pulled me into my bedroom and closed the door. I had no idea what they would say but I expected the worst.

"We found a letter from your boyfriend in the waste basket," my aunt confessed. She held up the offending letter, which I had torn up and discarded, and I saw that my uncle had obsessively taped it back together.

That kind of violation of privacy was expected from my mother but not from my former foster parents! My uncle must have found it and told my aunt about it because he was... jealous.

My uncle said, "What if your parents found out about these letters?"

They were pretty deep but none of his business. He shouldn't be snooping through my personal mail or anything else.

The burning question that remained hidden underneath my guilt was... *What if the cops found out about what you did to me and I showed them one of your letters as proof?*

He left the room after scolding me but my aunt remained.

"By the way, I have to tell you the good news about Uncle Bud.

Ever since you left, he stopped cheating on me. Everything is back to normal now," Aunt Sylvina said, content with the drastic changes in their relationship.

Uncle Bud didn't like me dating and attempted to put a stop to it while I was in New York under his supervision. Apparently, he was trying to do it in my hometown as well. I was sad to see my aunt leave but happy that my uncle had finally vanished.

That night, I tried to block that part of my life out again, as if it never existed.

I imagined going through a door to a land filled with green pastures, leaving the residue of *self-recrimination* behind me.

The next day, I waited patiently to see the familiar Mazda parked out by the curb. I had to get far away from here. Drake headed for the St. Matthew's United Methodist Church parking lot so we could have some quiet time. As the vehicle came to a complete stop, Drake selected some tunes from his cassette crate. Rain was beading up and running down the windshield. Drake pulled me close but all I felt were shame and regret. I physically and mentally pushed away the one boy I truly loved. Drake was left dumbfounded by my behavior.

I choked on my words as my eyes welled up with tears. Clearly something was not right and I owed him an explanation of what just happened. I needed to reassure him that he had done nothing wrong.

"Drake, remember when I left California to live with my aunt and uncle in New York in my Sophomore Year in high school? Well, I left a couple things out of the story. My mother never trusted my judgment as soon as I entered into my adolescent years. Her confidence level in me was just about zero. I couldn't wear a normal swimsuit, shorts or anything cute. She labeled me as *boy-crazy* which was an understatement compared to what she really thought of me. My anger escalated as a result of her distrust and she assumed I was experimenting with drugs and alcohol. Yelling and screaming was our only communication. My father wondered why I was continuously crying. It truly baffled me how he could be so unaware of what was going on. It was so obvious that no matter what I did, my mother was never happy.

When my Aunt Sylvina suggested I come live with her in Levittown, New York, I truly believed my problems were solved and a new life would commence," I said, explaining why I wanted to get away from my family environment.

I continued with my story… At the age of fourteen, I packed my bags and left for New York. I was thrilled to be able to concentrate on school and live with someone who did not yell at me. I knew my aunt would appreciate me and had faith in my decision-making. Little did I know, her love and acceptance were very conditional.

It was there I realized that if I focused in school and did my homework, I could obtain an honorable mention, and I did just that. I was very good at reading and memorizing, and along with my thirst for learning, I was able to excel. Although I came from an uneducated family, I developed a desire to pursue higher education. I had many missing gaps in my basic elementary education. My home environment was a major distraction and I also changed schools several times at a young age. Things became even more difficult once I entered fifth grade and my parents became incapable of helping me with my homework. My mother was illiterate and my father, for the most part, was too exhausted when he arrived home after a long day's work.

At Island Trees High School, I figured out that taking on extra credit would bump my grade up. It gave me the means I'd been looking for to be above average. I discovered how to navigate the system and I did it very well. I would consistently study until 11 pm, then help my aunt put my drunken uncle to bed at 2 am. I would get up at 6:30 am to get ready for school. I did everything imaginable to help my *new mother and father*. I would clean the house from top to bottom — dust, vacuum, pick up empty beer cans, empty the ashtrays, do the laundry and dishes. I helped out with just about any chore. I wanted someone to finally see me as a good kid — dependable, responsible and self-sufficient. I yearned to stand out because I knew I would get the recognition here, as opposed to my former residence. I was absolutely right in my positive thinking. My aunt would consistently praise me and was so grateful to have me around. Finally, I got the love I was seeking for years.

When I entered my teens, my mother would never take me shopping unless I was purchasing the clothes with my own hard-earned money. Although it was a good lesson in independence, some balance would have been nice.

My aunt took me shopping and it was a whole new experience. My mother conditioned me to believe that I was a *spoiled brat* if someone bought me something.

One particular time when I was nearly eleven, I was persistent about asking for something — the Barbie Dream Pool. My father said, "Is it your birthday? Is it Christmas? You cannot get it unless it is!"

My creative side got the best of me and every Sunday during Blessed Sacrament Church service (during the Act of Contrition), I would imagine a pool for my dolls. I thought about digging a hole in the shape of a kidney in the backyard. I dug one, only to find that it wouldn't hold water and my blonde-haired, blue-eyed beauty was covered in mud. The next Sunday, while sitting in my pew, I realized that plastic would do the trick. I cut up a kitchen trash bag and began designing my masterpiece. In my mind, my dollhouse was a town home. I had a vision of something grand and elegant. My father eventually built a dollhouse for me out of plywood.

It was my big day, my eleventh birthday, and I asked my father if I could have the pool I've been visualizing for months and he said, "Yes!"

All the way to the toy shop on Hollywood Boulevard, my mother screamed, "Giuseppe, don't buy her that dream pool! It's too expensive and we can't afford it! She's a spoiled brat! Don't go against me!" My mother's hysterical shouts were infused with venom.

"It's her birthday and I made a promise!" my father said, his decision firm.

Funny, when it was not my birthday, my father would always comment, "I find better stuff in the trash!" if I bought something new.

All the way to the Hollywood Strip, my parents had a screaming match while I sat in the back seat of our beat-up station wagon. I took a vow right then and there to never do this to my children. I had my perfect world and it included Barbie, Ken and Skipper. They were rich, had beautiful clothes and everyone was happy! I conjured up a paradise filled with promises.

Before I knew it, we were there. My father held the door open for me and I entered into a world filled with dreams and endless imagination. It was so spectacular that my mother even stopped screaming.

There I was on a shopping spree with my aunt, trying to inhale and appreciate every aspect of this new life. She practically bought me a whole new wardrobe.

Aunt Sylvina bought me a blue wool petticoat to keep me warm in the winter and several knit sweaters. I always liked oversized baggy tops that draped over one shoulder — a definitive eighties style. I remember a royal-blue woven sweater skirt that I always wanted to wear. I preferred mixing sets of clothes which in essence, doubled my wardrobe. My aunt frowned on my outside-of-the-box ideas… "You can only wear that if you keep it as a set or you cannot wear it at all!" she said assertively.

I guess it was a small compromise for being loved.

I became pretty popular in school. Suddenly, I was the *California Girl*. I was an alien being who had never saw snowfall. I remember my aunt waking me up… "Jeneen, come quick! It's snowing outside!" I ran as fast as I could, almost mowing down Buddy, their puppy.

Aunt Sylvina and I were inseparable. I would come home, do my homework and wait for her arrival at the entryway of the miniature tannish house, just like Buddy. I had more advantages than he did, though. We would grocery shop together and then she would cook. While she was busy in the kitchen, I would go back to studying.

She was an excellent cook but there were certain meats I didn't want to eat for health reasons. I also wanted to exercise during my stay to counter-balance my caloric intake but Aunt Sylvina didn't want me to do that. She said I was already too skinny. I liked working on my abs, and one time, she caught me doing sit-ups and forbade me to continue with my workout regimen. I'm uncertain what her reasoning was, but then again, I thought it was a microscopic price to pay for the love I was receiving.

I'll just tone up when I go home.

My closet back home was never filled with clothes that were new. I felt like Barbie in my own *dream house*. It was amazing and I couldn't believe the contrast in how I was treated. *It was nice to have a normal family for once.*

My uncle would come home intoxicated every night after work. In fact, I do not remember him ever being sober. Uncle Bud had dark, straight hair and a goatee. He would literally stagger through the door when he entered the house. He would always get irritated with me when I would warn him about future liver problems. Sometimes he would get quite angry. I didn't care about being an annoying pest; I was concerned. He showed me that he loved me and I wanted to show him that I loved him too.

At my aunt's request, I would often stay up to help put an intoxicated Uncle Bud to bed. It was evident that my aunt had to care for him as if he were an invalid. I would keep her company until 2 am. Many times, I heard his body collide into a railing while he was simply walking up the steps.

Uncle Bud would always say things to Aunt Sylvina about her weight. It was heart-wrenchingly cruel and I always found myself defending her. Ever since I was five years old, I idolized my aunt. She had a beautiful face and big brown saucer eyes. I loved her long, dark-brown, wavy hair. She was definitely a life-sized Italian Barbie to me. I liked the way she dressed and did her make-up and I hoped to someday be just like her. It made me so upset when I heard the man she loved put her down, making her feel less than her true worth. He was definitely not the worthy one; if anyone needed some work, it was him.

If he was so miserable, why was he in this relationship? Perhaps he was the insecure one… but what do I know? I'm just a kid!

That year, I took on the most advanced math class I'd ever attempted. I was tired of general math and I wanted to move forward, progressing to pre-algebra, but it was unavailable that semester. I decided to take on something more complex, in spite of my limited foundation. I nearly flipped out when I opened my textbook and saw negative and positive signs, at the same time, staring at me in the face. Panic set in as I turned another page following my instructor's notes on the blackboard!

What is this, and how do I know when to add or subtract?

I received a big fat D the first quarter. I took my *math-genius* teacher aside and asked if he could tutor me after school or during lunch. He could not and carelessly suggested I go back to general math. I wasn't going to give up that easily. Instead, I asked if he had any other ideas. He said, "You could get a tutor."

When I arrived home, I asked Aunt Sylvina if I could find a student at the school who could help me. My aunt immediately hired me a tutor. Before I knew it, I was asking questions during lessons and had other students wondering how I caught on in such a short amount of time. I ended up averaging a solid B throughout my Sophomore Year. I was now one of the top five pupils in a class that the instructor had nearly encouraged me to drop just a short time ago. Going against the grain has always been my strong suit.

It was getting close to November and my aunt wanted to throw me a party. She said I could have my fifteenth birthday party in the basement. She encouraged me to come up with a list of all my classmates and to invite my favorite cousin, Franco.

Aunt Sylvina decorated the entire basement with pink streamers and balloons.

There were party favors everywhere. I was so excited about seeing my friends. I could always tell that Aunt Sylvina really cared about me but tonight… she went over the top. I invited my friends Barbara, Dougy Fresh, Peter, and the whole *lunch gang* from school. My uncle was known as the *cool uncle* because he brought all the beer. I was never really into alcohol. Let's put it this way… if someone asked me for a screwdriver, I would have searched a toolbox. I was never a follower but I never judged anyone either. I only lectured when I was concerned about someone's well-being. Alcohol and drugs never piqued my interest. I was not interested in the taste of alcohol and I always liked being in control of myself. As I blew out the candles, I realized I was no longer a child.

After work, my aunt would sit on the plush brown sofa to unwind. I could almost feel the aches of her exhausted body being caressed by the soft fabric of the couch in the living room.

"How was school?" she asked.

"It was fun during lunch and I scored a 98% on my math quiz! By the way, thank you so much for the lunch money," I said with genuine appreciation. I never had the opportunity of eating cafeteria food in California. I always had a typical bologna and cheese or peanut butter and jelly sandwich in a paper bag.

I loved school because I felt that I could have proof of my intellect on paper, in the form of my report card. All I had to do was apply myself… and I did.

That night, while my aunt and I were alone (since my uncle worked swing shift), I shared something deeply confidential about why I needed to get away from my former life. I told her about being date-raped when I was fourteen years old. I told her that a sixteen-year-old boy from my study hall class threatened that if I didn't have sex with him, he would just rape me anyway — and he succeeded. Rape by coercion and intimidation is still rape. I screamed bloody murder but no one heard me, except for him. He heard me crying hysterically, knew I didn't want to do it and yet he callously continued. I had told him about my fragmented home life and he knew I did not feel loved by my family. He used my emotional vulnerability against me and got what he wanted.

I told my aunt how, when I confronted my mother with the story, she asked, "Did you fight?"

I said, "No..."

She said, "Then it wasn't rape."

I consented to it under duress... but that was rape. As I said before, rape by coercion and intimidation is still rape.

It was difficult for me to share this with her. I was afraid she would agree that it was my fault, as I'm sure my mother told her this story from her skewed perspective. I needed my aunt to hear my side of the story... mainly because it was the truth, and also because it explained a lot about my relationship with my mother. She listened sympathetically and I hoped she believed me. Aunt Sylvina eventually told the story to my uncle.

My uncle would take guitar lessons once a week and would practice in the basement. Often, he would invite me downstairs to sing along, using his amplifier and microphone. It was my time to unwind from, ironically, having to deal with him. My demanding school-load, babysitting an out-of-control alcoholic and dodging his sarcastic comments every day, was enough to make me want to hide for a while. I heard the sound of my uncle playing the beginning of Led Zeppelin's *Heartbreaker* over and over again on his guitar. The repetitive sounds echoed through the house as if it were a recording studio.

Prom was coming up and I could hardly wait. Although I was only a sophomore, I could attend if I were invited. Jamie popped the Junior Prom question in art class, catching me completely off guard.

Ramey, my other good friend, shrieked... raising the attention of the class, "Oh, man... I was going to ask her first!"

Before I knew it, there was a friendly squabble over prom night.

"Why don't we all three go together?" I said innocently, causing a new commotion.

"It's okay man, you two go with each other this time and I'll take her to Senior Prom," Ramey announced, coming to a compromise.

Aunt Sylvina had the perfect dress in mind for my special teen gala. The long bridesmaid's dress she borrowed from her sister-in-law (since she is my size) rested over her forearm.

"Go try it on!" Aunt Sylvina eagerly shouted. It was absolutely gorgeous and it fit me perfectly. The white chiffon A-line gown had embroidered blue flowers throughout. It was form-fitting on my upper body and then flowed downward into a bell-shape that truly captured my style. The full-time caregiver, full-time grocery clerk, and the now part-time stylist, applied her formidable talents to the task of getting me ready.

"Sit down by the light-up mirror so I can tweeze your eyebrows, apply your make-up and style your hair," my aunt offered generously. Within moments, I felt a sponge of foundation against my cleansed face. Brushes, with different colors from her palette, started to make their way onto my canvas.

"Don't look yet!"

She started blending colors until I had a nice combination of blues and pinks to match my spring gown.

When I looked in the mirror, I was transfixed and just stared at myself for at least five minutes. I had beautiful curls in my hair, flowers to match my attire and I felt like a princess. Barbie had nothing on me that night! I walked out the door, saying goodbye to my aunt with a big hug of gratitude. As I walked down the steps, the stretch-limo that was waiting for me made the scene complete.

Jamie was very studious looking and the closest description I could come up with was a sixteen-year-old, blond Clark Kent. His glasses perfectly suited his character. The chariot was filled with his classmates, and seconds later, the introductions and pleasantries were made. After dancing and socializing all night long, he told the driver to take us to Jones Beach. There were two other couples with us, and as you'd expect, they started to make out. Jamie attempted to kiss me but he was just a friend and it was like trying to kiss my brother!

"Yuck!" I thought silently.

Other than that slightly awkward moment, we all had such a great time.

The next morning, my Aunt Sylvina and I were talking in the living room when my uncle interrupted our conversation. They both then informed me that my parents were coming to visit. Like a bolt of lightning striking me down, he said "I can see why your parents didn't want you anymore!"

Where the hell did that statement come from? It was like being hit with a baseball bat. It was never out of the ordinary when my parents shot their mental arrows at me but this was completely unexpected and unwarranted. He knew I felt rejected and unloved by my parents and that's why I was trying to make a new home for myself. I remained frozen, perplexed by why he would say something so hurtful. Have I gone from the frying pan into the fire? I was starting to feel like no matter how high I jumped, it was inevitable that I was destined for flames.

Apparently, scrubbing the dishes, cleaning the whole house from top to bottom, laundry, a 3.5 GPA and my bubbly personality were not good enough for him?

On the flip side, Uncle Bud called me the *brainiac* because I studied so hard. I did like the nickname he came up with. My mixed emotions were all over the place. **What did I have to do to make him like me?** It seemed like nothing was good enough. I looked at my aunt for some sort of an explanation and all she could say under her breath was, "Don't worry about it, he's just drunk."

The next day was a school day and my uncle would have to take me because my aunt had to be at work early. The grocery store she worked in was in the next town over. My uncle came into my room to wake me up for school. Later, as he dropped me off, he ended up apologizing for his behavior the other night. "I love you and have a good day at school," he said as he hugged me. Immediately, I opened the car door and walked towards the only safe-haven that I seemed to have — school.

My aunt must have given him an earful last night!

I really enjoyed Island Trees High School. I loved my lunch crowd, especially my flamboyant gay friend, Doug E. Fresh. I defended him constantly when other students would bully him in the hall. Barbara, Peter, Chris, Doug and I would all go to McDonald's on our lunch hour.

After school, it was the same routine. I did my homework, completed my chores and helped my aunt with dinner. We waited for my uncle to get home from work. We sat down and had dinner with him and then I did the dishes while they both watched television. Since dinner was so off-the-charts delicious, it was the least I could do. My aunt made steak, mashed potatoes, green beans and biscuits.

I was lost in thought, finishing the dishes, as my uncle walked into the kitchen while finishing his last drink of the night. My aunt remained in the living room, fixated on a TV show. Suddenly, I felt hands cupping my breasts. I was shocked and outraged but never said anything to my aunt. I knew he was wasted, and in a weird, twisted way, it made me feel *special*. His unacceptable behavior made me feel that he wasn't mad at me anymore.

The next morning, as usual, he came into my room to wake me up. We spent some time talking and he was holding my hand. I was confused about why he was doing it, but again, it made me feel that he wasn't furious and wasn't going to lash out at me verbally. I never really received tenderness at home, so I thought he was just being affectionate. Often, when I was a little girl, my mother would yell at my father to stop hugging me so much.

"Giuseppe, stop holding her so much. That's enough!" My mother would scream while my father was embracing me. Affection was in very short supply in my family and I didn't know what was normal. Because of this, I thought my uncle holding my hand was innocent. I also chalked off my uncle feeling me up as just a result of his intoxication and didn't realize what it would lead to.

The next morning, he repeated his wake-up routine and while holding my hand he said, "Why don't you come into my room so you can rest a little more instead of sleeping on the couch?" Naively, I followed him into the bedroom. He lead me into his bed and when I pulled the covers over my body, he started to cuddle me. He held me for a long period of time. He was in his robe and I was in my pajamas. What followed was consensual sex between a minor and a twenty-seven-year old man. In legal terms, it's called statutory rape. This means that a minor **cannot** consent to sex with an adult. In spite of this, I continuously blamed myself, as if I were the only one in the wrong.

There were privileges that I purchased with my dignity. Uncle Bud treated me differently. There were no more verbal lashings. When he would take me to lunch off campus or write tardy notes for me, I felt like he was treating me like an adult. As a perk, his sarcasm dropped a good 30%. The illusion of love was powerful but I knew in my gut that this was wrong.

Since my uncle knew about the sixteen-year-old boy who date-raped me, he said that he wanted to show me what it was really like to have sex. Of course, he made me promise not to tell a soul because he would end up going to prison.

My aunt found out he was cheating with *a girl that just graduated from high school* but didn't think it was me. I had to stay at my grandmother's house for a while so they could work things out. Little did anyone know, I was the cause of their marital problems... *or* so I thought at the time.

The next week, I was back with my aunt and uncle. I often wondered when everything would come flying apart. My uncle decided he needed to take me for a drive so he could talk to me. That required me skipping school for the day. He called the school and told them I was sick and signed a note for me to give to the office the following day. He did this whenever he wanted to spend time with me.

He drove me towards the railroad tracks and parked right in front of them. He started crying and managed to fill me in on his private thoughts, "I want to kill myself and I want to take you with me!"

That shouldn't be too hard since he's usually drinking and driving me around. Quite frankly, it's a miracle I'm still intact.

He felt horrible about what he did to my aunt and that he no longer belonged in society. His guilt had him contemplating the railroad tracks for the two of us. They were, fortunately for my sake, meaningless words.

I blinked my eyes and mentally transported myself back to California. I was in the present but sitting in the car with Drake. He told me that I needed to get some counseling and repeatedly reassured me that it was not my fault. I wept in his arms and then he gave me a soft kiss on my forehead. He pulled up to the front of my house.

"I'll see you tomorrow?" I asked sheepishly.

"I'll see you tomorrow and I love you," he said solemnly.

PIECE FORTY SIX

C:\Jeneen\Heaven\Drake\St.Julie'sAnaheimTrip.doc

I WAS GETTING ready to memorize my Spanish vocabulary for a test that particular week. I couldn't help but stare at the cover of my blue folder which had the inscription, *I love Drake* inside a heart. I had drawn this masterpiece at the beginning of the semester. My artwork didn't stop with just one sketch. I had drawn its twin inside the folder that read, *I love God.* I flipped to the Spanish section tab. I had a couple of sheets to recite over and over until I locked them in permanently. I often talked to myself while studying to make sure I retained vocabulary properly. Once one knows how to pronounce the vowels, reading in Spanish is a cinch. It's logical and phonetic, as opposed to English. I looked at the word in Spanish and its English translation, visualized it, and then said it aloud in order to audibly lock in my efforts. The sound of the phone ringing is distracting but I try to stay focused. *Someone else will answer the phone!*

"Jeneen… It's Drake. Pick up the phone," my brother yelled from the living room.

I hurried into my parents' bedroom, almost tripping over myself. I closed the door for privacy.

"Okay, Giovanni, you can hang up now. Thanks!" I said as I heard an immediate click.

"Hello, Drake," I said energetically. "What are you doing?" he asked curiously.

"I am obsessively studying for an upcoming test for my Spanish class. What are you doing?" I asked, wondering what he was up to.

"St. Julie's is having a youth group seminar in Anaheim. I would love to have you come with me! What's your schedule like?" he asked, anticipating my answer.

"As long as it's on the weekend," I said putting my tests this week at a priority. "Yes, it's this Saturday," he said.

"What time should I be ready?" I asked with excitement.

"I'd like to get an early start. Let's leave about 7 am," he said, giving himself a little leeway.

"Sounds great, I'm looking forward to it," I said enthusiastically.

Saturday arrived quickly and I found myself springing out of bed despite the early hour. I was so excited to start the day because I was spending it with my love. I looked at the shelf above my bed and glanced at the alarm clock. It was 5 am. I made my way to the hall and then towards the bathroom. As I placed myself under the shower head, I could feel the warm beads of water invigorating me. It danced over my skin and took the place of caffeine, awakening my senses.

As I lathered up, I thought about how much Drake and I would go back and forth with our churches. Every Sunday, we had 10 am service at First Christian Church of Newbury Park and then we would have mass at St. Julie's in the evening. We attended youth group every Wednesday evening and loved our time with Miguel and Florence, its leaders. I felt like a Catholic version of a born-again Christian.

I started to apply Noxzema to my face. While I performed my regimen for anti-aging and preventing acne, I reminisced how Drake and I went up to Angeles Crest Christian Camp with our youth group.

I remembered earning a Bible scholarship to go on that trip

by memorizing verses of the Word. I took the initiative to do this because I did not want to take any money out of my savings or ask my parents for the funds.

I wanted Drake to get *saved* during our Christian weekend retreat... and he did. I accepted Christ into my heart and I wanted him to do the same. I was conditioned by the church that we were not *equally yoked*. Little did I know that I would be changing my views on theology in the future. Meanwhile, I couldn't wait to see our mutual friends at St. Julie's.

Drake decided that we should drive separately from the transportation offered in order to have some alone time. We would just meet everyone at the convention center.

It was a long drive but I enjoyed catching up with Drake regarding our school week. He told me about some articles he found in a Seventeen Magazine, including topics of relationships and love. He tore them out and I wondered if they were from Reenie's collection. He handed them over for me to read.

"I'll have to read this at a later time. My equilibrium is off and I get nauseated when I read in the car. Thank you for this. You are so sweet," I said, appreciative of him thinking about us. I knew in my heart that his character and behavior were strong ingredients for a great marriage.

He always created excitement by catering to my needs and making an effort to spice up our relationship. This time, he went above and beyond the call of duty when he decided to incorporate tips from a girl's magazine. It was quite unusual for a teenage boy to possess such nurturing qualities. I made a mental note, vowing never to take that for granted.

We arrived at the convention center and the first thing I thought about was grabbing his hand and dragging him on a detour to Disneyland. *After all, it was only five minutes away! We could relive our eighth-grade date.*

As we walked into the building, I could see our youth group

congregating in the entrance. We circled around, making social reconnections with our friends. We slowly made our way to an enormous theater for the seminar. We climbed high enough in the bleachers that the teenagers down below started to appear like ants. I grabbed the back of Drake's jeans so I would not get lost in the crowd. Our church was only one amongst many in this huge arena. In fact, we looked like a tiny speck in comparison to the rest. There were youth groups from all over California, coming together, searching in unison for divine knowledge.

In my case, it was an additional excuse to sit next to the boy I loved. As we were waiting for the seminar to start, I grabbed Drake's hand and caressed it softly with mine. Our eyes met and locked. He smiled. I glanced over his torn-up jeans and thought his exposed skin looked rather sexy. I played with the white, unravelled threads.

"Do you have any idea what the topic of today's discussion is about?" I asked, expecting something interesting and profound to come out of his mouth.

"I haven't the foggiest idea," Drake said laughing.

A bishop comes to the front of the stage and gets our attention. The all-too-familiar cassock distinguished him amongst the hierarchy. I took in the iron-pressed white angelican rochet, the traditional red chimere and the pleated white cuffs. Thoughts immediately surfaced of my childhood and I recalled the beautiful artwork painted on our cathedral's ceiling, the musky smells of incense that tickled my nostrils and the wall fixtures that held the holy water.

The contrast of this enormous arena, filled with chattering youth, was jarring.

At the sight of the bishop, the gigantic hall suddenly went dead quiet. I couldn't grasp how still this arena could get in a matter of seconds. A spa would have appeared to be more obstreperous.

He introduced himself, "I'm Bishop Connor."

Bishop Connor had much to say regarding the crucifixion. He went over it in great detail, giving us a vivid picture of the great sacrifice. Although I have heard the story a million and one times, I ended up crying uncontrollably. The way he told it, in explicit detail, allowed us to see in our minds how gruesome and horrific it really was. Since it was nearing Easter, it was fitting for the seminar. He was extremely animated and kept our attention.

He then started to switch gears with a different topic. He started to touch base on today's music and pointed out the genres that held a Christian value.

I could hear *Man In The Mirror* by Michael Jackson echoing throughout the arena.

Bishop Connor was using music that was relevant to us to make his point!

Teenagers from all over California started clapping and cheering. This was a pretty radical bishop and every teenager wanted him to know it.

Belinda Carlisle's *Heaven on Earth* was his next example. He turned up the volume a couple of notches.

All the teenagers started stomping their feet in appreciation of Bishop Connor's unexpected approval of today's music.

We Are the World was next, followed by Madonna's, *Papa Don't Preach*. I had to hand it to Bishop Connor — He understood who he was talking to.

Before we knew it, he started talking about movies that carried a life-changing message. Molly Ringwald's, *For Keeps* was now the center of attention. More cheers enveloped the arena. Lights suddenly went out and the *For Keeps* trailer appeared on a big screen. I looked over at Drake and smiled because we had already seen the movie.

He wanted to point out their decision to work through the troublesome times in spite of any obstacles, choosing… life.

As the seminar came to a close, Bishop Connor's heartfelt delivery regarding today's pop culture and movies left us with a very powerful message. His meticulous research, finding the good in the pile of rubble that is mainstream media, was an amazing example for mankind. We must continuously sift through our lives, searching for the diamonds that are hidden there.

PIECE FORTY SEVEN

C:\Jeneen\Heaven\Drake\JuniorProm.doc

I WAS STILL in bed and trying to fall asleep, looking at the new black velvet dress hanging on the back of my bedroom door. I bought my Junior Prom dress with the money I saved from working with my mother's friend, Nita. She worked for Carpenter's Insurance, located in the Los Angeles area, and called when there was extra work on the weekends. She trained me to do data entry which was a good job for a sixteen-year-old. I made five dollars an hour and worked an eight-hour shift. She would treat me to lunch and it was so much fun conversing with her on our long drives to and from the downtown area.

Nita had short, jet-black hair in a pageboy cut that complimented her face and was always dressed in a professional manner. She was generous with her time, remembered to give gifts on every occasion and carried herself as a smart businesswoman and leader. She will forever remain one of the most influential mentors in my life.

My dress felt wonderfully plush and I loved the texture against my skin. The scoop back exposed just enough to be flattering without being too daring for a sixteen-year-old. Every so often, the light would strike the sequined neckline, making it sparkle. Thoughts buzzed around in my head…

Drake is going to love this on me. I'm looking forward to seeing my old friends from Newbury Park High. I am also excited about taking him to my Junior Prom at Camarillo Cornerstone Christian in three weeks. This is one of many benefits of attending a different high school than your boyfriend. It will be dinner on a boat in the Ventura Harbor. It's going to be so special and I can wear this beautiful dress again.

Finally feeling drowsy, I snuggled my pillow, pretending it was Drake and thought about how blessed I was to have him. I fell into a deep sleep to these thoughts:

God… Thank you so much for sending Drake to me. He is so special and makes me happy.

He is my best friend and I can confide in him about anything. This is the one person in this world who helps build my self-worth, makes me laugh and appreciates me. It doesn't matter if I mess up or if we get into a disagreement; I can feel his love everywhere. I am so confident about the love he has for me. I love him so much. Thank you! Thank you! Thank you!

I woke up smiling to a ray of light coming into my room. Stretching, I made a wave on my waterbed and I imagined being aboard a boat. I wondered if it was possible to make myself seasick.

Maybe Drake could come over for breakfast. I dialed his number and paced impatiently as I extended the cord into the hallway.

Drake answered the phone, "Dominos Pizza."

"I'll take a sausage and mushroom to go," I replied with enthusiasm. "What's going on this morning?" I asked.

"Not much. I have to pick up my tux sometime before prom and get my hair cut, but other than that…"

We heard a click and Drake yelled, "Reenie, I'm on the phone!" I heard another click shortly after.

"Do you want to have breakfast at my house?" I asked, knowing the answer. "Sure, I'll be right over," he replied without hesitation.

Fifteen minutes later, I heard a knock on the door and my brother exclaimed, "Drake is here, Jeneen!"

I sprinted as fast as I could and rushed into Drake's arms at full speed. He lifted me up and I wrapped my legs around him and kissed him for what seemed like an eternity.

My brother facetiously said, "Okay, you love birds, enough is enough."

"Jeneen, Drake and Giovanni… breakfast is ready!" my mother yelled. We all piled into the kitchen. "Mmmm… that smells good," I piped.

The smells of French toast, scrambled eggs, orange juice and coffee permeated the kitchen and dining room. It was a Saturday morning, and although hungry, I barely touched my food because of my excitement for tonight's prom.

"So what time do you two have to be ready?" my mother asked.

"We should leave by 5 pm. The prom will be held at the Marriott Hotel in Woodland Hills," Drake informed us.

"Jeneen, I have to leave soon because of all the errands I need to run," Drake added.

I escorted him to the front door. I gave him a hug and the scent of fabric softener, mixed with the musky smell of sandalwood and spices, enticed my senses. He kissed me softly on my lips and headed for his Mazda.

"Mom, I made an appointment with Style Free, off of Kimber Drive. Can you take me?" I asked, my insides beginning to vibrate.

"Sure. Give me about 30 minutes," my mother said, making her way to the bedroom to get ready.

A half hour later, my mother knocked on my door and caught me with my microphone, singing Madonna's *Lucky Star*.

"Let's go, Jeneen. Are you ready?" my mother asked impatiently because she was ready to go right then.

The car had been running for at least five minutes and I nestled into the passenger seat. I noticed the *Godly* stickers on the dashboard: *I Love God! Forgive Others! Peace! Jesus Saves! Praise the Lord!*

We arrived at Style Free, and as soon as I walked in, my hairstylist greeted me. "Hi, Jeneen. I am Bridget, the one you spoke with on the phone."

I heard *Take Me Home Tonight* by Eddie Money playing in the background. I asked her if she could make my hair curly and put it up, halfway, in a bow. Of course, needed my bangs teased with a ton of hairspray — It was pretty much a requirement in the eighties.

Soon, Bridget inquired, "Who is going to do your make-up for you?" I said, "I am."

"Would you like me to do it?" she asked eagerly.

"Yeah, that would be awesome. Thank you," I responded with a singsong.

By the time we arrived at home, it was nearing 5 pm. I rushed to complete the final touches.

Wow, Bridget did a great job on my make-up. Good thing I added that service. It was worth my hard-earned money.

I put on my black cocktail dress and sprayed the powdery, musky smells of Primo all over me, clouding up the bathroom. "Mom, could you help me with my dress, please?" I called while coughing my lungs out.

I hoped Drake hadn't arrived yet but, then again, he should be accustomed to waiting by now.

"Mom, could you pass me my black lace *Madonna* gloves? They're in my bedroom on the edge of my bed. Thank you," I asked with emotion, completing my final touches checklist.

"Everything looks wonderful, Jeneen. Bridget really did a great job," my mother said, sincerely being complimentary.

The doorbell rang, causing my heart to go into overdrive. I ran to the front door.

"Jeneen, you forgot your shoes," my mother called after me.

"That's okay, Mom, Drake has seen me without any make-up on — I think he can handle me shoeless," I joked as I opened the door.

I embraced him and pulled him close.

Drake stepped back and his facial expression was so readable, he didn't need to speak. "Wow, you look… amazing. These are for you."

He handed me a dozen red roses and placed a white rose corsage on my wrist.

Now it was my turn to take a step back and admire my date…"I really love your spiked haircut and… wow, white tie and tails. You look so handsome!"

Seconds later, I playfully yanked on the tails of his *penguin-suit* as I ran back to the bathroom to retrieve my shoes. He took me by the hand and led me out the door. My mother and father said their goodbyes… after clarifying that curfew was at midnight. Somehow, Drake managed to finagle an extra hour out of them.

He opened the car door and helped me settle in for another memorable ride in his silver Mazda. I could hear *Your Love* by The Outfield playing. It was a sign of his thoughtfulness that his choice of music fit the evening. There wasn't any *Janie's Got a Gun*, *Bang Your Head* or *Shout at the Devil* on the playlist tonight.

We arrived at the Marriott. The extravagant entrance looked like a well-lit tunnel that beckoned us to enter. As we made our way inside, I noticed the vibrant floral arrangements and a black grand piano in the lobby. The smell of gardenias filled my nostrils. The pianist overflowed the room with sounds of relaxing smooth jazz. The warmth and sense of class were inviting to me as well as the many guests who had gathered near registration.

"Come on. It's this way," Drake sang with feeling. I saw a crowd of teens collecting in front of the ballroom designated for prom.

Flashes from cameras were going off in every direction and a professional photographer with a backdrop came into clear sight. We discovered a Disney-like line but decided to wait regardless because we spotted Amy Nestle and her boyfriend. I also found Mike Ginseng and his knockout girlfriend behind me.

Looks like his wit scored him a cheerleader. Well-played…

He was my ninth-grade pen pal in Spanish class and extremely brilliant. I presumed he had a crush on me because BreeAnna would deliver his letters to me almost every day. We were really good friends, and in spite of his high intellect, he remained humble.

It was finally our turn to get our picture taken and the photographer posed us in the classic couple's position.

We arrived on the dance floor and I heard *Push It (Real Good)* by Salt-N-Pepa.

Needless to say, I *pushed Drake real good with my booty* on the dance floor and he laughed. All night long, Drake knew I meant business on the dance floor. I didn't mess around and if your heart rate wasn't 120 per minute, you were not dancing with me.

The DJ switched gears to a slow dance. The song was Paul Young's *Every Time You Go Away.* I leaned in and rested my head on Drake's chest, feeling content. Immediately, my mind traveled back in time to our first slow dance to this very song at our eighth-grade formal. After this song faded, *Heaven* by Bryan Adams began to play. It was, evidently, middle school all over again. I stepped closer to him and nestled in the warmth of his embrace.

The DJ was now ready to cut loose and the music had taken an entirely different path. We both listened to the beat and lyrics of *Janie's Got a Gun.* I laughed so hard, I bent over to hide my tears.

"What's so funny? Are you going to tell me?" Drake asked curiously. "One day, I'll tell you. As for now, let's dance," I said, taking the lead.

PIECE FORTY EIGHT

C:\Jeneen\Heaven\Drake\Orion'sBelt.doc

I AM UNCERTAIN of how frequently the telephone rang throughout our house during 1988. It remains a mystery to this day. I recall racing like a well-trained athlete to pick up the handset before the call forwarded to the answering machine. I didn't want the hassles of deleting our recorded conversations. *That tiny tape could store enough conversation for the entire family for a year, providing free entertainment at my expense.* This was the fourth ring and by the fifth… I leapt and crashed onto my parent's California King while swooping up the phone as if my life depended on it.

"Hello," I gasped, out of breath, as if I had just finished a vigorous workout.

"Jeneen, do you want to come over and hang out with the boys this Friday night? I sort of want to show you off," Drake asked with anticipation.

How sweet of him to want to include me on the boys' game night. He wants to show me off.

He must be proud to have me as his girlfriend.

"Yes, that would be great. I would love to join you," I sang with a high-pitched chord.

"What time should I be ready?".

"7 pm-ish," he said in his sexy baritone voice.

The next day at school was test day. Although anxious, I was well-prepared. That morning, I combed over everything I memorized the night before, making certain I retained the information.

The day went so fast, and before I knew it, I found myself selecting from the assortment of coordinating colors of make-up displayed on my vanity counter.

I was finishing up last-minute touches when I heard a knock. I scampered through the hall, taking pride in beating everyone to the door.

I wasn't concerned about appearing eager. There were no games, no defense mechanisms, no hidden agendas, no expectations — just plain and simple love.

"Hi, beautiful! I'm almost ready. Give me ten more minutes. You can wait in my room," I said while I held his hand, dragging him in, pointing to the footboard of my bed. The base of the waterbed functioned as an oakwood bench and he had ample room to sit without taking a swim. There wasn't any other choice, actually... The bed was, in essence, taking up every inch in my average-sized bedroom.

I kissed him quickly on the lips and headed back to my bathroom.

I returned when I was done, giving him a well-deserved passionate kiss. Taking control, I started out slow, teasing him as usual. The advice columns from Reenie's collection of teen magazines were paying off and the passion erupted like a volcano.

"Why don't you stand up and turn around," He twirled his finger, making *the motion*. He examined my outfit while I spun around and my ruffled skirt danced in the air. My white blouse contrasted the turquoise skirt.

He said, "Wow, this is perfect. You look..."

Before he could finish his sentence, I made my way back to his soft lips. I wanted seconds, and this time, I was out of control.

Giovanni cleared his throat. "Didn't I tell you two to get a room?"

"Oh, hi Giovanni. We ARE in a room!" I said, overjoyed

with teenage love. "Hi, Giovanni," Drake said, nervously clearing his throat.

"Shall we go?" Drake asked while checking his watch.

"Sure, let's go," I said, kissing his hand that was intertwined with mine. My energetic happiness caused me to playfully swing our interlaced hands up and down.

"Mom, I'm leaving. I'll be at Drake's house," I sang in an almost soprano voice. "Say 'hi' to the McCallisters for me," she shouted.

We walked side by side to the passenger side of his car and I stood on my tiptoes to kiss his nose. Always the gentleman, he opened the door for me. The music was deafeningly loud, and as usual, outside my scope of interest. Since he loved it, I didn't mind compromising. It was a good contrast and added balance.

Okay, Quiet Riot is almost over. Oh, goody... time for Whitney Houston!

I hastily ejected the tape without giving it a chance to roll into the next song.

So Emotional started to play, and I started to sing while I planted kisses down his arm.

Drake usually gave me more choice during the back-and-forth battle of genres. His *Suicidal Tendencies* collection somehow got tossed to the side while Madonna took over. We were just different enough in just the right ways that we fit together like interlocking puzzle pieces. Nothing could pull us apart.

I loved his companionship. We had extensive conversations at night when we were on the phone or in front of our church after youth group. I felt so comfortable with him and it didn't matter that I was lacking, somewhat, educationally; he didn't judge. He was always willing to offer his insight and knowledge because I was hungry and willing to learn. He saw my potential and remained humble.

Drake liked my analogies and made an effort to constantly point that out. There was always a sense of intellectual reinforcement with him. His words of reassurance were meaningful because of how much I respected his intellect.

We arrived at his house and everyone was sitting in the living room by his upright piano, playing a game. The Dungeons and Dragons was spread out on the table and I took my position next to Drake.

"So, what character do you want to be, Jeneen?" Peleke questioned.

Drake's Hawaiian friend had straight, jet-black and bobbed hair. His sun-kissed complexion made you want to get on the next flight out of Los Angeles and visit the islands. Peleke had been close with Drake for many years and you could see they were on the same wavelength as the polyhedral dice exploded across the board.

"Lawful Good Human Ranger/Sorcerer (3rd/3rd Level)" I cheered, feeling quite sure of myself.

"And how did you determine that?" Drake inquired, quite impressed. "I have my ways," I beamed back, giving him a wink.

I whispered in his ear, "What's up with the psychological evaluation to determine what character you are? I took a 129 question test. For God's sake, what kind of game is this?"

I grabbed my share of junk food and let my extroverted personality go to work. The more I got a reaction from the small audience at the table, the more I wanted to entertain them with my sense of humor.

I tried to keep up with Samantha's witty spirit because Drake once told me he enjoyed how silly she gets. It didn't take much effort for me because our upbeat personalities were so similar. I took it to the tenth power that evening, without really caring about going too far.

When everyone left for the evening, Drake and I decided to take a stroll down Happy Trail Circle. Drake reached out to hold my hand but looked a little annoyed. I had never previously seen him that frustrated.

"Is everything okay? Did I do something wrong?" I asked, determined to fix the problem.

The streetlights illuminated the path along our leisurely walk. If you gazed into the lamps, you could see the hazy mist of the fog. He steered our bodies away from his house.

"You know, you didn't really need to act like that," he said. "Act like what?" I really didn't understand.

"Like an airhead, Jeneen. I told everyone how smart you are. Why did you act so silly tonight?" he questioned, feeling embarrassed.

"Who cares what people think. All that really matters is our relationship. Besides, people are usually so consumed with their own affairs that they probably aren't focused on anything else," I said, duplicating the confident nature that he projected.

We both looked up into the evening sky and noticed how clear it was. We could easily see Orion's Belt twinkling overhead. We talked some more and then headed back to his house with our hands interlocked. I knew everything was back to normal again because I felt the energy from his hands and body language and the way he responded to my kisses. I gave him a playful shove and he returned it. I held him in my arms and we slowly swayed back and forth, dancing to our own internal music. I buried my face in his chest. His arms wrapped securely around me and all I could feel was the rhythm of our love.

PIECE FORTY NINE

C:\Jeneen\Hell\Father\ProveIt.doc

THE STARTLING SOUND of the phone echoed through the quiet living room. I reached over to pick up the receiver. "Are you going to make an appointment to get some counseling?" Drake asked bluntly, as soon as he heard my voice.

"Whatever happened to 'Hello, Jeneen. How was school today and are you memorizing something else other than the *Raven*?'" I asked in a high-strung voice.

"Why don't you want to get counseling?" His tone was matter-of-fact. "I'll do it later," I said sharply.

I don't want to get counseling because my mother blamed me for the date rape when I was fourteen. I know in my gut that if I were to mention my uncle, history would repeat itself. It would be asking for trouble with my family. My mother thinks I'm a whore. It would be like banging my head against a brick wall while trying to explain my side of the story or educating her about the law. A counselor informed me that I need my parents' permission before I can receive therapy. Worse, a volunteer at a rape crisis center told me that I have to report it. Report it? I'm AFRAID to report it. I don't want someone to go to prison for something I know in my heart... I'm partly to blame. The volunteer also barked at me and insisted that if I do not file, my uncle will continue to do it to others. If I can get help without parental consent/police report, it would make my life a whole hell of a lot easier.

"Are you coming with me to youth group tonight?" I asked hastily. "Yes, I'll be right over to pick you up," Drake responded.

"I miss you, Drake. I cannot wait to see you," I said before we disconnected.

"I miss you too," he said solemnly.

I wrote Drake a quick love letter while I was waiting for him to pick me up. I folded it into tiny little squares and put it in my pocket. I heard him tap on the window and ran swiftly to the front door.

I hugged Drake tightly and then called to my mom, "I'm going to youth group with Drake."

"Okay, see you later and have fun!" my mom yelled from somewhere in the backyard.

The next day, my father knocked on my bedroom door while I was studying for an exam.

"Come in," I said.

"What happened with your uncle?" my father asked, as if it were the first question in a grueling hearing. I could see his stern face looking at me in disbelief. I was now officially on trial.

Drake… He must have said something out of desperation for me to receive counseling. I am horrified. Now I have to plead my case.

"I'm unsure if it was rape," I said, half blaming myself and half remembering what I knew of statutory rape.

"How can you not know if it's rape? I have never heard of such a thing!" he said mockingly and then laughed. His sarcasm converted to anger and the red flags started to waver in front of me. I immediately flashed back to my brother and me trapped on the studio couches by the man with the violin bow.

"Why don't you believe me?" I shouted angrily, risking much by standing up to him.

"You need to prove it," he yelled, losing his patience and obviously unconcerned with the truth.

By this time, I didn't feel like explaining the details of my seduction or how I blamed myself for an adult's actions. It's useless to try to communicate with someone who already has it etched in his mind that I am at fault or a compulsive liar.

I must have heard "prove it" a hundred times in this conversation. The shame and vulnerability I felt by my father's cross-examination, stripped me of all my dignity. He treated me as if I were under oath and about to be prosecuted. Without anyone to defend me, I felt weak and ambushed by my own father. I never felt more alone. I started going down my list of tangible proof that could support my case.

I erased all the phone messages my uncle left me and ripped up all the letters he sent me. All I had was a ring that he gave me. What was that going to prove? My aunt would think I just stole it.

The ring... the gaudy, gold ring surrounded by diamonds. I travelled back in my mind to New York. I could see the inside of the Boeing 747 before taking off for Los Angeles. I heard a loud commotion coming from the flight attendants. When I turned my head, I noticed Uncle Bud briskly coming towards my assigned seat. Since he worked for the airline, I supposed he had special benefits... and this was one of them.

"I just wanted to say goodbye. I have a letter and a present for you."

He handed me a card and a love letter. He hugged me and attempted to kiss me but I pushed him away. I desperately tried not to make a scene because I did not want anyone to know. I could smell alcohol on his breath. I'm curious if anyone was aware that he stole the miniature bottles from the airline every night.

"Jeneen, you know the U2 song, *With or Without You*? That's us and I'll be thinking of you whenever I hear the lyrics." His words imprinted themselves on my hard drive against my will.

"I'll miss you. Make sure you write me every week," he said as if he were a normal boyfriend my age.

Shortly after his disappearance, the plane began to taxi for take-off. Finally, I could see the runway whizzing by and felt myself being pressed back into my seat as we gained more speed. The jumbo jet shook as we lifted off and as the pressure eased, I felt a deep sense of relief.

The respite vanished as I crashed back into my room. Unfortunately, I was with a father who thought I was like the rubbish he compacted in his truck. I felt defeated, weak and lifeless. Loneliness consumed me. If my father felt this way, then the whole family did as well. After all, he was the leader of the pack. I was an outcast in my own home.

He left the room and I started to sob. There wasn't a hug or any tenderness and understanding. There was no serious conversation about what happened. Quite frankly, if there was, it would be entirely my fault anyway. Did it really matter? I felt abandoned and the phrase *complete disappointment to my family* started burning itself into my soul.

The next day, my mother performed her morning ritual of watching the 700 Club. I could hear her chatting over the phone. Our tiny home made it easy to overhear conversations. She was talking to a representative from the evangelical television show and I clearly could hear her complaints about me.

"I don't know what to do with her! She's out of control! Can you pray for us?" My mother pleaded as if she had a teenager heading for death row.

"Jeneen, I need you to talk to someone," she yelled across the house.

The phone cradled my face as a woman on the other end meekly said, "I hear you are having problems getting along with your mom."

I told her, "Yes!" and then started to explain, in detail, believing she could understand and offer some much needed empathy. Instead, the words she selected were "You must ask God to forgive you. You must be accountable for your actions."

Okay, let me wrap my head around this — you want me to ask God to forgive me for being a child in the hands of a drunken adult that manipulated me into having sex?

I did not voice my inner thoughts because I wasn't strong enough. Instead, I continued praying with her because she made me feel guilty in the eyes of God.

I heard my mother making more phone calls and talking about me to her friends and family. It was making me very indignant and angry. The more negativity that flowed from her, the more agitated I became.

"She must be on *cacahuna*," my mother said to my grandmother in Italian.

In a 1400 square foot home, it is easy to hear every word, including the disrespect that my mother had for me.

I yelled back at her defending myself. I understood a little Italian — enough to know when she said la figlia and droga (cacahuna was their slang version). I pieced it together…"My daughter is on drugs." I muttered under my breath, "You are such a bitch!" There was no other word that could accurately describe her demeanor in such a delicate situation.

That same evening, my mother continued getting under my skin by relentlessly gossiping about me to other family members. She decided to call my Aunt Sylvina.

My mother screamed, "Pick up the phone. It's your Aunt Sylvina."

I reluctantly picked up. A sinking feeling came over me that I would be speaking to yet another set of deaf ears. I still continued trying to defend myself, however, to whomever would listen.

"Jeneen, what's this about you and Uncle Bud?"

I told Aunt Sylvina about the statutory rape. She said softly, with very little emotion…"You are just trying to get attention. You are lying!"

No matter what I said, I could not be heard until I blurted out, "I know what the paper towels are for on the end table in your bedroom."

She exploded at me…"That's just a coincidence. You're a liar! You're a liar!

You're…"

It took everything in me not to hang up on her. Instead, I bravely told her the truth about how he would take me out of school.

"Go to the Island Trees High School's office and check my sick days and tardies — all with his signature on the excuse notes."

Why am I even explaining? I'm exhausted from fighting this pointless battle. The truth will never come out because I didn't have any tangible evidence and I'm already labeled as a 'bad girl' by my mom. Now it's my aunt's turn to write me off in order to save her dysfunctional marriage.

"Talk to my former counselor at the school!" I blurted.

I was seeing a school therapist at the time to help me deal with being date raped. I wanted Aunt Sylvina to know that there is a form of violence called *date rape* but I believe she misconstrued that to mean I informed the counselor about my uncle. I also wanted her to be informed about statutory rape. I was grasping at straws. I never said anything to the therapist about Uncle Bud because I knew that I would be taken out of that family and sent back to my immediate family in California. At the time, I thought it was a better situation.

I heard one more time, "You are lying!"

"Fine. If that's what you want to hear… *I AM lying!*"

I slammed the phone down so hard, I thought it cracked.

I shortly overheard my mother dialing my aunt again. "Hello, Sylvina. I told you, she's wild!" she said decisively.

I tried to tune their voices out of my head but I couldn't.

My aunt does not believe me and thinks I'm just trying to get attention… On top of that, I have a mother who believes I'm a tramp.

I ran into my bathroom and started crying. More anger erupted when I heard my mother saying to Aunt Sylvina, "I told you she was trouble, Sylvina. I warned you about her before I sent her to New York," my mother said in her normal voice, which was so loud I could hear every word.

Before I knew it, I lifted the toilet seat and slammed it so hard, it cracked. I felt guilty that I let my frustrations get the best of me, but it was too late — the damage was already done. There should have been a punching bag in my garage but there wasn't.

My mother grounded me for the toilet crack. She took away my radio and locked it in the trunk of her Ford. This parenting technique owed its thanks to "Because We Love You", a tough-love program my parents were involved in. They religiously attended in order to *fit in* with other parents of troubled teens.

Why didn't they pick up a hobby? Gram, Drake's dad enjoyed Morse code. Why didn't they sign up for a cooking class, or better yet... a parenting class?

Once a week, my parents would try a new method of punishing my reactions to their tyrannical behavior. It's a pity these programs never consider both sides of the story.

I told Drake what was going on. He said, "I have a counselor for you and she can meet you at your school." For a sixteen-year-old, he had more common sense than any adult in my life. He was insistent about pointing me in the right direction. I met with a licensed therapist at school, on my lunch hour.

Her name was Bolivia. She had straight, sandy-blonde hair that curled at the bottom. She wore a simple, professional suit and carried herself with confidence. She informed me that her daughter, Penny, is a student at Cornerstone and is in my Junior Class. Penny had sun-kissed freckles that accented her long, platinum-blonde, wavy hair. Not only did I know Penny from school, but when Mrs. T was on maternity leave, she was my tutor for Algebra II.

Bolivia reassured me it wasn't my fault; it was my uncle who made the moves. I kept thinking of every way to blame myself but she insisted that I cannot carry the burden of an adult's illegal behavior.

"You were a child in his care and he should have protected you," she reiterated.

I told her about my parents and how isolated I felt from my family. She was the first adult to tell me it wasn't my fault. I cried in her arms. I had a feeling that seeing her once a week as planned was going to be the remedy I had been praying for.

I wish Bolivia was my mother. I told her everything and she heard me without judgment.

She hugged me and told me that everything was going to be okay.

Every time I entered my house, all the counseling was being viciously unravelled by how my parents treated me. To them I was a liar and the town Jezebel. There was no way to get them to accept the truth and no way to protect myself from their bitter accusations. I was sure that no one could help me — no one.

The atmosphere in my house was so negative that I suffered extreme anxiety. I felt isolated and despised. All I wanted to do... was run.

PIECE FIFTY

C:\Jeneen\Hell\Mother\Runaway.doc

I WANTED TO hide myself in the corner of my room so no one could see me. I securely locked my bedroom door hoping it would block out the noises inside my mind. I found a place on the far side of my bed and covered every inch of my body with a blanket. I thought about *To Kill a Mockingbird*, my tenth grade English book assignment. Mayella Ewell had a better chance than I do.

Where was my public defender during my unjust trial?

Tears were now out of control and a normal parent passing my door would want to comfort a daughter in despair. Not my mother. She ignored me, whistling and singing, thinking it would suffocate the problem.

I wonder if her group, 'Because We Love You', suggested something like that as a quick fix for a rebellious teen. She did this on several occasions — in the middle of an argument or during a discussion she didn't want to have.

This situation was always the same — She would verbally attack me, I would react with anger as anyone who is falsely accused would, and then she would whistle because she didn't want to hear my side. How convenient, Mom.

What else is going on in that stupid group? If I were in another family, I would not have to endure this indignity. I should not be on trial in the first place. I hate this home.

I dialed Drake's number as if I were dialing 911. "Hello, Drake… Please come quick," I said, the tone of my voice telling him everything he needed to know.

I stayed by the window, locked in my room until I saw his car pull up. I ran out of the house while my mother continued to whistle and sing. She never noticed my exit.

I walked slowly with the heavy weight of a family burden on my frail shoulders. I managed to move my body forward towards Drake's silver Mazda. I sobbed uncontrollably.

Drake assertively called out, "Get in the car."

I jumped in, fastened my seat belt, and soon we were zooming down Potrero Road. The further we drove from the house filled with utter disgust and disappointment, the better I felt. The sense of freedom washed over my spirit giving me a glimmer of hope.

"Why do you have white spots on your nails? I've been reading up on it and I think you might need vitamins. I'll give you some when we get to the house. I'll put a whole bunch in a Ziplock bag so you can have one every day."

Oh, joy… If my mother finds them, she'll think I'm popping pills!

He searched his car for napkins to wipe the tears streaming down my face. "You can use my shirt. I'll just wash it later," Drake whispered soothingly.

I grabbed the end of his T-shirt to wipe the stream of sadness off my hot flushed cheeks. I leaned my head against his arm as he drove. He stroked my face.

"If you act happy, eventually, you will be happy," Drake said, offering me more self-help philosophy.

My emotional outbursts continued, "I'm afraid of going home. I don't want to go home!"

He said casually, "Then you don't have to. You can stay at my house."

He drove up to his house and parked by the mailbox. We walked hand in hand to the front. I glanced at the rose bushes. They gave the face of his home a colorful curb appeal. I imagined that this is where Drake collected all of my roses. The thought of it lifted my spirits.

Drake opened the door to his home. We walked past his parents' room to our left and then I looked into his living room. His upright piano, sitting on the right-hand side of the room, rested in silence.

We slowly tiptoed by Reenie who was busy in the kitchen. I inhaled the scents of chocolate and cookie dough baking in the oven. This preteen had some serious talent for creating scrumptious desserts. I saw in my peripheral vision that she was frantically searching for a utensil in a drawer. She never saw me.

As we passed the junior chef, we made a left turn, cutting through the living room. We rushed down the hall towards his bedroom and made a hard right.

Good Lord! I wasn't informed that tornadoes existed in southern California.

This was nothing new to me, however, it was a shock every time I saw the catastrophic ruins. I always managed to give him a hard time about the disaster. One time, I cleaned his room as a gift. This boy needed a full-time maid.

He informed me of his plan: "You can sleep in my closet so my parents won't know you're here."

I opened the sliding doors very slowly. I didn't want anything to fly out and accidentally hit my face. I took a quick peek and felt I was in the clear. I made an area for myself. As I sat down, I felt something stab me in the butt.

Ow, that hurts! What the hell?

I lifted up the offending object. Sure enough, it was a Star Wars spaceship. Action figures, comic books and spaceships — oh my! I was surrounded. There were clothes scattered all around me.

Why aren't these on hangers? Oh, my God... This is an all-day project.

Mrs. McCallister calls for her son, "Drake, I thought you were taking out the garbage today."

"Coming, Mom," Drake responded as if he didn't have a girl in his closet.

Can I camouflage myself if they accidentally hear a noise? All I have to do is throw all of these action figures and articles of clothing on me and they would never know I'm in here.

Are those the army pants he wore in eighth grade when he hounded me in front of my locker? You have got to be kidding me.

That evening, Drake brought me dinner and I ate in the closet right next to Luke Skywalker. Between Reenie's and his mom's cooking, I had the best meal on this planet. Mr. Skywalker kept me company as I patiently waited for Drake's return. After he helped with the dishes, he came back in to check on me.

He informed me, "Everyone is going to sleep. In a couple hours, I can bring you into my bed so you are more comfortable."

Although, sad to get away from my new friends, I was not reluctant to make my way to the comfort of a bed.

"Come close to me," he said caressingly. Of course, we had no other option — It was a twin bed.

He held me in his arms as we slept in our clothes from the night before. He caressed my arms and wrapped his around my waist. He gave me soft kisses on my neck, and soon, I fell fast asleep. His father was the first to wake up at 5 am. As soon as Drake heard the shower running, I went back to the cramped closet and took my position, this time, next to Darth Vader.

Reality hit when everyone left for work and school. I feared the repercussions from my parents. I tried to enjoy my freedom with Drake but I knew the thrill would come to a screeching halt.

I'd rather be with the Star Wars clan surrounded by the tornado that was Drake's closet as opposed to living in a dark, clean castle with the Wicked Witch of the West.

There were no phone calls from my mother in the middle of the night. His parents had no idea I'd run away because they never came into his room or questioned him.

After Drake called his school and told them he was sick, he tactfully said, "You might need some deodorant. Do you want to use my brand?"

"Sure, but no Old Spice."

Being cooped up in your closet all night has taken its toll on my endocrine system. I am no Princess Leah this morning. These are desperate times.

Although reluctant to smell like a sailor, I succumbed to his offer.

Drake decided to practice the piano providing a private concert for me while I freshened up.

Bang, Bang, Bang, Bang… We were both startled by the aggressively loud knock on the door. Who could that be at 11 am?

Drake let me know that a police officer wanted to speak to me. "They want to take you back home, Jeneen," he said disappointedly.

Why couldn't my mother pick me up? She knows where Drake lives. You have got to be fucking kidding me.

Drake kissed me lightly on the forehead and told me to call when I could. The female officer escorted me towards the police car and drove me back to my domestic hell. I felt like a criminal.

It is despicable how my own parents have no interest in protecting me. Now I'm a bad girl in the back of a cop car — the deviant black sheep of the family. I have been emotionally exiled, and yet, my physical body is forced to remain captive in the home.

All of this could have been prevented if my mother picked me up herself. My parents could have avoided this crisis altogether by believing me. They could have said 'It wasn't your fault!' but they didn't. They could have shown me a tiny sliver of support and understanding but they did nothing of the sort.

"You know your mom is only concerned about your well-being, right?" The officer couldn't be expected to say anything else.

I saw the black and white vehicle drive away from the actual crime scene.

My mother started yelling, "Don't ever run away again! Do you hear me, Jeneena?"

"Why, not Mom? You don't even love me," I fired out like an automatic weapon. I slammed the door so hard that I thought it would come off the hinges. I cried myself to sleep. I needed a good day of rest.

My mother barged into my room. Her belligerent hollering was deafening as she went down a list of all the things I had done wrong.

Happy to be in the position of control, she made the announcement, "You are grounded, young lady. There are consequences for what you did. I'm taking your prom dress and you are not going to prom!"

She angrily grabbed my dress and yanked it forcefully off the hanger.

"What are you doing with *my* dress that I bought with *my* money? Give it back!

Give it back! You have no right to take what I have earned away from me!" I cried.

I curled up into a ball and started sobbing hysterically.

She continued to taunt me with her ruthless power, "I'm burning it!" Her anger had the ferocity of a wild animal.

For some strange reason, my mother loved to burn my belongings — or at least she enjoyed saying it. Years later, she confessed it was locked up in her car's trunk. Is that where she hid my radio and bikini too?

I was looking forward to attending my Junior Prom at Cornerstone Christian. I already bought the tickets for the cruise and dinner around the Ventura Harbor. It was going to be a memorable evening for Drake and me.

Now, my dinner plans lay in flames, shot down by my lunatic

mother. I felt defeated. Every time I tried to captain my own ship, it was hijacked by this ruthless villain.

Where is my Luke Skywalker, with his lightsaber drawn, ready to rescue me from the evil Darth Mom?

PIECE FIFTY ONE

C:\Jeneen\Hell\Mother\HolyOil.doc

IT WAS ANOTHER beautiful day in southern California. There were few clouds in the sky and the temperature was in the mid-eighties. The light, cool breeze grazed my skin as I walked out of school at the end of class. It was the week of finals and I had about six books in my hands to take home. Giovanni and I walked over to where my mother was parked. We could easily spot her enormous yellow Ford Fairmont in the crowd of smaller Toyotas and Hondas.

She walked over to meet us and escort us back to the car. The resentment and anger I felt towards her jabbed me every time I saw her dark short hair. The sounds of her calling me *una puttana* (a whore, in Italian) and my aunt calling me a liar played over and over in my mind. It crawled under my skin like an infection.

I asked, "May I change the channel of the radio station to pop?"

Giovanni said, "Why do you always have to get your way? Keep it on the fifties station for Mom."

I am so pissed off right now. Why is he trying to score points with the monster?

I started yelling at him, "Why are you such a mama's boy?"

We both started arguing back and forth, all the way up the high, twisted hill of Potrero Road. My mother decided to stop the car at the top of the hill and deal with the heated squabble in the backseat.

Mommy Dearest actually got out of the car and came to our window just to yell at us. She started screaming at the top of her lungs, "You are grounded!"

I shrieked, panicking at how dangerous what she just did was... "Get back in the car! We are going to get hit! We are going to get hit! No one coming up the hill can see us and someone will hit us!"

Keeping her position, she continued her rant... "If you believe in God, then He'll protect us. You must have no faith!" she said angrily.

It took her what seemed like an eternity to get back in the Ford. Soon I heard the click of her safety belt and we were on our way again.

I have faith that you are one hundred percent crazy.

When we got into the house, my mother began yelling again, "You are punished! There are consequences for what you did in the car!" I got so mad that I started yelling back at her. She grabbed some holy oil and started applying it to my forehead, making the sign of the cross. She grabbed me and shook me while saying, "Devil, get out of her!"

The thought of my own mother believing that something evil was residing inside of me enraged me even more. She may as well have poured gasoline on an already lit fire.

She came at me with the *blessed oil* as if she were performing an exorcism. This time I blocked her and pushed her away because I refused to submit to this ludicrous nonsense.

She yelled, "I'm going to tell Dad what you did to me! You must have the devil inside of you if you pushed me!"

I ran to my bedroom and started crying. My mother promised me that she had changed when she wanted me to come home from New York. *She changed all right... but into what?*

I buried my head in my books. *How am I going to study now? I have finals coming up. I'll just put the radio on and try to tune her out. It's important that I get accepted into a university and I am not going to let anyone stop me.*

I started going over the numbers one through one thousand

and all the expressions and verbs for my Spanish final. I went over all the formulas we covered for algebra and memorized homework from my English Literature class.

My dad knocked on my door. I shouted, "Come in."

"Mom tells me you pushed her," he said, frustrated and disappointed.

"You don't understand..." As I tried to explain my side, I was immediately cut off.

"You were disrespectful to your mother and that's the bottom line so you have to be punished. Your mother will come up with something."

I'm sure she will. What could she possibly take from me now — my study material for school?

As soon as he left my room, I threw all my books at the wall. I immediately regretted my actions and I picked each subject up one by one. Throwing in the towel and giving up on my dreams of a higher education will only make my life worse. I cranked up *Like a Prayer* by Madonna and tuned everything out. I studied until midnight, as I usually did.

That week, during finals, I miraculously aced them all. I was so excited. It was the end of my Junior Year and I needed only one more year maintaining a good GPA to get into a university.

Giovanni and I waited, as usual, for our ride by the curb. I chose to stare out into the distant future. My heart started racing as soon as I saw the miserable middle-aged woman coming towards me.

Is she really my mother? Why does she think I'm such a bad child? I thought studying, working hard and excelling academically would be sufficient but that's definitely not how it works with her. I could be Miss America and I would still be a tainted reject. I wish... I wish I could be placed into another family. I could study so much easier and I wouldn't have to deal with all the yelling. I know deep down that some other family would love me but this one sees me as a liar and a devil child. Oh no... here she comes.

This is where I lost it. Everything leading up to this point — the negative emotions, pain, injustice and abuse — finally broke me. Like a bolt of lightning striking me, I suddenly realized there was no escape. Social services just makes things worse. I'm trapped and no one cares to free me from the destruction caused by my own family.

I didn't care that I was in front of my peers on school property. I couldn't take it anymore. Between my parents not believing me about my uncle, the guilt and stress over finals, my books came crashing down to the ground. The wind carried my loose papers away, scattering them so that all of my hard work was lost.

After months of tears and arguing, the walls my family put up in order to keep me isolated parted slightly and my father finally understood that there was something wrong.

My father took me to see a counselor who informed me that if I felt suicidal, they would arrange for me to get counseling as an inpatient. It was the only way to get away from my family, get therapy, and have it covered by my father's insurance. I voluntarily admitted myself into a Kaiser Permanente behavioral health program. The first thing they did was run tests to see if I was on recreational drugs... but of course, I was not. They administered medication before I went to sleep but I didn't tolerate it well. I woke up at two in the morning and headed towards the nurse's desk outside my door. My body felt weak and I blanked out. It was like someone pulled out my plug. I just fainted. After they brought me back around with smelling salts, I told them that I no longer wanted any medication.

They soon brought in a sixteen-year-old who tried to kill herself by carbon monoxide poisoning. She was now my roommate.

I went up to her bed. "Hi, my name is Jeneen. Do you believe in heaven? You know, there is a purpose for you to be here. Please don't do it again."

"I'm Debbie." The teen that resembled a young Justine Bateman reached over to shake my hand. Instead, I hugged her.

Debbie went on to tell me her story. She came from a loving

family. Her parents were divorced but both remarried and remained really good friends. She said it was not her family but stress in general that just got to her.

The staff brought in another roommate later on that day. Her name was Elle and she was not thrilled to be in this mental institution. Her parents were forcing her to spend the week.

During the next couple days, she showed me how to pull my hair back without teasing it in the front. Elle was a model and we all gave her our undivided attention when she shared beauty tips. I was unaccustomed to this new look. Elle told me she wanted to fix my hair when Drake came to see me on my first visit.

I said cheerfully, "Elle, that would be wonderful. I can hardly wait."

The inpatient program was nice because I was able to receive counseling and I had a break from my parents. I could call Drake whenever I wanted on a nearby payphone. He was happy that I was finally receiving help.

"I can visit you in three days," Drake reassured me.

"I'm in the San Fernando Valley. Hold on for just a second. Let me get the address." I rushed over to the front desk for the information.

Our conversation soon came to an end. He promised he would come up to see me. As I hung up the phone, I realized I had an appointment with Dr. Logan and my parents at 2 pm.

At the appointed time, I headed for his office. My parents were already sitting down and introducing themselves. Immediately, my mother gave me a hug and expressed how much she misses me. She behaved like an entirely different person. I took a seat next to Dr. Logan.

He asked, "What seems to be troubling you?"

I told him everything. He reassured me that it was not my fault. This is now the second adult who confirmed I was not responsible for an adult's actions. I left the room for a while as he privately spoke to my parents.

Then it was time for all of us to come together again. He asked me once more, "What seems to be troubling you?"

I said, "My parents do not believe me about the sexual abuse in our family."

My mother chimed in and tried to embrace me, "Yes, we do. We've always believed you."

Dr. Logan said furiously, "No wonder your daughter is going crazy. You just told me that you didn't believe her when you were alone with me. Now you are telling her you believe her?" He shook his head in a disapproving manner.

My mother cried because she felt singled out and attacked. I saw the Kleenex pass me by like the offerings basket in a church.

A mixture of feelings overwhelmed me. I finally have an adult going to bat for me and it made me feel empowered. The second feeling was guilt. I almost felt bad for my mother. He continued to chastise her about her behavior as a mother.

Dr. Logan explained it to my parents by using this scenario: "If a teenager is stark naked in front of a twenty-seven-year-old, the twenty-seven-year-old should tell the teen to put some clothes on. You do understand that the man has to be the adult?" It finally clicked with them. I believe that Dr. Logan told this to my parents earlier and then said it again in front of me to reinforce my position with them.

At least this man was trying to educate my parents, but ultimately, it still didn't change their behavior. They will always think I'm a liar or a whore — whichever came first. The damage was already done.

The next day, Elle spent time with my hair and makeup. It was a bit odd to see my front bangs slicked back, as opposed to the teased, eighties look.

Drake came by to pick me up. He asked, "Where do you want to go?" "Let's go someplace where we can talk that's near Reseda," I said.

Drake found a nice park. He grabbed a blanket out of the trunk and carried it out to a spot under a tree. We spread out the quilted fabric, laid down side by side, and held each other.

"How is it going with the program?" he asked.

"It's going well. The psychiatrist is educating my parents about statutory rape."

I stared at the eucalyptus tree right above me, using my hand to block the glare. The leaves wrestling with the wind caught my attention. It was warm outside and the month of June was starting to show its character. The birds were singing a gentle, high-pitched melody. I could also hear the faint laughter of children playing in the park.

"Dr. Logan told me it was not my fault," I said in a low tone.

"It wasn't. That is what I've been trying to tell you," he said matter-of-factly.

"I feel better in this 'mental institution' than I do at home," I said earnestly. Drake laughed.

"How is everything going with school? How did you do on finals?" I asked, expecting a predictable answer.

"I did fairly well," he answered modestly, with a smile. He reached over to kiss me softly.

"I missed you!" he said in a whisper that sent chills down my spine.

"I missed you too," I said kissing him again, feeling his soft supple lips with my own.

Being with Drake was like being in another world. It was like night and day from being with my family. It was a place where I truly felt loved and I could reciprocate with open arms.

My escape slowly comes to an end. The winds that carried me away from Victory and into this memory have come full-circle and returned me to hell.

I grab my hoe and continue with the task at hand for Brother Green. It was torturous coming back to my physical body after flying away for hours. I felt guilty for thinking of Drake. The brainwashing is like a computer virus, corrupting my memories and my emotions. I am starting to feel shame for fantasizing about my love. I'm just going to have to shut this part of my life down. I have to get through this program. I have to stay sane.

PIECE FIFTY TWO

C:\Jeneen\Hell\Victory\HappyBirthday.doc

It is now the crack of dawn. I hear the piercing sound of the alarm signaling the start of another day of captivity — another day of hellfire and recrimination burning away my identity.

"Get on your knees... NOW! It's time to pray!" The *Helper* demands.

It sounds like Bernadelli but I'm too groggy to figure it out. Today is my seventeenth birthday but what good is that when I'm locked up in a cage against my will? I am forced to pray, get ready for the day and I am timed and walked through every ritual of this military hellhole. *Looks like I made it into boot camp before Drake. I have a feeling if we compare notes in the future...Victory is much more unpleasant.*

This is supposed to be my Senior Year of high school where I attend homecoming with Drake, study like mad, purchase a yearbook and indulge in a case of 'senioritis' without allowing my GPA to slip. All of it is outside of these gates, beyond my reach.

Hello, God! You know what I want for my birthday. I don't have to spell it out for you anymore. You should be able to read me by now. Maybe my parents are feeling guilty for having me locked up against my will on my birthday. Nah, we are talking about my parents.

I shuffle my feet towards the line for the usual inspections. We are now dismissed, row by row.

I cannot wait to sing our eerie 'Christian' songs and recite our verses today.

As Ms. Arizona approaches me, I try to figure out what mistake I made today. "Happy birthday, Jeneen."

She hands me a gift.

Wow, it's from Nita. She never misses a cherished moment. She is a normal part of my life but she can't see the abnormal behavior from my parents... or can she? I bet if my mom would have dumped me off at her house, I would have been better off (as long as my mother didn't visit). Anakin is a bit high-strung, but overall, it would've been much better. Pity, she can't come and visit me. Nita would have seen the exterior barricade topped with barbed wire and freaked out. She would have been greeted with surveillance cameras and would have noticed the angry preacher screaming at the top of his lungs. My parents believe this is a good program, because now, I don't react to mother's verbal abuse. Well, halle-fucking-lujah, QC, your ministry is working! Now my mother can say what she wishes to me.

The girls crowded around me like pigeons in a park. The wrapped-up gift is everyone's highlight of the day, including me. "Open it up. We want to see it!"

I unravel Nita's big surprise. I am hoping it's something that will link me to the *world* so I could feel it again. I open the box and find a new King James Bible. My other one has four months' worth of tears staining the cover.

I'm curious, do Nita and Anakin know where I am? Do they think I deserve this? What did my parents tell them?

After chapel, Brother Green collects his volunteers to work outside the gate. It represents trust, honor and work ethic to all of the *prisoners* in here. In my case today, I just want my grueling time to go by like a speeding freight train. I just want my birthday to be over so I can chalk off *another day in paradise.*

I raise my hand and I'm chosen… but what else is new?

Happy birthday to me!

I give myself a pep talk, focusing my anger in order to continue digging ditches out in the field. My stomach is growling and I feel weak because I'm not eating enough but talking to myself gives me the right amount of strength to complete the task. Brother Green looks at me and smiles. I know he's pleased.

"How's everything going with your parents?" Brother Green asks with concern.

"Fine, sir," I say robotically with my usual Victory expression. *I won't tell him anything about how I really feel because I will be locked up in isolation or demoted. So what's the point of this conversation?*

"Good, I'm glad to hear it. It looks like everything is working out for you. I'm ecstatic to be a part of a ministry that brings families together," he recites charismatically, as if he really believes in the cause.

I'm surprised that Brother Green did not mention a possible job after I complete my one year at Victory. He has offered girls who have graduated staff positions as a way to give back to the ministry.

I couldn't imagine in a million years coming back to this nightmare.

"Thank you so much, Jeneen, for helping me work on this project. You are a hard worker," Brother Green complimented.

"Thank you, sir," I say as I pick up my hoe again and slam it towards the ground.

It's actually considered a privilege to be out here feeling the wind. Brother Green pats me on the back, so to speak, with his empty words. When you have been brainwashed, it's very easy to take this as positive praise. I am slowly reaching this state of mind.

What I really need, instead of empty praise, is some water.

I continue to have a conversation with myself because I can't speak honestly to anyone else.

It's amazing how we are taught in this church to stuff our passion and humanity down a dark hole. In spite of this, QC quite passionately condemns abortion, celebrating his pro-life stance. If you are going to celebrate the life of a baby, shouldn't we celebrate the love and passion that leads to creating new life? After all, a baby is the aftermath of passion. It's as hypocritical as radical pro-lifers who kill abortion doctors. It doesn't make any sense. How can you love the product of a natural process that you condemn?

The sun is setting and everyone heads towards the cattle lines for dinner. As I make my way into line, girls who are permitted to speak are saying, "Happy birthday." The girls who are not cannot even smile at me.

I grab my food and head towards the table. I take my half-plate and inhale all the food on it. I eat fast, not only because I'm timed, but also because I'm starving from working so hard. I want seconds right now but I cannot get them; my decision was *etched in stone*. I chose to avoid the risk of throwing up and then being forced to eat my own vomit. I'd rather have hunger pains and feel depleted.

Brother QC makes an announcement: "It's Jeneen's birthday today. I want all of you back here in an hour. We'll have cake and ice cream and play some games. It will be like Friday night."

I could hear everyone clapping and cheering at the privilege that QC allowed.

Even girls that had seven demerits could attend. This is a big deal at Victory.

We all scatter to our dorms after being dismissed by QC.

I sit alongside my bunk using the frame to support my back. I write my demerits to catch up, in case I don't have time to get it done later.

'I will not be rude and interrupt someone while they are speaking.' — one hundred times. 'I will not ask a stupid question. I am not a phony so stop acting like one.' — one hundred times. I will not be in the same location as someone I am on separation with.' — five hundred times.

"Girls, line up! Dorm One, Dorm Two and Dorm Three!" *Helpers* yell throughout the halls.

Everyone is happy and in good spirits. We march like soldiers towards the kitchen. I swish by QC, hoping to avoid the demonic minister of the century. As usual, he performs his creepy inspection.

"Your parents don't have a lot of money and they bought you cake and ice cream for your birthday. They have you at Victory on a sliding scale because they want to help you in spite of the fact that you caused them nothing but trouble!" he yells causing everyone to look in our direction.

"I heard you told your parents a *s t o r y*," he smirks and shouts loud enough for my peers and all of the staff to hear. All eyes are fixated on us, waiting for something to happen, however, my tail is between my legs. At this point in the program, I'm just a horrible excuse for a human being.

I'm feeling his insinuation stinging me. I want to collapse, disappear or respond in my typical sarcastic fashion… but I cannot. All I can do is remain silent, stand up and march in robotic formation.

Within moments, Ms. Arizona brings out the cake. She displays it so all of the girls can see how wonderful my parents are on this special day of the year.

Now, I really want to throw up. God?

I blow out the candles on my Victory birthday cake. *My only wish? Come on now!*

I watch the melting candles dripping into the vanilla frosting. Celebrating my birth in this place just doesn't appeal to me. It was not a good year and there's nothing to be happy about. There are no outside visitors, no free day-pass or phone calls. What I do have is a secret passage in my mind…

I grab the knob on a hidden door and take the secret steps down to a different time. November 30th, 1987 was the day of my sixteenth birthday.

"Jeneen… Get dressed up because Drake is coming over to take you somewhere special!" my mother gasped.

It was just another excuse for me to wear my sequined, royal-blue dress I had worn to homecoming. I painted my nails silver-sparkle to match. I made sure my hair was in a white-laced bow and scrunched it with gel to make it curlier. I blow-dried my bangs, teased the living daylights out of the top section and gave everything a final glueing with hairspray. I completed my ritual with light-blue eyeshadow and dusty-rose lipstick.

"Jeneen, Drake is here!" My mother's screams echoed throughout the house. "Hi, Drake," I said with eagerness.

"Well, don't you look stunning? You're wearing your homecoming dress. Am I underdressed?" he inquired, feeling a bit out of place.

"No, you look perfect," I said, reassuring him that he looked just fine.

Drake was wearing a turquoise checkered shirt with gray cargo pants and a vest. He grabbed me by the hand and escorted me to the car. I hopped in and then he kissed me softly on my rosy lips.

"Happy birthday, Jeneen," he said, closing my passenger door.

We drove down the spaghetti like spiraled road, making our way to the beach.

We continued along PCH until we finally found a spot at County Line Beach.

I looked out the car window and I saw the beautiful Pacific Ocean. The waves were making lovely curls and breakers against the rocks that were alongside the walking path. Drake opened the door and held out his hand to pull me up. We walked down the rocky maze leading us to the sandy beach. I immediately hopped on his back and he carried me until we got to a rock-free location where I could take off my shoes.

We dug our bare feet into the warm sand. Our fingers locked as we started walking along the ocean. The sun was slowly dropping down below the horizon, leaving behind its trail of vibrant colors in the sky. As it started to get colder, Drake draped his jacket over my shoulders. I grabbed him tightly and gave him an aggressive kiss.

"I have something for you. Why don't you open it up?" he said, handing me a beautifully wrapped box.

I unraveled the paper and saw my first box of perfume called Primo.

"I like this fragrance and I picked it out especially for you," he said, beaming proudly.

I sprayed some on myself, testing the unfamiliar scent. I must have inhaled some because I immediately began coughing and choking.

"Are you okay, Jeneen?" he asked, afraid that his birthday present was actually going to kill me.

"Yes, I'm fine. Um... You like this scent on me? Do you want to take another whiff?" I offered.

He sniffed me like his hound dog, Droopy, and gave me his stamp of approval by telling me that I smelled delicious. "Mmmmm... intoxicating," he said as he took in the fragrance and gently kissed my neck.

"Well, in that case, it must be good," I said, cherishing his gift.

"We'd better head back," he said as he grabbed and kissed me. No prince from a Disney fairy tale was ever more dashing.

In no time flat, we arrived back at my house. We rang the doorbell and my mother yelled, "Jeneen and Drake are here!"

"Surprise!" Everyone cheered... and I do mean everyone.

I saw so many classmates from Cornerstone Christian. The first two I ran into were John Boarderston and Penny Wilkenson. John had his Miami Vice attire on: white jacket, slacks and a turquoise shirt. Penny had a beautiful royal-blue dress on that had frills at the bottom.

As I made my way around the room, I ran into Tammy, Jennifer, Marc, Jamie, Samantha, Anakin and Nita.

The furniture had been rearranged and I saw Justin Mills from our Junior Class situated with his equipment. *I cannot believe my mother hired a disc jockey! What an amazing surprise.*

Half of my Junior Class was here and I just couldn't believe how my mother put this together. The crowded, small residence was filled with an energy of warmth and love. Against the dining room wall was a narrow table covered with a pink plastic tablecloth. It was filled with paper cups, plates, dips and chips, a punch bowl and a birthday cake. Streamers and balloons were hanging from the ceiling and music was blasting throughout the house. I grabbed Drake's hand and we danced in the living room near Justin's DJ stand.

After our dance, Drake made his way, socializing with my classmates and chatting with Samantha. I went around the house, fluttering and mingling and then asked Justin if I could belt out a song. I sang *Holiday* by Madonna. With her singing in the background, it was easier to deal with my stage fright. I was nervous as hell but I went for it anyway.

Everybody applauded and I enjoyed my moment of stardom in the privacy of my own home. I took a bow and then made my way to the kitchen.

Shortly after, a slow song came on and out of the corner of my eye, I saw that Drake was dancing with Jamie. I remembered him asking my permission at a previous function. I was not worried in the least because I was confident about what Drake and I had, however, I was highly concerned over what my mother might have whirling around in her head. She could not comprehend that opposite sexes could be friends.

When the next fast song came on, Drake grabbed me and we hit the dance floor. We danced our goofy eighties dances like we were on Soul Train. We took a quick punch break and then went right back to it.

I looked around and noticed my parents and their friends. I was completely surrounded by my Christian companions and the non-alcoholic punch. The only thing smoking at this wild soiree was Justin's fog machine.

As we all congregated around the cake, everyone waited with

anticipation to have me blow out all sixteen candles. The feelings of love and camaraderie were everywhere.

As they say, "All good things must come to an end," and now, instead of sixteen candles… there is one more. I find myself back in the darkness of my seventeenth birthday, surrounded by fellow *criminals* and *cast-offs*.

If I stare too long at the silver tray the cake is sitting on, I'll notice my reflection. I cannot avoid my image and start to choke on my tears.

PIECE FIFTY THREE

C:\Jeneen\Hell\Victory\Christmas.doc

CHRISTMAS... A TIME to give with all of your heart to friends and family. It's the day to explore a kiss with your soulmate under the mistletoe, an occasion to exchange gifts of love and the perfect excuse to cook comfort food. I cannot dwell on how much I miss the warmth of Drake's lips and how much I miss the smells of home. Spices, pine and fresh-baked pumpkin pie are merely things of the past.

Bam! I'm wide awake and staring at rows of bunk beds. I'm not in my own room, there isn't a Michael Jackson poster on one wall or Madonna on the other and no sounds of birds outside my window.

It's Christmas at Victory. I take extreme measures to suppress holiday memories and associations so I don't slip and say the wrong thing. I wouldn't want to spend any more time in *the Get Right Room*. Girls are in in there for weeks and months at a time. I wonder if anyone is occupying that dark hole on Christ's birthday. I'm sure it's either Jade or Sissy. How they can endure sleeping on the hard floor and listening to that screaming lunatic of a preacher on a recorder for so long is beyond me. At least when you are in the *SHU (Special Housing Unit)* in minimum/maximum security prisons, you aren't subject to brainwashing and you get a bunk. What would Jesus think of this?

Enough of this bullshit! I should be with Drake driving to Point Magu. Extravagant locations, flowers, luxurious cars and shopping for fashion never had any importance to me. Spending time together, safe in each other's arms, was the thing of most importance to me. It was never about the top-notch restaurants he surprised me with (Wendy's and Taco Bell). It wasn't the designer perfume he bought me (Primo). It wasn't about the gold ball necklace he gave me that his mother most likely picked out from an Avon catalog; it was about how we interacted with each other. Conversations would last for hours. It was always the *here and now* for us. The separation in eighth grade was water under the bridge. We reunited at the St. Julie's Dance in our Junior Year and picked up as if we were never apart. Maybe that's why this separation doesn't make me lose faith because we will always reconnect. This Victory time-out is just a test of our true love.

It's around 6 am and I cannot get off my bed until 8 am because the damned laser alarm will go off. We are allowed to sleep in for Christmas. *Oh joy, what a treat! I have to go to the restroom so badly right now. This should be a no-brainer.* A necessary biological process is now a stressful decision — *Should I take a five demerit punishment or suffer in silence?* It's the same feeling one would get when watching a movie in a theater, except there, you can get up and missing a scene is the only repercussion. *I have to urinate now but I can't think about it. If I ask permission to use the restroom, I'll be punished.* The punishment for asking permission to use the washroom is writing 'I will not wake up my Helper to use the restroom' — five hundred times. It is considered one of the bigger offenses.

I will think about Drake to keep occupied. I can't wait to get out of here. I know Drake loves me and Jessica is just filling in until I get home. I'm not going to dwell on what the wicked witch said to me on my three-month visit. I'm going to solely focus on the fact that our love is so strong that no one could tear it apart. There is not a shadow of a doubt that he is waiting for me to come home. We can just pick up where we left off, right?

As I reassure myself of Drake's loyalty and dedication, I hear the alarm and *Helpers* yelling for us to get off our bunks and down on our knees. I start my prayer to the Almighty:

God, please get me out of here. It's Christmas. I should be with Drake where I feel loved. His adoration for me was evident and I felt it deep down inside of me.

I hope the new girl at Victory is really an undercover cop. It's just a matter of time until someone tells the authorities how cruel it is in here. It cannot be possible that every graduate is so brainwashed to believe she deserved this and that Victory saved her life. I don't want to be here anymore. Please help me. Please help me. Please help me.

God?

"Okay, ladies, you are excused to get ready," our *Helper* announces.

I hastily scoop up my items. I run to the bathroom, making my way to the toilet at maximum speed. I rush to get myself prepared this morning but it's really not *my day*. I'm just part of the property. I am no one special to these people. I'm just another problem child.

"Line up, everyone," *Helpers* start shouting. "Open your drawers," Alexandra yells.

Helpers scrutinize every aspect of each girl's drawers as if their lives depended on the end result.

Here come the same old inspections. If a *Helper* wants to give you grief, she will make your life a living hell. My Christmas present today is passing my bunk check. Being perfect doesn't necessarily mean you pass their test. It all depends on someone's mood or if you are pegged as a trouble-maker. The mania of Victory is unpredictable and I'm unsure when the attacks will strike.

"Dorm Three," Alexandra yells, as we patiently wait for girls from that dorm to march into chapel. "Dorm Two," Shelly orders and we wait for them to pass. Finally our dorm is called. We parade into our circle so we can sing the repetitive Christian songs: *It's a Happy Day, Victory in Jesus* and *You are My Hiding Place*.

Drake and I used to sing, *You are My Hiding Place* when we

attended youth group together. It will never have that positive meaning again. I hear Ms. Arizona's distracting piano playing.

We continue our morning reciting Bible verses. The mundane and meaningless rituals continue. *If this happened in a public school, it would make the news, however, paying an outlandish amount of money to a private Christian organization to torment your teen in secret is somehow okay?*

"You didn't memorize the whole scripture! You get a demerit! Demerit for you, Cynthia! Jade, here's a demerit!" Shelly yells again. I cannot help but notice Jade's red matted hair and it wouldn't surprise me if she's serving time in *the hole* this holiday season. *Helpers* continue to check us at random. *Give us a break! It's Christmas!*

Helpers stopped checking me because they tested me numerous times and I passed with flying colors. Unfortunately, my memory is a double edged-sword. It helps me with scholastics and I can recall the good moments of my life as if they happened yesterday, however, I have a sickening feeling the memories of Victory will haunt me in excruciating clarity for the rest of my life.

We head into the food line. Scrambled eggs, biscuits, gravy and pancakes somehow have to fill the void in my life. Drake's affections for Jessica come into my mind like a freight train at full speed. It takes everything I have to push that coal polluted toxin out of my engine and fill my energy source with… French toast. I seem to have a handle on my unpredictable digestive system now because I have convinced myself that Drake and I will be together when I get out of here. Plus, my mother said she would not bring him up again during my once-a-month visits.

How gracious of her.

We are excused from breakfast and are now allowed to prepare for chapel. We repeat the same line calls and make our way from our dorms into the sanctuary of destruction. QC performs his usual smirking inspection as we all make our way down to our assigned seats.

Maybe QC will say something nice today. After all, it is Christmas morning. My optimism never ceases to amaze me.

"Ladies, open your Bibles to Ephesians 6:1." QC yells, as he slams his King James on the pulpit.

Children, obey your parents in the Lord: for this is right.

"Do you know why you are here, ladies?" QC scours the congregation. "Tina Somule, can you answer that?" he questions sarcastically. "Because we didn't obey our parents?" Tina responds timidly.

The holy Bible violently meets the podium again and wakes us all. "Yes, Tina... because you didn't obey your parents. That's all you had to do was listen to them. Instead, you decided to cut class, smoke, tease the boys, dress provocatively, fail classes, run away and talk back to your parents. This is why you are here on Christmas. You are a bunch of home-wreckers who caused your parents nothing but grief, and now... you pay," QC yells.

I can hear girls next to me sobbing. I can't comfort them in any way. There are girls crying uncontrollably and I can't avoid hearing the sounds of their weeping. I can't feel anything because of the fact that I've already been conditioned, before I came into this hellhole, that I was already a family disappointment. I have been stung by a venomous scorpion. I suffered excruciating pain, and now, my infected area is numb.

Merry Christmas from QC to the girls locked up in his reform school. Please just get me out! This is my only Christmas wish. I will be free again to give and receive love, with all my heart. I will be free to express myself with writing and speech. I will help others feel worthy because I know what it's like to feel unworthy. Once the door to my cage is opened, I will soar through the air.

It's Christmas here at Victory and all I desire is a way out so I can live again... because in this place, I am dead.

PIECE FIFTY FOUR

C:\Jeneen\Hell\Victory\LaundryHelper.doc

I LOOK AT the pages of a calendar inside my mind. I stare at another dreary day that I just crossed off. It's the 15th of January, 1989. My Senior Year of high school continues to play out while I stand frozen in time. *I wonder if my school will hold me back a year like they did with BreeAnna. Obviously, there isn't really any education going on in this 'academic institution'.*

I hear the sound of the dryer tossing underwear, shirts, culottes and nightgowns. I am waiting for clothes to finish out their cycle. It's like a factory in here but without a paycheck. I am folding towels in a systematic fashion, filing underwear and meticulously arranging clothes into perfect squares, which I will then distribute to each individual student on her bunk. Each clothing item is, of course, labeled with a name. I like to keep busy because it makes the time go faster... and I have less idle time to think of Drake. It's hot in the laundry room but I like it because it's cold outside and chilly throughout most of the building. It's also my temporary hideout from daily torment. My status has changed to *Laundry Helper* and now I can give out demerits and talk to girls on *Buddy*. In fact, I *have* to give out demerits. If I don't, I'll get punished or lose this privilege.

I flash back to when social services came to visit. *I truly believed it is because of Carey... but why did it take them four months to come?*

Was this death not important enough? Are they afraid to investigate a 'religious' institution? Here's a creepy thought... Are a lot of teenagers dying in places like this and it just took them this long to get to Carey? Whatever the reason, I'm glad they're finally here and I silently thank Carey for her sacrifice.

Social services tried to question the girls, however, we were all terrified to say anything because we would either get thrown in isolation or find ourselves back on *Buddy*. At Victory, the humiliation of *Buddy* is more than just the physical distance. It's looked down upon because it represents that you are rebellious — a lowlife. If you're new to the program, you are *of the world* and if you are a veteran in the program, you must be a heathen or backslider... the list went on and on. Once again, the emotional manipulation in this program is just as twisted as the physical.

QC demanded we sit in chapel so he could prep us for more questioning. He looked completely paranoid while he called *Helpers* traitors and demoted them to *Buddy*. He wanted them to be an example for all of the girls.

"Let me tell you about Sara. Stand up, Sara. When social services interviewed her, they asked her if everything was okay. She looked the other way and made some sort of eye motion," QC yelled, slamming his King James so hard I saw a paper fly out.

"Sara, you are on *Buddy*. I cannot trust you anymore. You are like Judas! Caroline, please have her follow you!"

Caroline didn't have any ranking. In fact — Sara, at one point, was her *Buddy*.

Caroline is now promoted. As the decision was made by the unfit judge, no one could miss the uncontrollable sobs coming from Sara. She risked everything just so she could try to free us from this miserable place.

On and on he rambled, demoting *Helpers* to *Buddy* and promoting other girls without a rank.

"Jeneen, I want you to be *Laundry Helper.* You are in charge now," QC shouted.

A lot of girls looked at me with smiles communicating their approval.

I didn't see social services because I was always busy with Brother Green, working out in the field. Had I been approached, I would have passed with flying colors since I'm so good at wearing a *'Victory smile.* I would never jeopardize my current standing because I knew my life would be made worse than the living hell I was already experiencing.

I blink my eyes and continue to fold clothes alongside the two girls who are helping me. Karen and Susie are under me in rank but I try to make it fun while we are being productive. In this *sweatshop,* we solely talk about God and what we plan on doing for Him today. There are monitors — *eyes and ears* — all around us. One slip-up could land us right into isolation, stamping a label on our pretty little foreheads. It's the only safe conversation, other than the task at hand… and even then, I worry about speaking. *I can't even talk about Disney or his cartoons. That is considered the work of the devil. It's like my mind is on hold for a year.*

I gather underwear from the hot dryer that finished its cycle. I am ordered to inspect them and toss any old ones into a separate drawer. It's a recycled underwear container for girls who do not have any panties. I open it, toss the dingy undergarment in and shut the drawer as if I really didn't do it. I realize how unsanitary this is but I try not to focus on it. I have no say in anything. If the demonic disciple says to do something, you do it.

I'm a bit OCD about folding the towels, and if something is out of place, I start over. I want to make everything perfect for the girls so they have something to look forward to. I also want to make God happy today. *It's the least I could do to compensate for my wicked soul. I am a Christian but not like I used to be. It's different. I believe in a different God now. It's a God whom I associate with the negativity that spews out of our preacher's mouth. However QC feels about me, that's how this God feels about me. As far as I'm concerned, even if I'm saved a million and one times, I'm going to blaze in hell when I die because that's what QC has instilled in me. I'm not worthy of salvation... and I know I'm not alone in this feeling. I see girls every night, getting saved over and over again because they don't feel it either.* The buzzing sound from the dryer snaps me out of my reverie, briefly.

"Okay, Karen... let's fold these sheets together," I say in an upbeat fashion, keeping spirits high. We shake the sheets in order to get the wrinkles out and fold the ends.

Corners! Corners! Corners! Five, four, three, two, one... I throw myself back in time. I just arrived at Victory and I'm given my introduction to making hospital corners by a twelve-year-old girl.

"You are not allowed to make your bed in the traditional way. You have to perfectly top it off with hospital corners... and if you don't, you get a demerit. We have hospital corner checks at random. Do you understand?" Alexandra informed me.

The work continues — endless loads of laundry without a single cent in compensation. All of our work is like this — tedious and thankless.

"I have to go to the bathroom. Karen, could you watch everything? I'm leaving you in charge," I say assertively, making my way to Dorm Three.

I stumble upon Ms. Arizona in the hallway. She nods approvingly and chirps, "Ms. Jeneen."

I reply with, "Hi, ma'am."

Seconds later, I see Sissy coming out of *the Get Right Room* with her *Buddy*. She has been locked in there for at least a full week. Her hair is matted and she looks desperate. Her soul is drained from the non-stop recordings of sermons she has to endure inside that confined *hole*.

QC proudly informed us during chapel that he's feeding her baby food. "If you want to act like a baby, then we'll treat you like one! You have the devil inside of you. If you can't come to know Jesus, you are just a lost cause. You will probably end up doing drugs and then prison time. You are never going to make it without this program!" he says with wrath as he throws his Bible on the weather-beaten pulpit.

Once again, I find myself in another situation of witnessing something that is inhumane and I can't do anything to help. Guilt showers over me like a storm. It hurts like fucking hell because I know this is wrong.

I can almost feel my blood starting to boil but I shove that feeling back down. I shove it down hard.

How did social services overlook this? What did they do, hide her for the day? Did she have a free day out of isolation with a shower to boot? I can't fathom this satanic cuckoo's nest. It's so ironic that QC imposes gothic judgments on girls for having worn the 'goth' look in their past. He judges Disney movies as if they were the forbidden apple. Disney, for God's sake! What about his movie, 'Nightmare on QC Street'?

Poor Sissy. It must be so awful for her to continuously be in the closet by herself. I often wonder how she will cope when she gets out of here. I suddenly remember QC bragging about her and Beth being locked up in a chicken coop for the entire day in the hot sun while other girls mocked them.

I cringe every time I see either Sissy or Jade locked up in isolation, sometimes for several grueling weeks at a time.

I stare long and hard at the numerous out of place crosses hanging everywhere. *The religious quotes over the girls' bunk beds make me sick to my stomach. It all has a different meaning now — ALL OF IT.*

I return to the laundry room. Karen looks at my face with concern, most likely because the color has completely drained from it, "Is everything okay, Jeneen?"

I reply with my *Victory smile* as I fold another hand towel on autopilot, "Everything is just fine."

PIECE FIFTY FIVE

C:\Jeneen\Hell\Victory\MyNervousBreakdown.doc

IT IS ANOTHER day in the pit of destruction.

Parents are deceived into believing that this is a teen program for positive transformations — a church where their daughter can choose to know Jesus, a place to meditate, a safe-haven from the cruel world and a reformatory for their wayward child. After all, it's a *Christian* academy, right? The *Christ-like* faculty operates this *loving home* for troubled girls as if they were missionaries. Parents are sleeping soundly tonight, knowing they did the right thing for their child. What could possibly go wrong when you have people that *love the Lord* behind anything?

I pass through a hallway and stare at the drywall. I imagine taking cans of spray paint and creating graffiti that tells the truth about this place. As my artwork takes shape in my mind, I notice our mugshots. They identify the city and state we are from and our arrival date in this *joint*. That also means they show how much longer we each have to stay in this purgatory.

The ongoing conditioning and verbal beatings have finally penetrated to the depths of my soul. QC has full ownership of my thought processes and I am afraid to think on my own. I feel shameful when I start to have thoughts that make me... human.

Now, I'm programming myself with self-destructive reinforcements. One of my self-punishing acts is giving myself demerits every day. Every written penalty is another corrupted file on my hard drive. I am now my own virus, eating away any sign of affirmation. My storage unit is nothing but damaged files and corrupted subdirectories. One day, someone is going to have to get in there and help me fix things. I hope they're very, very good.

I fully take on all of the responsibility for my family issues. I do not deserve a kind God and QC reassures me that my parents do not love me because I live in the house of Lucifer. I am nothing more than a Jezebel. I'm just a worthless piece of shit. I hear it in biblical terms every day, so it sounds more authoritative.

Dear Mom and Dad,

You didn't want me anymore… and worse, you wanted me to change. This is what I have morphed into. Do you like the new me? Do you? You better because I'm sure it cost you a pretty penny.

Jeneen

Well, that letter's never getting written. God forbid I make an honest attempt to try to work on my relationship with my parents. I see myself wearing a beautiful, vibrantly-colored dress — one that Drake chose to represent our love. I spin around and the dress begins to fly apart, piece by piece. I stand naked and exposed, unable to hide myself. This is the letter I choose to write…

Dear Mom and Dad,

I lied about everything. It's my fault about Uncle Bud. I made the first move and I'm 100% to blame. I shouldn't have worn provocative clothing. When he told me he wanted me in his bedroom, I shouldn't have followed him. I am just a temptress and a home-wrecker and I ruined a marriage. Please forgive me. It's because of my actions that our family fell apart.

Genesis 3

2 - And the woman said to the serpent, "We may eat the fruit of the trees of the garden;

3 - but of the fruit of the tree which is in the midst of the garden, God has said, 'You shall not eat it, nor shall you touch it, lest you die.'"

4 - Then the serpent said to the woman, "You will not surely die.

5 - For God knows that in the day you eat of it your eyes will be opened, and you will be like God, knowing good and evil."

6 - So when the woman saw that the tree was good for food, that it was pleasant to the eyes, and a tree desirable to make one wise, she took of its fruit and ate. She also gave to her husband with her, and he ate.

7 - Then the eyes of both of them were opened, and they knew that they were naked; and they sewed fig leaves together and made themselves coverings.

Please throw out my underwear, swimsuit and pants... In fact, just throw out all of my clothes. You have my permission to tear down my Madonna and Michael Jackson posters. Clear out all my music and anything else that is 'of the world'.

My clothes, makeup, wardrobe and body language are the reasons why it is all my fault.

2 Kings 9:30-33 KJV

"And when Jehu was come to Jezreel, Jezebel heard of it; and

she painted her face, and tired her head, and looked out at a window. And as Jehu entered in at the gate, she said, Had Zimri peace, who slew his master? And he lifted up his face to the window, and said, Who is on my side? who? And there looked out to him two or three eunuchs. And he said, Throw her down. So they threw her down: and some of her blood was sprinkled on the wall, and on the horses: and he trode her under foot."

Please forgive me. Jeneen

I hope *Mommy Dearest* reads this letter to Drake's mother, Anna. At least she would have the common sense to know there's something wrong with this program. She would be able to see right through the message and piece together that I'm being brainwashed. Anna would question why I wasn't getting any better. It's the perfect plan — if it gets to someone who's sane and educated.

I believe this is why my parents sent me here. They wanted people who they could count on to blame me for my own sexual abuse. They didn't like what Dr. Logan had to say, so they went shopping for someone who would be certain to blame me. QC fit the bill.

Hours later, Ms. Arizona pulls me aside and says, "Jeneen, I would like you to follow me to my room. We really need to talk."

"Yes, ma'am," I reply instantaneously.

This is the first time that Ms. Arizona and I spoke to each other in a conversation since she tore down my hopes of learning to play the piano.

I follow her through Dorm Two, making my way down the hall to Dorm Three. From the corner of my eye, I see a *Helper* standing guard outside *the Get Right Room,* making sure the *flavor of the month* doesn't escape.

"Jeneen, I would like to talk to you about the letter you are wanting to send to your parents," she says in a soft, sweet voice one could easily mistake for Snow White.

"Yes, ma'am." I gulp hard because I'm frightened that it's not going to pass through the staff's scrutiny and be mailed out. I feel a horrible repercussion about to come my way. *There is no doubt that I fully blame myself for what happened, however, I want someone normal to see what they did to me. This could get me out of here but it's risky because if Ms. Arizona figures out what I'm trying to do...*

I calculate a 50/50 chance. These people truly believe that women are at fault in rape, no matter what.

"Are you sure you want to send the letter?" she asks, waiting patiently for my reply.

"Yes, ma'am. It's the truth and I want to make it right with the Lord," I reply while swallowing hard.

"You've come a long way, Jeneen. I'm so proud of you. I remember when you first arrived here with your bad attitude and we had to escort you to *the Get Right Room.* You have made so much progress with this program," she responds, hugging me.

It's the first human contact I've received from any staff member, aside from being pulled by my wrist. It makes me feel good that Ms. Arizona is proud of me, but by the same token, I walk with my head down and my shoulders slouched. I am not proud of myself for what I've done.

"Let's pray, Jeneen.

Dear heavenly Father, I want to thank you, Lord, for really working Jeneen's heart so she can truly understand your messages in the Bible. Lord, you've touched her in so many ways and I'm so proud of her honesty. I see what a kind spirit she's become. Please continue to work through her. In your name, I pray. Amen." Ms. Arizona sings like a blue jay from a fairy tale in a land far, far away.

The next morning during breakfast, I'm feeling ill and can barely stand. I am physically weak and fear fainting onto the floor.

It started when we were in a circle reciting Bible verses. My body is now aching and I'm moments away from collapsing. I try to get a *Helper's* attention.

"I'm feeling sick. I need help," I call out in a worrisome tone.

"Ms. Arizona, please come quick! Something is wrong with Jeneen. She is not feeling well," Bernadelli yells, getting the staff's attention.

Ms. Arizona and Ms. Josella come to my table. "Do you want to lie down on your bunk bed?" Ms. Arizona asks, wanting to help.

"Yes, ma'am," I respond.

My head is tilted down and my eyes are fixated on my French toast. I am so hungry and it smells so appetizing but the weakness is overriding my appetite.

Tears are streaming down my face as they both guide my frail body to my dorm. I look to my right, catching another glimpse of that God-awful sign, "*Home is Where the Heart is.*" Something triggers in me and connects me to what I once was...

In an instant, I involuntarily cry out in hysterics, "It's all my fault! I'm a bad person. I ruined everything. It's all my fault! It's all my fault! It's all my fault! It's all my fault!" Tears of despair continue to stream down my face and Ms. Arizona hands me a Kleenex.

They both lead me to my bunk bed, unravel my hospital corners and place me underneath the sheets.

"Do you think she is schizophrenic?" Ms. Josella asks Ms. Arizona, as if I were not present.

Interesting... you people drove me crazy, not deaf, you stupid woman!

Ms. Josella was a graduate of this reform school and now she's part of the staff. She thinks I have a mental disorder? I'm more concerned about *her* mental state since she voluntarily chose to come back to this place after serving time here.

PIECE FIFTY SIX

C:\Jeneen\Hell\Victory\7MonthVisit.doc

JUVENILE HALL — a place for minors to rehabilitate. In order to attend this fun sleep-away camp, you have to commit a crime. There must be due process of law and a court order. According to your schedule, you are able to watch movies (G or PG), use the pay phone, freely write letters and play games. You could even have a pizza party (as a reward). There is no child labor period — because the youth are in school. The average visitation in a detention center is with your legal guardian or parent but it can be with anyone. It is every Saturday and Sunday, in a two or three hour time slot. You also have the right to refuse visitation.

At Victory, you are accepted without committing a crime, there-fore, you have no due process or legal representation. The only media allowed is pre-approved Christian movies — their version, of course. You cannot make phone calls, write letters freely, read anything besides your Bible or continue your education. There is forced hard labor... unpaid, naturally. You must accept Jesus or be punished. You have no free speech, friends, freedom of art or poetry... not a single connection to the outside world. You cannot have visitation for the first three months. Afterward, it is monthly, and it must be with a parent or legal guardian. You cannot refuse the meeting with your parents.

On a seven-month visit, you are granted one overnight stay with your parents. It's the only time you can leave the premises, unless of course... there is a funeral for an *inmate*.

I would have rather had the liberty of an uncensored letter delivered to a certain mailbox along a certain cul-de-sac. Drake just needs to hear from me. I would have preferred one chance at talking to my love over one day off the premises with my *biological guardians.*

By this time, my mind is no longer my own. I am a zombie. QC and company have opened my head and messed with the wiring. My lifeless shell goes through the motions, as programmed, without normal human feelings. I now truly believe that I am a bad example of a Christian. I have been programmed to believe that pants are against God, the clothes I used to wear are trampy and secular music/ TV are of the prince of the power of the air. I'm going to hell, I'm a troubled teen, a criminal, liar, druggie, alcoholic, cheap whore, a temptress and a home-wrecker; I'm doomed to spend everlasting eternity in hell for my crimes.

I take full responsibility for my statutory rape. I am accountable and Mrs. Wagster made that crystal clear. The icing on the cake is when QC made a point to tell me on my seventeenth birthday that I made up a story. How did he know about that? Did my parents tell him I made up a tale?

Victory does not need proof of a criminal record or the results of due process. Parents can just drop their child off here (with a fee), tell QC they made up a fictional story causing family problems and children can slide right through the blazing gates of perdition.

The last time I left Victory was when I attended Carey's funeral. It was so agonizing to come back. Now, I have to taste the thrill of freedom again. This time, I have to spend it with the enemy, hide my fear of Victory, then have them drop me off and abandon me for the second time. Only this time, I have to hug them. If I don't show any improvement, I most likely will serve additional time.

I continue to walk slouched, with my tail between my legs. I need to wear layers of clothing to hide my body. *No one trusts me and everyone in society hates me.* I feel shame and worthlessness to the highest degree.

This is exactly where QC wants me... right under his boot. By this time, 90% of the girls are at this level. The 10% that haven't yet been broken, get locked up in isolation. It's the perfect mindset for a day pass out of Hades. QC can be sure we will carry our captivity with us wherever we go.

Running away on my visit is out of the question. It's evident to me that my parents can do as they wish. I wouldn't dream of telling them what really goes on in here. After all, telling the truth regarding abuse is what got me locked up in the first place. If I make a run for it and get caught...

The only obstacle I have right now is my mother mentioning Drake. I don't want to hear any of it. I can't bear any more pain. It's not over for me. The spark of hope is what keeps the candle burning in my hollow shell. It's my survival mechanism, getting me through the war of Victory.

I have my nightgown and toiletries packed. All I can think about is *the fucking car dropping me off here tomorrow. This isn't a road trip to freedom but a reenactment of my parents getting rid of me once again.*

I am escorted by Ms. Arizona to the office to reunite with my darling parents.

My brother is here! It's been seven long months.

Does he notice anything odd about me? How does he feel about me being locked up against my will? Does he realize this is a reform school? Does he notice the razor wire? Does he think I deserve this? Does he even care? I wonder what my parents told him. Maybe he'll tell me something positive about Drake to give me some hope. He knows how much I love him.

I pray for a miracle.

I see the open arms of what appear to be happy, normal parents. As we embrace, I feel the façade wrapped around me. I cringe, fighting to catch my breath, gasping for air. I have to keep it together. I disassociate myself so I don't feel the knife in my back.

Let's get this charade over and done with. I just want to checkmark another day in the kingdom of the shadowy palace.

"We are going to take you to the San Diego Zoo today," my mother sings, convincing herself that she is *mother of the year.*

So now, I get to see more animals locked up? Oh goodie! I can hardly wait to start this field trip.

My mother rolls her car window down and I taste the flavor of freedom. It's bitter and I cannot enjoy it at all. I am frightened by being out in the world around other people. QC and the staff condition us, every day, to see how unfit we are for society. I am trained to believe that I cannot function without them. The world outside is full of sin and I am just going to backslide. QC, Brother Green and Brother Wagster reinforce this every day.

I go over the ground rules with my mother, "Please do not talk about Drake at all. I am not allowed to talk about boys. Please do not put any music on either. We cannot listen to the radio. Thank you."

There goes the chance of my brother saying anything positive about Drake. Sacrificing this is necessary to prevent 'Mommy Dearest' from rubbing Drake's and Jessica's romance into my open sores.

I flashback to QC's sermons…

"If you go into a bar or a liquor store, you are a bad example of a Christian. Even if you are not partaking in drinking, you are, in essence, consenting to it. Birds of a feather flock together. I don't want you to hang around your friends from your past. This is why you got into trouble in the first place. I do not want you to keep in touch with any of the girls after Victory. You will probably revert back to your old ways and fall from grace. We can't risk your progress. You are not to communicate with each other… period," QC ordered.

"I am such a bad person. Please forgive me," I tell my parents, hoping they could tell something is definitely wrong with me.

"All the girls at Victory are in the same boat, including you. The staff really loves and cares about you. They love you in spite of your mistakes." My mother is as clueless as she is heartless.

I'm in a misty haze of pretension — acting happy, shoving the real problems underneath the carpet and looking at other animals behind bars.

Diagonally across from where I'm standing, I notice a couple kissing. It's different now to see that display of intimacy. I catch the tender moment and Drake flashes right before me, with his soft lips touching mine. My heart races, triggering my body to overheat. I panic and push the image away. All I think about is my training and how lust of the flesh is wrong and sinful. The suppression of physical intimacy has definitely taken its toll over the past seven months. The dreamlike sweethearts by the sculpted elephant tree, physically touching each other, makes me uncomfortable.

Drake is no longer in the forefront of my mind. If I think of him, it's a sin.

I end up praying and pointing out scripture from the Bible when we arrive at our motel room.

The next morning, I'm awakened by the light shining in. I squint. I panic. Immediately, I come to the realization that it is the day I go back to that God-awful misery. My heart starts pounding, like the beating of a drum, marking the rhythm of my anxiety.

As we near Victory, the wind against my face dies down. I can't control my emotions as we approach the dirt road. The *corpse* suddenly has a pulse and I completely lose it. I cry uncontrollably, without speaking. It lasts for about fifteen minutes and any other parent would immediately catch on that something is not right.

"Please don't take me back. Please... Please do not take me back." I shake nervously and plead. I am so frightened to explain what really goes on inside the academy from the living hell.

They choose to ignore my cries for help and say their goodbyes. I immediately take charge of my emotions, like the tough soldier I have become. I flip the switch, walk back into the murky pit and continue to fight for my survival.

PIECE FIFTY SEVEN

C:\Jeneen\Hell\Victory\Separation\BreeAnna.doc

I HEAR THE sound of someone's sorrow coming from Dorm Two.

Who is crying? Is she okay? Did one of the Helpers cause another fellow 'convict' to come unglued? The voice is familiar… Something is horribly wrong.

The whimpering continues.

This is making me insane because I can't walk over to investigate. I am invisibly restrained in my bed. Although there are no signs of straitjackets or shackles, we are all immobilized by our fear of punishment. *How absurd is it that we can't even pee if we have to? If I were a zoo animal, I could at least pee on a rock somewhere! In this place, that would be considered a huge perk.*

Helpers whisper (since they're the only ones allowed to speak), "BreeAnna, it's going to be okay. Let's pray."

I wonder what's wrong with BreeAnna. I wish I could go over there and talk to her, like a normal human being.

BreeAnna Stafordson, my best friend from eighth grade, is back for the second time around at Victory. She was not a *bad girl* at all and was extremely humble and meek. BreeAnna confided in me that she hung around a bad crowd at Newbury Park High School and was a rebellious teen. Now that I'm experiencing the persecution at Victory firsthand, I believe her self-recriminations were just QC's brainwashing. She was not your average teen; she was mature, honest and unusually happy. She was one of the most positive people I know. She was my rock. We prayed together all the time and I'm shell shocked that she is back in here for a second helping.

So why has she returned to Victory? Did she misquote Bible scripture to her parents? Did she actually have a mind of her own and accidentally voice her opinion? According to Drake, 'She was a complete nun with a good heart.' BreeAnna would attend youth group and then the three of us would hang out. I can't believe her parents. If they think BreeAnna is a bad girl, they must be insane.

I cannot look her way, speak to her, hug her or cry with her. It is an automatic and immediate *separation* between two girls that were friends prior to this incarceration. We are forbidden to have a relationship inside this criminally insane establishment. I have not uttered one syllable to her since she arrived in January. I cannot smile at her or slightly nod in her direction. It's almost as if she does not exist and is merely a figment of my imagination. No one can share anything with me regarding BreeAnna because everyone is aware we are on *separation.* No student or staff member can deliver messages between us, however, there is indirect communication of a sort. It is dorm silence. Even the tiniest sound is accentuated. I can overhear more whispers from around the dormitories, "We need to pray for BreeAnna. Her grandmother just passed away."

Hello, God? Please watch over BreeAnna. Shield her with your light of peace.

What is their justification for blocking our friendship? Are they afraid we will buy drugs from someone in this cult? Do they think we'll have a party with the powdered milk — sneaking into the kitchen and mixing up a batch after hours… or worse, snorting it plain for a special high? Do they think we will plot against them? Do they think we will have sex? Do they think we would risk getting our bodies cut up by the wire on the twelve-foot fence while trying to escape? Do they think we would have discussions of the abuse that is taking place, and God forbid, try to put an end to it? Are they afraid we would discuss our passion for the outside world? What are these barbarians afraid of?

I wonder if BreeAnna will be able to attend her grandmother's funeral? 98% of us are not permitted to visit a dentist or a doctor off-site because the staff fears we will run. Imagine that! Some girls have medical conditions which require outside attention but the staff calls them phonies and liars in order to protect themselves.

I am now marking the end of seven months in this *pit of anguish*, and so far, I haven't needed any doctor/dentist visits. Then again, I really don't give a shit! I despise going past the gate and then having someone drop me back into this filthy, foul dumpster. The stench is unbearable especially after being exposed to the air in the real world.

PIECE FIFTY EIGHT

C:\Jeneen\Hell\Victory\JadeandtheGoodSoldier.doc

FRIDAY NIGHT... A few hours of normalcy in our bizarre existence. The assortment of peanut butter and banana sandwiches, ice cream, cakes, candies and soda pop are nicely organized and accessible... for some of the girls. We are all smiles and looking forward to the sugar rush as we take our treats from the kitchen window. *This reminds me of the films of Vietnam War soldiers, playing football along a beach, right before being assigned to another mission.*

The normally noiseless hall surprisingly echoes with the sounds of humanity — laughter and excitement in the midst of despair. It's our only time to binge on junk food... and we do, without regret. Since I'm locked into half-portions and working off way more calories than I consume, Friday night is my time to fuel up.

Every Friday night, there is a separation. It is the girls who make it to Friday night with six demerits or less and the ones who do not. The girls who have seven demerits or more have to go back to Dorm Three. *It is nearly impossible to go through Victory without making a mistake and receiving a demerit. You try it! You might get a punishment for breathing the wrong way.* One girl got locked into isolation for one week because she forgot her pencil for school. Her pencil? *You have got to be fucking kidding me!*

As long as you are a perfect little *Christian Stepford child,* according to their tainted view, you are in the clear. I remember my God being divine, like a rock for me. Now, he has become a monster that will send me straight to hell, regardless of my salvation. The lesson that Victory has taught me is that I am an untouchable, plain and simple, and I will always be. That being said, I have seven demerits this week. Brother Green does a double take. I am a *Laundry Helper*. *Helpers* usually have each other's backs.

"What? Jeneen? How are you not getting to attend Friday night?" Brother Green questions loudly in front of all the girls. Other than the staff, I am at the highest status in rank. I have finally arrived, so to speak. I do not cause any problems and follow QC's game plan to the letter. I hand out demerits, but for some time, I have been going slightly against the grain. I do things in an unorthodox fashion — I do it with love. I say things like, "I have made that mistake before. You'll get it." I try my best to soften the blow while enforcing the ludicrous regulations.

The only girls that can give out demerits to a *Helper* are other *Helpers*. Each demerit for a *Helper* consists of five hundred lines, instead of the minimum one hundred. If the normal punishment is five hundred, then it's one thousand lines for asking permission to use the toilet, however, *Helpers* look out for each other and rarely give other *Helpers* demerits. So what heartless *Helper* gave them to me? **I did.**

I started giving them to myself some time ago if I left a hairbrush out, if I accidentally walked too close to BreeAnna (which was nearly impossible to avoid in such close quarters) or asked a stupid question… or any other numerous infractions. I gave myself seven demerits this week.

"Okay, everyone, it's Friday night. All of you girls who get Friday night, line up in the food line. All of you girls who do not, go to Dorm Three," QC shouts, wearing his usual evil smirk. He goes into explicit detail about the goodies that we will be missing out on. His eyes blatantly scan up and down our bodies and I can feel the negative vibe of his disapproval. I also feel naked as he inspects me under my steel armor, continuing his manhunt for my vulnerability. We remain in silence and march in single file back to the dorm.

One of the privileges of being a *Helper* is the opportunity of leading the Bible studies. I enjoy doing it because it's my private ministry — my opportunity to reach the girls and make them feel worthy. It's also cathartic for me to lift someone's spirits because I feel like the scum of society.

If I could just make these girls feel valuable, then maybe... I will heal too.

It's a silent understanding between my fellow inmates and me, that I am always indirectly speaking of the judgment at Victory. The *Word of God* is my only means to relay my thoughts. The girls who are punished for making Victory mistakes, feel defeated. I want them to know the softer side of God through Jesus. Jesus teaches us how to reach everyone and how to talk to the *untouchables,* according to society. He specifically gives us instructions **not** to segregate. I want these students to realize they are something special and the Bible is the perfect tool, and the **only** conduit, I have left. In spite of how I feel about myself, I want these young girls to feel worthwhile. I want them to get in tune with God's love.

"Everyone, please turn to Luke, Chapter 18. I will read it for you..." I say softly.

Luke 18:9-14

9 - To some who were confident of their own righteousness and looked down on everybody else, Jesus told this parable:

10 - "Two men went up to the temple to pray, one a Pharisee and the other a tax collector.

11 - The Pharisee stood up and prayed about himself:

'God, I thank you that I am not like other men — robbers, evildoers, adulterers — or even like this tax collector.

12 -I fast twice a week and give a tenth of all I get.'

13 - But the tax collector stood at a distance. He would not even look up to heaven, but beat his breast and said, 'God, have mercy on me, a sinner.'

14 - I tell you that this man, rather than the other, went home justified before God. For everyone who exalts himself will be humbled, and he who humbles himself will be exalted."

I want to use this as an example of what that psychopath should be preaching in chapel. The parallels are extremely clear.

Obviously, QC is the Pharisee and we are all, as he puts it... Jezebels. We are, according to our ruler, just a bunch of whores and home-wreckers.

"Girls, please open your Bibles to Luke, Chapter 7. Let me know when you are there and then I will read it for you," I say, keeping my voice soft.

Luke 7:36-50.

36 - Then one of the Pharisees asked Him to eat with him. And He went to the Pharisee's house, and sat down to eat.

37 - And behold, a woman in the city who was a sinner, when she knew that Jesus sat at the table in the Pharisee's house, brought an alabaster flask of fragrant oil,

38 -and stood at His feet behind Him weeping; and she began to wash His feet with her tears, and wiped them with the hair of her head; and she kissed His feet and anointed them with the fragrant oil.

39 - Now when the Pharisee who had invited Him saw this, he spoke to himself, saying, "This Man, if He were a prophet, would know who and what manner of woman this is who is touching Him, for she is a sinner."

40 - And Jesus answered and said to him, "Simon, I have something to say to you."

So he said, "Teacher, say it."

41 - "There was a certain creditor who had two debtors. One owed five hundred denarii, and the other fifty.

42 - And when they had nothing with which to repay, he freely forgave them both. Tell Me, therefore, which of them will love him more?"

43 - Simon answered and said, "I suppose the one whom he forgave more."

And He said to him, "You have rightly judged."

44 - Then He turned to the woman and said to Simon, "Do you see this woman? I entered your house; you gave Me no water for My feet, but she has washed My feet with her tears and wiped them with the hair of her head.

45 - You gave Me no kiss, but this woman has not ceased to kiss My feet since the time I came in.

46 - You did not anoint My head with oil, but this woman has anointed My feet with fragrant oil.

47 - Therefore I say to but you, her sins, which are many, are forgiven, for she loved much. But to whom little is forgiven, the same loves little."

48 - Then He said to her, "Your sins are forgiven."

I make eye contact with everyone and then comment, "This is how we should be as a true Christian. We should follow Jesus and not cast judgment on anyone else. We should treat others how we want to be treated and make an effort to follow the *golden rule.* Jesus is the perfect example. He sees everyone as clean, pure, whole and worthy to enter into the kingdom, no matter what the charge."

I am clearly referring to how things are run here in this bottomless pit of destruction. I can almost see the ideas sinking in and taking root.

"Would anyone like to add to this?" I ask, interested in hearing other interpretations.

Jade immediately raises her hand. She waves it, indicating that there is something urgent she needs to share with the group.

"That's how they treat us in here. They judge us and they shouldn't do that. They are going against Jesus' message!"

I gulp. I gulp again. *Yes, that is where I am going with this but we are forbidden to have that kind of discussion. I will be demoted to Buddy, risking months in isolation. I still have five months left.*

My heart sinks because I know she is taking a stand. Jade definitely received my message but there are ears everywhere. Aside from monitors, girls will tell the staff — not to mention, we are right next to Ms. Arizona's room. The girls in the group are so brainwashed that they will rat me out for my opinion, seeing it as an opportunity to go up in rank. I will be locked up in *the Get Right Room* and find myself three feet behind a *Buddy* in a heartbeat. If I say anything negative about the staff, my head will be in the guillotine. I am in a state of paranoia… and for good reason.

The only thing I can utter to Jade, because I have no other recourse, is "We can't say that in here. You need to watch your mouth!" I throw back sternly, only thinking about saving my rank.

I am dying. I just killed a little butterfly for speaking her mind. I am no better than the staff. I am merely a soldier following orders, hurting anyone I have to, just to survive. I have to be selfish and look out for myself.

She just wanted to spell out the obvious and vent a little of what is bottled up inside of all of us. After all, she is only thirteen and subtlety is a bit beyond her.

What I want to say, but cannot, is…"Yes, Jade, that is what they do to us in here. You are absolutely correct. Bullseye!"

God, can you see my tears? They are inside me because I cannot allow them to fall from my face. If they did, Jade would know I love her but then the staff would punish me for having integrity. God, could you let Jade know I love her? She's a beautiful soul whom I intended to help with my private ministry, but one slip of the tongue has undone all my efforts. Hellooooo, God?

What kind of ministry is this if I cannot speak the truth? What good is the Word when I can't use it as a tool to help someone? I want to rip out all the pages. I want to tear up *his bible* of the Old and New Testaments. I want to read my Bible study to QC with Jade by my side and show him what Luke really teaches. *This is my sermon, you bloody bastard! I will shed light in the dark crevices of your soul and remind you about Jesus' teachings. You call us whores every day but Jesus would have treated us differently. You are supposed to be our parent-figure but you are just a demon, masquerading in sick righteousness. You use the highest source western civilization has for defining what is right and good, as a tool to torment our already broken souls.*

PIECE FIFTY NINE

C:\Jeneen\Purgatory\TheProdigalDaugherReturns.doc

I AM CREATING meticulous rows of tracks on the carpet as I repetitiously push a Hoover back and forth. I try not to let my mind drift — the memory of volunteering for First Christian Church of Newbury Park comes to mind. I freely gave up my time to do work like this for my former church. I wanted to help out and be part of something positive, however, this... this was different. There isn't anything I do here that is for the greater good.

I hear an unexpected voice behind me. I'm a bit startled because no one is allowed to come close.

"Jeneen, I need you to stop vacuuming. I need you to come with me... RIGHT NOW!" Ms. Arizona shouts over the loud motor. She starts walking rapidly and I follow her to Dorm One. There is not one girl in sight. All of the inmates are busy working.

She starts opening my drawer and I see my toiletries neatly arranged, military style.

Do I have a sock out of order? I start frantically looking for something that might be out of place.

She says, in a low tone, "I need you to pack your things before the other girls see you. Start packing. Your mom and dad are here to pick you up."

My heart starts pounding and I immediately think… *Drake! Drake! Drake!*

I get to see my Drake again. I cannot believe this is happening! Is this happening? Is someone going to pull the rug out from under me? Is this another one of my crazy nightmares where I'm finally free and happy and then I just wake up staring at the same blue concrete wall? I don't care, I'm just going to pack and go with this dream, just in case it's not a figment of my imagination.

I try to hide my smile.

I shove everything into a box. I'm shaking with excitement.

I see my parents by the front desk where QC originally introduced himself. I catch sight of the prison-like barbed wire fence. The electrical gate is open and *Mommy Dearest's* yellow Ford Fairmont is parked on the dirt road. My mother and father reach out to hug me and say, "We are taking you home."

Someone must have finally told everyone from Cornerstone Christian School how horrible this place is. It must have been BreeAnna. They took her out earlier and no one knew about her disappearance. She just vanished and no one spoke of it.

My parents were not going to take me out of here early on their own. No one knew I was in a reformatory for troubled girls until more of Victory *graduates* started attending my former high school. There were already two survivors from Victory attending Christian Cornerstone in my Junior Year. I just never thought in a million years…

I don't care how it happened. I'm going to see my Drake and that's all that matters. He's the only one who kept me sane during my imprisonment. Now, I am free to love and to be loved again.

The car moves slowly over the gravel and I keep my eyes fixed on the road ahead. I do not dare look back at that horrific *torture camp*. I can finally feel the wind on my face, smell the scent of flowers and taste the deliciousness of my liberty.

I blurt out, "When I get home, I will kiss the ground! I am free. I am free. I am free!"

My father looks at me in his rearview mirror, smiles, and says dramatically, "The *prodigal daughter* returns. It's Easter week and this month is about forgiveness. This is why we took you out early."

It took everything in my power not to lose control of my sanity.

What the fuck is he talking about? Does he know what the 'prodigal son' is about? This is not a good analogy for the last eight months of my life. There was no share of an estate to have. I didn't have any options or get to make any decisions. I would have chosen wisely. I would have stayed at Drake's house until I graduated and then prepared for college. Instead, dear old Dad, you sent me to a prison. Forget about the abuse for just a second… you took me from my life. You didn't give me any money, nor did I choose to leave of my own free will.

You do not have any servants and there will not be a feast waiting for me. Do you think I'm unworthy of being your daughter? You are not the father in the story of the 'prodigal son', so don't think that parable describes our relationship. It doesn't fit. In my book, you just didn't want to deal with the situation and this was your easy way out. You punished me for someone else's misdeeds because you couldn't handle the truth. You took me out of the equation on the assumption that our family problems would dissipate if I was gone. My question is, how's the family doing now?

I'm not going to react over this thoughtless comment. I've come this far. Daddy Dearest might just flip the car around and take me back if I sound off. I will not do anything to jeopardize being with my love one more time.

I was well-trained by my stay at Victory. I just continue doing what I always do — stuffing the anger from the abuse deep down.

I look out my window and take in the beautiful scenery. I missed seeing the palm trees. I start to fantasize about Drake. I long for his tender kisses and the passion that he once had for me. I thirst for his positive reinforcements, his tenderness, our intimate conversations and being held in his arms. I yearn to inhale the confidence he gave me to stand on my own two feet. I want to be in tune with the way he made me feel about my intellect and my beauty again. I need to know that he will be the one to rescue me from my toxic family. I will have a normal life once I get away from my parents.

The exterior of our cottage-like home remains unchanged. The familiar plants and flowers are in the front and the country-style door sits straight ahead, waiting for me to open it. As I pass the welcome mat, my mother shouts, "I thought you said you were going to kiss the ground?"

Luke 15:11-32

New International Version (NIV) The Parable of the Lost Son

11 - Jesus continued: "There was a man who had two sons.

12 - The younger one said to his father, 'Father, give me my share of the estate.' So he divided his property between them.

13 - "Not long after that, the younger son got together all he had, set off for a distant country and there squandered his wealth in wild living.

14 - After he had spent everything, there was a severe famine in that whole country, and he began to be in need.

15 - So he went and hired himself out to a citizen of that country, who sent him to his fields to feed pigs.

16 - He longed to fill his stomach with the pods that the pigs were eating, but no one gave him anything.

17 - "When he came to his senses, he said, 'How many of my father's hired servants have food to spare, and here I am starving to death!

18 - I will set out and go back to my father and say to him: Father, I have sinned against heaven and against you.

19 - I am no longer worthy to be called your son; make me like one of your hired servants.'

20 - So he got up and went to his father.

"But while he was still a long way off, his father saw him and was filled with compassion for him; he ran to his son, threw his arms around him and kissed him.

21 - "The son said to him, 'Father, I have sinned against heaven and against you. I am no longer worthy to be called your son.'

22 - "But the father said to his servants, 'Quick! Bring the best robe and put it on him. Put a ring on his finger and sandals on his feet.

23 - Bring the fattened calf and kill it. Let's have a feast and celebrate.

24 - For this son of mine was dead and is alive again; he was lost and is found.' So they began to celebrate.

PIECE SIXTY

C:\Jeneen\Purgatory\Parents\Drake\Emptiness.doc

TIME TICKS SO slowly when you're waiting for the one you love to call; it's like waiting for water to boil. Hours have passed but no phone call from Drake. I try to erase it from my mind but all I think about is how happy my mother said he is with Jessica. I don't want to intrude on his new life so I wait for him to make the first move. It shouldn't take long for my mother to spread the word that I am back in town. I will wait… I know he'll call.

I catch a glimpse of a soap opera my mother is watching. Erica Kane and Travis Montgomery from All My Children are kissing each other passionately. Since I've been deprived of physical contact and television for the last eight months, seeing this stirs up mixed emotions of guilt, shame and desire. Part of me feels guilty, thanks to QC's teachings about the lust of the flesh, and the other makes me think of the boy who has my heart.

The phone rings. My heart is beating like a drum — this can go either way…

Does he still love me? Is my mom wrong about him being happier with Jessica? Will we go out for the evening and fix everything that is broken? All we need is one drive into the past to make everything whole again. He'll know I still have strong feelings for him no matter what came between us.

I grab the phone and he cheers, "Hi… how are you?" "Fine. How are you?" I say robotically.

"Do you still walk funny?" he says as if he were the comedian of the decade. *Is Jessica right beside him?*

Drake? What happened to you? Hello? Who is this and what have you done with my boyfriend? The other Drake adored me. Hello?? Drake?

At this moment, it feels like my heart is going to stop. *Isn't he happy with me anymore? Am I not entertaining enough? Did I do something wrong? Maybe he just thinks I'm an airhead and doesn't believe I'm stimulating enough.* I flash back to the display of Orion's Belt in the starlit sky on Happy Trail Circle.

"Do you want the necklace back so you can give it to Jessica?"

"No, you keep it. It's yours," I say emotionless.

The conversation couldn't have been more than five minutes. There isn't a discussion of what happened at Victory and I do not receive the resolution I had anticipated. He didn't exactly break up with me either. I am left hanging in midair — over a cliff.

My boxing gloves are down and I forfeit the fight for the boy I love. I'm defeated and worn out; I'm going to throw in the towel. It's not the same. QC broke me down into pieces and took away my faith in my own self-worth.

If I could turn back the clock, I would have invited Drake over and insisted on a long drive up the coast. I would have convinced him that our relationship is worth saving.

I can't believe he's gone. Drake was the magic potion who kept me from falling apart. It was almost as if I was Buck Rogers, frozen for 500 years. The world moved forward while I remained frozen in time; everything in the real world is different now.

I run to the bathroom and throw up. Then, I cry. I vomit. I cry. I vomit. I cry.

Why is he so different? How can he just forget what we had? Those magic kisses were amazing, and now, they are just dust in the wind.

I flush the toilet.

I walk into my bedroom and look all over the place for my diaries. *Where are my diaries?*

I check my bedroom with a fine-tooth comb, hunting for my private words. I frantically search every nook and cranny... and nothing. I dash into my brother's room without knocking.

"Giovanni, where are my diaries? Did Mom take them?" I ask abruptly. "Yes," he says.

"Well, did she read them?" I ask frightened. "Yes," he responds, matter-of-factly.

"Did she read them to other people?" I ask again, terrified. "I think so," he replies.

Wasn't this the same mother who told me that my treasured thoughts should be written in a private book and kept out of reach? Wasn't she adamant that I keep it hidden? She gave me my first journal with a lock at nine years old. She probably read them to justify sending me away. My guess is that she read it to Drake or told him about it. If she did... that was beyond wicked.

I angrily confront *Mommy Dearest.* "Did you read all three of my diaries?"

"Yes, and you should never write such filth again," she shouts callously.

"You broke us up! If it were not for you, I would be with him. I was happy and you took my life away from me!" I yell with utter sadness in my heart.

"He doesn't love you anymore and you need to face it! You need to be strong and just get over it. The truth hurts!"

My father heads towards the dining room after my heated discussion with my mother. I stare at the 1970's brown flower-pattern design on the white dish in my hands. I am prepared to raise the dish and break it into a million pieces. I stop myself because my father is now in the kitchen.

"It's a real shame that your lover couldn't wait for you. He should have waited." His words would be soothing if they came from a concerned parent. Instead, it feels like a knife in my back.

Okay, so now it's Drake's fault? You are going to blame my boyfriend for this?

I analytically process everything in silence, for fear of being sent back to that wretched place.

I truly hate my parents. They ruined my life and they're proud of themselves.

As I'm blaming them, logic comes to the forefront. Drake has free will and his hands are not tied. He could come over here but he chooses not to. I only want someone who wants me. I do not want forced love. Honest love is what I am after. I had it once and I can have it again.

The pain kicks in again. *Oh my God! This hurts like holy hell.*

I am numb from my anguish and walk slowly to my room in order to wallow in self-pity. After all, they are my emotions… and Ms. Arizona can no longer stop me. I pick a corner, squat on the floor and cry so many tears that I thought the house would flood. The waste paper basket is filled with tissues. My eyes are completely bloodshot and my nose is bright red. Round and round we go… my parents will probably make the assumption, once again, that I am using drugs.

PIECE SIXTY ONE

C:\Jeneen\Purgatory\LifeAfterVictory\WakingUp.doc

THE DISTURBING RINGING sound rattles me out of bed in a cold sweat. I flip on a light switch expecting to see blue brick walls. It takes me a while to come to grips with reality. I start to look around for something familiar to ground myself. I search left and find my Madonna poster taped to my wall. My heart rate starts to slow down to normal until… the heavy weight of acceptance that Drake is no longer in my life, causes a malfunction. The pain feels like a sharp weapon stabbing me in the chest. My heart has been trampled on, squashed by numerous people, tossed around like a hot potato and put through a grinder. I'm anxious, empty and emotionally drained. I lackadaisically reset my alarm for a later time. Why should I bother to spring out of bed? There's nothing for me to look forward to anymore… nothing!

Suddenly, a knock on my bedroom door startles me. I almost choke on my own fright when I hear the shrill voice…"You need to get ready for school. We're driving you down to Camarillo Cornerstone Christian. We have a meeting with Mrs. T before we register you back into school."

Mrs. T… I miss her so much! Maybe she can help me find my identity. Unfortunately, I still feel like a mindless automaton.

I reluctantly drag myself to the bathroom. I figure if I take a shower, it will energize me somewhat. Everything moves in slow motion as I turn the water faucet to hot and then add a little cold.

I start to think about the *Helper* with the whistle as the beads of water repel off my olive skin. *Oh… I almost forgot — I'm not timed. I can finally shave everything at slow speed and not risk cutting myself!*

I feel the moisture from the steam and it keeps me warm.

One hour later, my mother starts the car to warm up the engine. She leaves it unattended and comes back into the house.

"Let's go, Jeneen and Giuseppe," she yells like a military sergeant, not realizing my father is right beside her. The irritating, whining sounds that originate from her lips are always tinged with disapproval. It's enough to make your skin crawl. She always sounds annoyed and makes me feel that nothing I do is good enough for her. I do my own laundry, clean, set the table and have resumed my studies. Evidently, this has all been overlooked.

"I'm right here. Why do you have to yell like that for, huh?" my father questions in his New York guttural accent. *Why should he be surprised? This is her normal means of communicating.*

"I'm not sure if I should get in the car with the two of you. You might send me back to Victory." *I am really scared to fucking death to get into the same vehicle with them.*

"Don't worry, we won't send you there again," she tries to reassure me — as if I could ever trust her word again.

I'll just remain fully alert at all times, preparing myself to jump out of the car. I have no qualms about risking my life to stay away from that satanic cult they called 'Christian'.

If my mother were driving without my father, I would not worry at all. My mother doesn't know how to drive to Ramona and she's too afraid to figure it out.

We settle in for the drive. I notice the religious sticker collection on the dashboard and crinkle my nose. *The proverbs make me ill. I am reminded of the cruel God that hates, the punishments I had to endure, being locked up and the light that was snuffed out of my soul. I stare in disgust and cringe. Now, all I see is ultimate hypocrisy.*

My brown eyes blink and I go into a trance while I become fixated on my sad reflection in the window. We stay on target, bound for Camarillo. I put myself on guard, making certain there are absolutely no detours.

As my mother pulls up in the parking lot of the school, I reminisce about the last time I attended Cornerstone. I was popular, had many friends, respected by faculty and my nurturing boyfriend kept me centered.

What exactly did my parents conjure up to tell the faculty and staff regarding my disappearance? I most certainly suspect reform school was not the story they told, otherwise, both would have received a mouthful from my instructors. I can almost hear the lies, as if I were listening to a recording... 'We didn't know what to do. We were so desperate and we had to help her. She was very unhappy.'

We make our way to Mrs. T's office and I carry my Bible like a briefcase. I'm afraid to be without the *twisted scriptures* because I'm still operating on QC's programming. I refuse to leave home without it.

Mrs. T! I notice her right away but my social skills are now destroyed. I see her arms reach out as she offers me a hug. It's the first genuine contact I have received since my ordeal over the past eight months.

"How are you, Jeneen?" she asks, very concerned for my well-being.

"I'm fine, ma'am," I say on autopilot, partially hoping she will see what Victory has done to me.

"Jeneen, you don't have to call me ma'am. Mrs. T is fine," she says with a smile.

Moments later, we all settle into our chairs across from Mrs. T.

There is no longer an expression on my face. I rock back and forth as I space out, in order to tolerate sitting next to my parents.

"Thank you so much for meeting with me today, especially under short notice on Easter week. We can definitely accept Jeneen back to Cornerstone Christian without a problem. Jeneen has been an excellent student in the past and we would like to keep her, however, the school committee deemed it necessary for her to attend counseling.

That is our only stipulation," she states, concerned about my future.

My father stands up and grabs my Bible, places it in front of her and angrily says, "No. Do you see this? God is her counselor."

Oh my God. He sounds like QC! No wonder he likes the miserable preacher from hell. They are both the same kind of crazy. This is unraveling right before my eyes!

They go back and forth on this. My father repetitively throws the *Word of God* in Mrs. T's face. *It is so obvious that he is terrified of what would come out in my counseling sessions. Since my father is so adamant about following the Bible, maybe he should reread Luke 15:11-32. I wonder if he realizes that this is a Christian school and that these people know the Bible better than he does? Does he understand that I have always received A's in my Bible classes? Hmmm. Did he ever see my report cards... or was he too tired from work?*

My father makes an impulsive decision, his ego overriding my best interests... "We'll just put her in public school."

I look at Mrs. T without voicing my opinion. I am unable to describe what was done to me at Victory or back her up on how much I really need professional help to save me from self-destruction. I just stand there, like a statue. After all, I *am* merely a robot.

I hug Mrs. T for the last time.

Maybe it's for the best that I can no longer attend this school. My mother gossips about how horrible I am. One student in my science class confessed that my mother told everyone in the office that I was on 'the pill'. She also told everyone how rebellious I was at home and that if I didn't make changes, she was going to do something. Maybe they will believe anything negative she tells them about me. I'm tired of walking with my head down in shame.

On the way back home, my parents have a ludicrous conversation. They remain blissfully ignorant — dumbfounded as to why I need counseling.

"Mrs. T doesn't know what she's talking about. They need to mind their own business. I can't believe they are kicking our daughter out of that school. Those miserable Christian bastards!" my father yells ironically.

Meanwhile, I am flabbergasted by the fact that I have to attend the same high school as Drake. I swallow my anxiety like a bad pill. I would be able to hear my beating heart if it weren't for my obnoxiously loud family.

Newbury Park High School... Unwanted images of watching Drake kiss Jessica come to the forefront. I swallow my salty tears as my hopes of recovering from Victory are dashed. The daily torture continues...

PIECE SIXTY TWO

C:\Jeneen\Purgatory\LifeAfterVictory\MyNewGPA.doc

HEART... THE VINDICTIVE anger coming from Ann Wilson as she sings, *If Looks Could Kill*, is blasting through my boom box, however, I would never in a million years get satisfaction by seeing Drake in pain, lying on the floor. *It's not my style. Besides, he didn't cheat. I was taken away and then he moved on.* I press the fast-forward button hard, not realizing the extent of my bitterness. I randomly land on another song.

Maybe if I can sound like Heart's lead vocalist, it might bring him back. I start to memorize the lyrics to *Stranded. Now, that seems fitting.*

The waterbed takes up the better part of my room, so I set my karaoke speaker on the built-in bench at the foot.

The echoing, haunting sound of Heart has become my wallowing in sorrow and heartbreak music. I grab my microphone and sing *Stranded* in hopes of Drake tapping on my window. Hours pass in slow motion and there isn't one sign of him. I leave my window open a crack... just in case. Like a raven, I released him, letting him go so he could spread his wings and fly high. I'm hoping that, eventually, the raven will somehow transform into a homing pigeon.

Like a parrot, I pay attention to every detail of Ann Wilson's voice. Maybe if I sing the chorus really loudly, Drake will hear me three miles down.

I adjust the audio.

Wow, maybe I should have been singing this a long time ago. I wonder what Jessica is doing to impress him right now. My homing pigeon seems to have forgotten where I am.

Perhaps he wants to live like a normal teenager, without the stress of my dysfunctional family.

Suddenly, my mother barges into my room, shows me my report card and yells, "Turn your music down. What is this? You are failing one of your classes — Political Science!"

"Hmmmmm, Mother… Let's do the math on this one, shall we? I was selfmotivated and studious. I had good grades and was prepping for a university before you locked me up in a reform school. I was well-liked by my peers and had a boyfriend who was every parent's dream. You sucked the vitality out of my soul when you took everything away from me. I have nothing now, and every day, I am reminded of it when I see Jessica and Drake holding hands and kissing at school.

You took my life away and I want you to get the fuck out of my room so I can be alone. Get out! Now!" I shout and then start to sob in a corner near my closet, fully expecting my father to forcibly haul me back to Victory like recycled trash.

My mother replies angrily, "You are not going to graduate unless you pass a test. I think it's called the GED. I have you scheduled for Monday."

"Fine. Get out of my room please! Thank you," I shout, risking getting locked up for another round of the *good gospel.*

The months of pent up anger finally erupted. My rage is like a fully loaded automatic weapon. I'm armed to the teeth and I don't know what to do with it. I take my schoolbooks and slam them against the wall. My scholastic future seems bleak. I don't give a shit because that takes too much energy. All I want right now is to get through this pain.

I crank up the music to drown out my mother screaming at my father, "I don't know what to do with her! I give up! I give up!"

What is she going to do now… call QC for guidance? It's only a matter of time before they dump me off by the wayside again.

I crank up my boom box, completely drowning out my mother's yelling. This means, I'm blasting it on the highest level possible.

I can barely hear a faint knock at my door over the blaring music. I open it… "Chris? Let's just get out of here," I demand in desperation.

I shout to my hot-blooded parents, "I'm leaving now!"

I lock the door behind me and leave the intense arguing behind.

"Chris, hurry up and get in the Nissan before my parents have a chance to stop me from going out. I'll explain in the truck," I say hastily.

Chris Meshkan. I have known him since my Freshman Year. He is a lanky eighteen-year-old, six feet tall and has fair skin and straight brown hair that falls over his freckled face. I started calling him *Chrissie* in ninth grade and he would always smile at me. Our flirtatious bantering kept up, until one day he asked me for my phone number.

We took many drives together. I talked about Drake and he talked about Michelle, his former girlfriend. It was a perfect fit — two wounded souls trying to survive a loss. There wasn't any jumping in his arms by the ocean or a sparkle in my eye. The only intimacy we have is talking about our past relationships and of course, my current troubled home life.

We drive for hours while I explain all of my pain in explicit detail. He keeps a supply of Kleenex just for me, because one night, I came out with a roll of toilet paper. We have nothing but time and Chris likes to drive for hours. We drive past Malibu, Santa Monica Pier and then back to Ventura. The lights on PCH are mesmerizing. It's unfortunate that I can't give my heart to Chris because it's been shattered into pieces. Somehow it works because he cannot do the same. We are both spent. What he does give me is his time, his ear and his understanding. I'm so thankful for this and I don't know what I'd do without him.

I stare into the fog and notice how it distorts the light from a street lamp. Five, four, three, two, one… I fly backwards to a memory of Camarillo Cornerstone Christian. It was during a time when my grades were outstanding. I was studying during finals, staying up until 1 am and drinking an occasional coffee or popping a NoDoz to stay awake. My mother somehow managed to find something to yell at me about while I was studying.

"Would you please keep the yelling down? I'm trying to study," I barked back on high volume, in order for her to hear me.

I turned up my music to tune out her annoying, high-pitched screeches. Every time I spoke with my mother, it turned into a screaming match. She would always drown out my voice with her sheer volume. She could only hear me if I raised my voice a couple of octaves above hers. Our *opera buffa* was a daily occurrence.

"Jeneen, you are too stressed out! You study too much and I don't think college is for you. You put too much pressure on yourself. *College is not for you. College is not for you. College is not for youuuuuuuuuuuuuu.* I'm going to have a talk with your teachers as soon as possible!" she said, as if my studying was the root of our family problems.

'*College is not for you!*' continued to ring in my ears but I opened my literature book and continued anyway. I will not allow *Mommy Dearest* to get in the way of my success.

On Friday mornings, our Bible class would take a walk to McDonald's for breakfast. On this particular stroll, my Bible teacher, Mr. Mahogany, wanted to speak with me on the way back.

"You know that college may not be the best solution. You may want to think about something that's not going to stress you out. College isn't for everyone," he said, concerned.

What did my mother tell him?

"Well, maybe I'll work for a company right away and put all my energy into that. It will be an on-the-job education for me," I said to Mr. Mahogany, enthusiastically.

"This is what I'm talking about, Jeneen. You are putting too much pressure on yourself," he said, trying to get his point across.

My next class was Algebra II. As I stepped into the classroom, I spotted Mrs. T writing formulas on the chalkboard.

Mrs. T said in a cheerful voice, "Jeneen, I need to speak with you after class." "Sure thing, Mrs. T!" I responded in an upbeat manner.

Before I could blink, class was over and I joined her by the chalkboard as soon as the students cleared the room.

"Jeneen, I would like to talk to you about college. It's much different than high school. You have approximately three classes a day instead of six. You have been an outstanding student and I have faith that you can do this. You will be a success at whatever you put your hands to." This was the kind of support I needed; too bad it never came from home.

"Thank you, Mrs. T. I'm looking forward to it… I can hardly wait! Thank you for always encouraging me," I said with confidence. Mrs. T has always been a shining star in my life.

I blink my eyes and I'm right back in the Nissan truck, staring at a different light.

"Thank you, Chris, for always being there for me. I could not get through this without you," I share, reassuring him how much he has helped me in my healing process.

"It's the least I can do," he responds with a smile that I am able to notice in the dark, thanks to the city lights of Santa Monica.

The next morning, I wake up and realize, once again, that I'm not staring at a blue brick wall. It's like reliving the same day, over and over. I sit up. Panic spreads through me like malaria. There are no longer butterflies fluttering inside of me. There are, instead, restless bats trying to escape.

I force myself to get ready for school. I didn't even bother to study for the GED. *Well, the one good thing I have going for me is that I'm not nervous, primarily because I don't give a rat's ass about anything anymore.* In the past, I would study for every test. My goal was an A on everything. Failing was absolutely out of the question. Those used to be my standards. *Now, I just can't seem to muster up the motivation for anything.*

The test is held at the library. I pass the student store and make my way to the book room. Mrs. Mueler hands me a number two pencil and my test begins.

I have to pass this test. If I pass this exam, I can graduate and leave the 'house of pain'.

With that thought, I realize there *is* a way out of my situation. There *is* a glimmer of hope.

My algebra skills surprisingly pop up from some corner of my subconscious.

It's as if it never escaped my hard drive, despite the damage that was done at Victory. As I plow through the essays, I realize my English skills remain intact.

"Mrs. Mueler, can you let me know if I passed?" I ask with renewed excitement for a promising future.

"We'll call you in a couple days. You just have to be patient. Thank you," she says with a soft, pleasant librarian's voice.

PIECE SIXTY THREE

C:\Jeneen\Purgatory\LifeAfterVictory\ MyCollegeApplication.doc

My mother storms into my room and cheers with excitement, "Jeneena, I've got great news for you. You passed the test and you can graduate. Now you can start looking for a job. How about applying for a live-in nanny position so you can live for free where you work? This way, you don't have to live with us anymore," she points out. Her suggestion is not exactly like a parent handing a young adult an application to a nearby college, for example… Pepperdine University.

A live-in nanny? Are those the expectations you have for me, Mother? Is it because you never finished high school and you don't want to see me surpass you in education? Is it the fact that you want me to have everything I worked hard for destroyed because you resent me? Is my unhappiness your pleasure? How did you become so wicked? How could you lie to everyone, telling them that you have an out-of-control teenager who's heading down the wrong path when, in reality, I had a good head on my shoulders? That's what really rubbed you the wrong way, isn't it? You did your best to turn me into a monster and now I regret to say that I own a piece of what you created. I will fight it everyday so you WON'T win because you are right… I AM rebellious. I will fight what the evil queen, my abusive father and Victory Christian Academy have placed on my hard drive until… the day I die.

"I'm going to live with Kara and her parents until I get on my feet, and then, I will be on my own," I say with a combination of confidence and annoyance at her presence.

"You will NEVER make it! This is a cruel world and I know you'll fail out there! Do you hear me?" she yells, as if concerned. There is no concern because she is blatantly kicking me out of the house with her live-in nanny game plan. She thinks she knows the world but her understanding is distorted, tiny and skewed.

She lived with her aunts until my dad married her at the age of 19. She didn't have to work and never lived a day on her own.

"Cruel world you say? Well, it can't be any more difficult than what I've experienced thus far, living in this home with you. In fact, you have thoroughly prepared me for how atrocious the world is out there. I am no longer ignorant to wolves in sheep's clothing. The world should be a walk in the park. Well done! I have graduated at the top of my class from the *school of hard knocks*," I say with utter sarcasm.

I dial Kara's number. "Hello, Kara? How soon can I come to live with you and your family?" I ask, desperate to get out of this place where I feel unloved and unwanted.

"I can pick you up tomorrow," Kara says reassuringly. Today is the day. I have taken my first step. I've jumped off of the satanic merry-go-round. I reached for Kara's hand as she pulled me out of the flames. From this day forward, I refuse to live in fear, with no control over my life.

The next morning, I awake excited and eager to start my new journey. I start to shove all my toiletries in a plastic garbage bag and grab my clothes off the wire hangers. I toss them into another bag. I look at my Junior Prom dress and feel the black velvet material. Before I can pull up a happy memory, I angrily shove it into my bag. I find my cardboard box of love letters from Drake. I force myself to read just one to experience the magic again. I wonder how something so beautiful can just vanish into thin air. It was an innocent love without any baggage, hurts or fear of abandonment. I felt secure and confident that no one could separate us, no matter how hard they tried. I refold the letter exactly how Drake originally had it, place it back in the box and set it on the edge of my bed. I will not forget my treasured fairy tale. I hope I can feel the same way again… one day.

I hear a honk outside and eagerly gather what little I have, leaving my king-size bed behind — along with all the negative energy that resides in this room. I look out the window and spot a Toyota Camry parked by the curb. Leaning up against the vehicle is my rescuer. She has shoulder-length blonde hair and is wearing a miniskirt. She is also a seventeen-year-old Italian and I have labeled her as my guardian angel. She is a true, nurturing spirit.

"Can I help you put everything in the car?" Kara asks.

"This is pretty much it. My clothes, toiletries and one shoebox," I say, combing over my possessions.

"What's in the shoebox?" Kara asks curiously.

"The most valuable possession I own. It's worth millions!" I say lively, looking forward to my new journey.

As we listen to *Mad About You* by Belinda Carlisle, we can feel the cool breeze mixed with the warmth of the sun. I stick my hand and arm out the window, feeling the energy of freedom. I inhale and exhale very slowly. Kara and I sing along with the music, very loudly, all the way to her house.

A couple guys in a vehicle to our right whistle at us. We giggle and then it turns into hysterical, tear-filled laughter.

We arrive at her cookie-cutter house in Newbury Park. The landscaped front curb is picture-perfect and when we open the front door, I can hear the laughter of children.

"My mom has a daycare center," Kara informs me. I introduce myself to Kara's mother, Mrs. Patrini.

"Hi, I'm Jeneen. Thank you so much for letting me stay here. I am so grateful."

"You can call me Judy," she responds with warmth.

"Hi, I'm Lisa!" a ten-year-old girl cheerfully calls from her room.

"This is my sister, *Hammy*. Let me show you to our room," Kara chimes. "We can share my closet and you can sleep on the floor in my sleeping bag. I hope you don't mind," she says, feeling guilty that she couldn't offer more.

"Mind? Are you kidding? This will be one big slumber party all summer long," I respond, wisdom dawning in my mind: *What good is a waterbed when it lies in the midst of burning flames located in the depths of hell?*

PIECE SIXTY FOUR

C:\Purgatory\LifeAfterVictory\Bonnie&Clyde.doc

IT IS NOW mid November, 1989. Due to the traumatic beginning of my Senior Year, I barely graduate from Newbury Park High School. I'm a minor who left home without being legally emancipated from her parents. I am set free from the darkness of my former life and I have a new address now...

Kara and I met at Newbury Park High School during the last semester of my Senior Year. She has big, beautiful, brown eyes, a splash of freckles on her face and platinum-blonde hair. She drives me to and from work as if it's just an extension of her normal routine. I'm extremely grateful to have such a nurturing, compassionate friend.

Bill and Judy, Kara's parents, are trying to help me obtain my driver's license on my birthday, November 30. They're fully aware of my family situation and are doing all they can to help me move towards my immediate goal of getting out on my own.

I need to cross one last item off my checklist for my driver's license — my birth certificate. My parents have my important papers in an envelope in their armoire.

How am I going to get it when I'm not speaking to them? Anxiety creeps up on me like an eerie chill on a foggy night.

After living at Bill and Judy's for a month, they were understandably concerned that my parents were worried about my whereabouts. They knew I was not in contact with them and wanted to reassure them that their daughter was safe.

They sat me down in the living room. Bill began to tell me about the phone conversation that took place. "Jeneen, you have been communicating about how abusive your mother is but I really don't think you have come to grips with your father's behavior. We have something to tell you…"

"Your father specifically told me, and I quote, 'Why is she at your house? I want her on the street so she knows what it's really like.' You have been protecting your father since you've been here," Bill said, delivering the news with the anticipation of an emotional reaction.

"That's odd, Bill… He lived with his parents until he got married at the age of twenty-seven. I left home at seventeen and he wants me on the street? I'm not surprised. I believe you. I think I've become numb to all of it and I'm not going to cry over it either. I never felt loved or protected and it's impossible to expect normal reactions from them," I say, detached as if I were discussing someone else's family.

I believe Bill was in utter shock that a parent could actually be so removed towards his own child. The heart-to-heart conversation regarding my whereabouts turned out to be an unexpected lesson for the Patrini family. Bill wanted to reassure my father but instead got a clear picture of my dysfunctional bloodline.

I am not going to allow the cold, hard facts about my parents rule my life. I am happy to be free from them and I owe my new attitude to the Patrini family. I am in a better home now, feeling stronger every day, and that's all that matters.

Kara and I spent the summer together. We did errands for her mother (since she was overwhelmed by her childcare business), played on the swings in the park off of Wendy Drive, talked for hours on end and double-dated. We were inseparable, and I felt so at ease… without a care in the world. It was a much-needed respite from the guilt and self-hate.

Kara's summer love was Charles McManigan. Charles towered over both of us, made us laugh with comedy and came from an extensive family in Moorpark. We never stopped laughing through the entire season. Unfortunately, Charles broke up with Kara at the beginning of autumn.

Now it's November and I'm anxious about my next step towards independence. Time is of the essence because I want my driver's license on my eighteenth birthday. It's easier to get around with a car and I no longer want to depend on Kara's family.

I'm on a mission and no one can sidetrack me from reaching my goal.

My mother gave me her old clunker for graduation because she bought a new car. Her father bought the used car for her and now she is passing it down to me. I thought that was commendable, honestly, but it came with a price.

I remember my father giving me *the lecture* in the dining room, "You know you can't drink or do drugs while you are driving, right? You do realize you can really hurt someone!" I stood frozen because I was appalled that he thought I could be that kind of person. He really didn't know who I was at all and he had no interest in finding out.

Five, four, three, two, one… I go back to the day before I left home.

"Why did you send me to a place for bad girls?" I asked, hoping for a logical answer.

"Well, that's what you are and that's why we sent you there!" he growled like a pit bull.

"Do you know what they did to me in that horrid place you threw me into?" I asked. I had assumed incorrectly, once again, that I had a remotely normal family — one who would hear what I had to endure and show some remorse.

"Do you always lie? You know, Jeneen, sometimes I think you believe your own lies. I really do," he yelled, causing my pent-up rage to rise to the surface. I slammed my fist on the table, nearly breaking my knuckles.

"I'm not going to bother telling you anything because you are not worth it! Do you hear me? You aren't worth it!" I yelled so loudly that I was surprised the Montgomery family, two doors down, didn't hear me. Perhaps they did.

As I walked away, my father said his final farewell... "You are either going to kill someone or kill yourself." I ran to my room, slammed the door as hard as I could and cried facedown on my waterbed. I thought of Kara, my ticket out of the constant ridicule.

I reminisced to my friend, Kara during lunchtime at Newbury Park High School. Amy Nestle, Eric Adamston, Sheila Paulette, and occasionally, Mike Ginseng who studied with Dorothy Patterson. Everyone in our lunch group was aware of the *torture camp* I was thrown into and they all suggested seeing the school counselor to cope with Victory.

Rose was my therapist for the remainder of the school year. She was encouraging me to move out of my house after graduation. She also suggested not living in another family environment. She was afraid I would go from the frying pan into the flame, however, I needed a stepping-stone... otherwise, I'd be on the street.

Kara offered me a place to stay until I got on my feet. I accepted and intuitively knew things would only get better. *Besides, how much worse could it possibly get?*

I sail through the seas of time, back into the present. I'm working full-time at a company called Henson Aviation. They sell small aircraft engine parts. I have a hefty sum of money in my savings account. Judy and Bill never asked for a penny during my stay. I started out making five dollars an hour and eventually worked my way to twelve dollars as a receptionist/invoicer.

It's nearing 5 pm and Kara comes into the office to wait for me to finish work and then drive us home.

"Henson Aviation... How may I help you? This is Jeneen speaking. Can you please hold? Thank you," I grab another line and repeat the process, sounding so upbeat you would have assumed I won the lottery.

Moments later, Kara says, "Wow... I'm impressed! You sound so professional!"

After we arrived home, I call Chris. "Chris, can you take me over to my parents' house tomorrow? I need your support in case I get emotionally ambushed by my family. I don't need any setbacks right now," I say, trying to keep my composure.

"Yes, of course. I'll see you tomorrow at 2 pm," he says, without hesitation.

It's Saturday and there's no traffic but the drive up to hell's gates seems like it takes hours, though it's only ten minutes away. I knock and ring the doorbell several times, hoping for someone to answer.

"It doesn't look like they're home," I say, worried about not getting my birth certificate in time for my birthday.

"You still have a key on you, right?" Chris says, wondering why I didn't think of it in the first place.

"Well, I just don't want to barge in uninvited," I say, feeling like a burglar. I slowly get the key out of my purse and try to put it into the keyhole... I try again. *Am I not doing this right?*

"Chris, can you try to do it, please?" I ask, panicking.

"It doesn't fit, Jeneen," Chris says, matter-of-factly and ready to take the next step.

I can't breathe. I feel panic, abandonment and loneliness. *Somebody help me!* Everything that Bill told me about my father finally hit me like a bullet to my heart.

"They changed the locks on their door because they think I'm such a bad kid — that I'm on drugs, out of control, a thief, a liar and a bad seed," I cry out loud. Tears are streaming down my face.

"Jeneen, it looks like your bedroom window is open. I'm going to remove the screen. You crawl in there, unlock the front door from the inside and then we will look for your certificate," Chris says, giving me a look that says time is crucial.

"Holy shit, Chris… My parents already think I'm a criminal," I say, shaking in my boots.

"You are forgetting something again… It's your house, Jeneen. Besides, I already took off the screen. Get in!" Chris orders, after his quick justification speech.

He gives me a lift up to the window. I jump onto my bed and run as fast as I can to unlock the front door.

"Now, where do you think your birth certificate is?" Chris immediately asks.

I lead him to my parents' bedroom and to the armoire. We rummage through paperwork like a couple of thieves.

"I found it!" I cheer as if I just hit the jackpot.

We run as fast as we can towards the front door, lock it from the inside, then run to my room and close the door. We climb out the window and Chris securely replaces the screen.

No one would ever suspect we broke into the *house of pain*.

If they found out, I wouldn't be surprised if my parents attempted to have us arrested. After all, my mother has called the cops on me before.

"We did it! Thank you, Chris," I say, breathless from our unexpected stunt. We run to his Nissan, hop in and flee like Bonnie and Clyde.

My house key not opening the door was proof positive that I was no longer a part of this damaged family or locked inside their insane world. Now, I could move forward with no regrets.

I have a brand-new key now. It unlocks my future where I am the captain of my own ship and I will chart my own course… because now, I'm on the outside.

PIECE SIXTY FIVE

C:\Jeneen\Purgatory\LifeAfterVictory\PinkFloyd.doc

COMFORTABLY NUMB... THAT'S what I am. I have freed myself from my past physically but my emotional state doesn't match. There is a wall around my feelings, built by my self-doubt and guilt that prevents me from really being part of my new world. I have to tear down this wall I built in order to fully heal, but every time I remove a block, it is immediately replaced. It's like some kind of sadistic video game. You can't win but you're forced to play. The really sick part is that you're playing against yourself. The layers of blocks are stacked high and I stand guard day and night, repairing the wall and barricading myself with my own demons. *I am not good enough. No one loves me. Everyone at work thinks I'm incapable. I'm all alone.*

Chris pulls me into his vehicle. The stereo is blasting Pink Floyd's, *Wish You Were Here*. For some reason, the British band has an empowering effect on me. Their music is a weapon against my demons. I climb into a brown Nissan pickup truck, sink into the passenger seat and habitually fasten my seatbelt.

The gears have switched on the spinning cassette and *Comfortably Numb* surrounds the cab. Chris bought his *pride and joy* with money he saved by working for Miracle Appliances. He is a hard worker, frugal with his money and focuses on his goals.

Sadness seeps out of my pores as I tune into the blaring music.

I follow the lyrics closely in my mind. I roll down the window and feel the damp air as we pass Camarillo State Hospital. I am curious if there are any vacancies.

My dependable boyfriend, Chris, is eighteen years old. He makes no judgments and I lean on him through the roughest waters. He tries his best to stitch my war wounds back together. The sutures keep coming undone, however, because Chris can only do so much for a patient like myself. My wounds go deeper than he can reach. Still, without his help, my wounds would be open and predators could easily prey on my weakness.

I am so fortunate to have someone in my life to help me through the battle of my pain versus my optimism. It's a fight to the death and too strenuous for me to endure alone. I stroke Chris' arm.

My mood matches the thick misty fog and the darkness outside. It's hard to believe this is the same Potrero Road that at one time was magical and lead to happiness. Now, for this damaged driver and passenger, it's filled with shadowy eucalyptus trees, isolation and dreary clouds blocking the vision of the path ahead.

Once upon a time, I was loved by Drake, and now… it's gone.

I am left *comfortably numb*, unable to feel anything from Chris and incapable of giving him the love he deserves.

I just want to jump out of this pickup truck right now. The urge increases and takes over my body like an unknown entity. I can't breathe and waterfalls of tears block my vision. Now, I feel something — the piercing stabs to my flesh — causing me to cry out loud.

I was waiting for Drake the whole time I was imprisoned. I thought Jessica was just a temporary fill-in. I held on to the idea that we would pick up where we left off… just like that. Hope was the only thing that got me through prison camp. It was my shining light against the darkness. It's hard to feel loved by anyone anymore because I have been reprogrammed. The words untouchable and unworthy have been branded on my soul. My parents did not love me, nurture me, protect me, trust me or believe in me. This is not about the loss of Drake — that was just the last straw. The agony on this earth is so unbearable, I can't hold it all back.

I blink my eyes and think back to my Senior Year. I listen to my mother's *words of comfort*. It only sounds like nails on a chalkboard.

I confided to my mother about Chris' breakup with Michelle. I continued about how he has been my support system after my loss of Drake.

"That's great because you two can lick each other's wounds," she said, in her special way of sounding heartfelt and sinister at the same time. Those would be words of wisdom and comfort coming from a normal mother. Now, I'm angry and disgusted. *How the hell does she have the audacity to first break up my relationship and then give me heartbreak advice?*

I immediately leap back into the present because that memory is too heavy. I can't go there right now.

Comfortably Numb is still flying through the air and it touches my lips. I can taste the lyrics on my tongue.

I can no longer feel the wind rummaging through my hair or smell the ocean breeze. All I can see ahead of me is a dead end with no way out. QC laid the foundation for this damned wall in my soul and now I am continuing his work. The torment didn't stop when I left the gate. It haunts me every day and *the lunatic* resides in my head.

Comfortably Numb transitions to *Hey You* and I have an epiphany of how to cope with my severe depression without resorting to alcohol or drugs.

I unfasten my seatbelt.

Chris yells because he intuitively senses what I'm about to do, "Put your seatbelt back on now!"

I open the door and look down. I can measure how fast we are going by looking directly at the road below. The asphalt on the Ventura Freeway is passing below us at high speed and it's making me dizzy. I can feel the wind pressing against my cheeks, hitting my face and taking control of me. I hear Chris yelling, "Get in the car, Jeneen! Get in the car! Shut the door! You are going to fall out!"

The music continues soaring through the air and all I can think, at this very moment, is a way out of this turmoil. I decide to shut the door and sob hysterically because I could not follow through with killing myself.

Guilt sets in as I begin to understand the ramifications of my impulsive behavior. You see, Chris' brother killed himself and here I am trying to do the same, without any regard as to how much I might be hurting Chris. I realize the incredible insensitivity of what I just did, but now it's too late. The damage is done.

I examine Chris' profile and he looks like he has been through a war. I'm amazed at how he continued to stand by my side. I can see his solemn facial expression in detail... the moonlight has etched it into my mind. It will only be a matter of time until he has had enough and I'm left alone again.

I can identify with a soldier who went into battle, came home and the life he/she once knew had vanished into thin air.

I, like a soldier, have been to war against the forces of psychological evil. I have been through abuse by my parents and relatives and experienced physical and mental torture as a prisoner of hell here on this earth. I am a surviving GI of the fight for freedom, dignity, the truth and faith in humanity. I wait patiently for someone to take all of my broken pieces and put them back together. I want to be whole again. There is only one person who is capable of putting these intricate fragments back together — ME.

I am a soldier in a different kind of war... but I refuse to be defeated.

PIECE SIXTY SIX

C:\Jeneen\Purgatory\LifeAfterVictory\TheGift.doc

I LEFT MY safe-haven at Kara's after my eighteenth birthday. Before I *flew the coop*, Bill gave me a crash course in driving.

My big *yellow boat*, built by Ford, sat patiently by the curb outside their suburban home.

My driving lessons took place in the Conejo Valley. Bill was extremely generous with his valuable time. For a solid month, he sacrificed long hours after he finished work to give me lessons. My terrible eyesight (even with glasses) didn't make his job any easier. If you remember the old Mr. Magoo cartoons… well, that was me.

"Watch where you're going!" he often scolded, fearing for his life. "I just can't see!"

"Well, if you can't see, I suggest you slow down," he advised, with the patience of a saint.

Bill drove me to take my written and practical driver's tests in Thousand Oaks on the day I turned eighteen. In such a short time, he helped me in so many ways to reach towards independence. My wings developed so fast, and before I knew it, I was ready to leave the *Patrini nest*.

Many times Bill would say, "Parents should want to be a springboard for their children, guiding them into the next phase of their life. It's a shame your parents didn't want to do that."

Now, I am completely on my own. It's December, 1989, and I am renting a room in Newbury Park. Ironically, it's only half a mile away from my parents' house but I choose to no longer contact them. I live with a middle-aged woman who has been recently divorced. Her name is Mariam, and like myself, she is also making a new beginning. She is compassionate and approachable and we talk for hours. She is also responsible for getting me hooked on *Days of Our Lives*. She frequently bakes, so the house is comfortably warm and smells like Christmas cookies every time I come home.

I remain working full-time at Henson Aviation and co-workers have informed me that we receive generous raises every six months. I have $2,000 in my savings account because Kara's parents did not charge me to stay at their house. It's getting close to Christmas and our company just had a holiday party. I received a thousand dollar Christmas bonus and I have only been with the company for five months. I'm curious what the bonus will be next year. I feel so fortunate to have landed this job right out of high school; I am starting to believe I have guardian angels watching over me.

RASAC (Rape and Sexual Abuse Counseling) is part of my weekly routine and I'm on a sliding payment scale. I'm taking one psychology class per semester. Mrs. Davidson, my co-worker at Henson Aviation, encouraged me to take at least one class at Moorpark College every semester. She said, "If you take one class a semester, it all adds up. Before you know it, you will have your bachelor's."

Joe Donaldson sits next to me in my psychology class. He makes me laugh uncontrollably during lectures, sometimes to the point of tears. We have become best friends and I feel I can trust him with my story. He is thirty-two-years-old and usually wears a dress shirt that hangs over the waistline of his jeans. I like the contrast of dressy and casual. His dark-brown hair is styled with a light gel and one cannot miss his inviting smile. We study together on the weekends.

I know he would be perfect to partner with on my mission this holiday season.

I tell him my plan to help the homeless in Santa Monica.

"I want to do something special for someone who is struggling to survive. I have been so blessed after leaving home, between moving in with Kara's family and my job with Henson Aviation, my life has changed completely. I definitely don't want to do this alone, in the middle of the night. Joe, could you accompany me this Saturday?" I question, knowing his answer.

"Sure, I would love to. It will be best if we take my truck," he says, enthusiastically.

I purchase two-hundred dollars worth of pizza and we both make our way to distribute the tasty slices of heaven. The wonderful aromas of meats and vegetables permeate the cab as we drive down Pacific Coast Highway. It's cold and dark by the beach and I'm only expecting homeless adults but I see a child amongst the crowd. That really hurt because I know that I'm only putting a band-aid over the problem. There were times when, while driving to Hollywood to see my grandmother, I pulled my car over and gave out food to the less fortunate. I understand that there are many with mental health disorders but I'm willing to take the risk in order to help, trusting my angels to look after me. It's my way of saying, *thank you.*

My love life… well, that went into the grinder. Chris finally had enough and I am left without anyone. I can't say that I blame him. I intentionally pushed him away. I have friends to keep me occupied, so I try not to think about the past.

Everything is wonderful by day but the shit hits the fan when I am left by myself at night.

Loneliness hits me like a bullet to my head. The negative recordings of my family and QC play in my mind like an ongoing nightmare. I turn on my boom box and play music to drown out the voices.

I grab my *little pink book* as if I were going through heroin withdrawals. I panic because I know the feeling of isolation too well. I make an impulsive decision to fill the void with companions — *fast*. I go down my list, like a telemarketer, looking for a *yes*.

I do this daily. I'm either on the phone with someone or at his house. I am sacrificing my dignity to get me through the night.

Financially, I am independent; emotionally, I am lost. I yearn to fill the emptiness. Silence triggers my associations of abandonment and I flip out like a drug addict looking for a fix.

You are never going to make it! That's why we sent you to Victory! You are a bad girl! You are going to kill someone or yourself! Drake doesn't love you anymore! College is not for you! You are a liar! You are a whore! You are a Jezebel! You should be ashamed to call yourself a Christian! You should be ashamed to call yourself a Christian! You should be ashamed to call yourself a Christian...

I start to shake when those voices play through my mind. I grab a Kleenex. I make my calls and the cycle continues.

I have so many male companions, one would assume I'm an escort. If I were, I wouldn't be renting a room or driving a Ford Fairmont that stalls in the middle of an intersection. I just don't want to be alone. I use men, while keeping myself detached. One time, after one of my self-destructive trysts, I walked out while saying, "It was nice. Thanks. I've got to go." I was not seeking companionship this time but merely a way to feel powerful and in control. I leave first before anyone considers leaving me. I am quite the robot, without a heart to crush or tamper with, and I'm making sure that I'm safe this time around. This next part of my life is going to be different. No more serious relationships for me equals no more pain, no risk of a damaged heart and no more abandonment. I have become a free spirit of the night.

The phone rings. I wonder who it is this time. "Hello?" I ask, hoping to fill the void.

"Hi, Jeneen. It's James Garcia... your brother's friend from youth group. Do you want to go for a drive?" he asks, without hesitation.

"Sure... It's been a while," I reply, curious about how life is treating him.

He picks me up at 7 pm and then drives me to First Christian Church of Newbury Park. We walk outside the front entrance. Memories of Drake flood my mind.

"What did happen, James? What happened after my parents locked me up... How did Drake respond?" I ask, searching for answers.

"He started to ask where you were and questioned everyone at youth group. He had a hunch your parents were not being straight with him. When he got the final answer, he got very angry, jumped into his car and peeled out of the parking lot. The screeching sound of his tires was his final farewell. He was extremely pissed," he says, giving me the information I needed to hear.

He did love me...

I start to cry uncontrollably and James holds me in his arms. Unpredictably, he leans over towards my lips and kisses me. I start to enjoy it and then I stop. Tears of loss run down my face.

"I wish you never loved him, Jeneen. I pray you could just get over him," James says, hoping for a miracle.

"I wish I could too, James. It's blocking me from moving forward. I wish... I wish there was a magic potion that I could take to wipe the memory away. Then again, do I really want to do that? It was the most magical time of my life and it's the best memory I have. If I can tap into my greatest love story, I can learn to give again. Right now, I'm still in mourning, solely focusing on the darkness. One day, I'll step out into the sunshine and start to live. Thank you, James, for snapping a missing piece into my complex puzzle." I hold him in my arms for what seems like an eternity. I am forever grateful for his friendship.

PIECE SIXTY SEVEN

C:\Jeneen\LifeAfterVictory\RayofLight\Pepperdine.doc

HENSON AVIATION HAS been the first rung on my unorthodox ladder of success. I have been dedicated to this *mom and pop* business for about a year and a half now. I am nineteen years old, I've had three raises and my last Christmas bonus was $2,000. The generosity of these people takes me by surprise and I continually have to pinch myself.

I'm frugal with my money and deposit everything extra, after paying my bills, into my savings account. This explains the holes in my socks. I pretend my savings doesn't exist. As for my wardrobe, Bill gave me a bagful of hand-me-down office attire — a gift from a secretary who works with him. The dresses are beautiful and I wear them every day to work. I'm grateful for the new professional style I am developing. Bill works for GTE and had a secretarial position lined up for me. He suggested I use him as a reference and I did. He put his reputation on the line because he had faith in me, however, the job at Henson Aviation came through first and I took it immediately.

It's nice to have that Christmas bonus as a cushion, now that I'm on my own financially.

I ended up taking my grandmother on a mini shopping spree, since she has been there for me during my loneliest times. Besides, the expression on her face was priceless. I drive to her house almost every other weekend. She still lives in Hollywood, next door to that old house… you remember… the one with the bars.

Sometimes, I would take Grandma Vera to Florentine Gardens — a famous Hollywood nightclub. Not surprisingly, she was the only grandmother on the floor.

I remember one special time, a young club enthusiast, in full hip-hop regalia, thought it was so cool that I brought a more mature flower into the gardens. He ended up escorting Grandma Vera to the dance platform. I watched my dear grandmother have the time of her life as she boogied the night away.

When I returned to work after this fun-filled weekend with my Italian nana, I ended up sharing some personal information with my colleagues. I confided in Joy and Janis about the abuse that is taking place at Victory *Christian* Academy. They are both mothers in their mid-forties and are completely stunned that this is happening in modern-day America… especially in our liberal state of California. My heart goes out to the girls trapped there and I feel a sense of responsibility to report it to authorities to prevent further torture. After leaving that intense hell, I didn't want to relive any of it ever again. It continues to burn me up inside that I have this knowledge and didn't bother to do my part.

The guilt of being on the outside and allowing those criminals to continue doing terrible things is gnawing at me. I need to rescue these children — *now!* I know I am going to have to face my demons all over again but it's for the greater good. I will gladly walk through the fire to make sure it doesn't happen to one more soul, otherwise, what I have endured would have no meaning.

Janis and Joy encourage me to get in touch with CBS, 60 Minutes, 20/20 and my local politicians. It is the perfect time to involve local politics because we are nearing an election.

Both of these women are my adopted mothers in the workplace. I spend many weekends at Janis' house (when I'm not dancing the night away with Grandma) earning extra income by cleaning her house from top to bottom. It also keeps me busy and I don't have to be alone in my rented room during my time off. Her son, Melvin, and daughter, Molly, also work at Henson Aviation and we have become like family.

She often tells me, "You must have angels looking after you, Jeneen."

She should know... she's one of them. Janis has endured domestic violence in her past and survived. She found happiness in her current marriage and now she is paying it forward by helping another survivor — me.

Janis introduced me to self-hypnosis through meditation. It's an excellent tool to overcome anxiety and depression. I also use these methods to cope with rage.

Months after sending out letters to my local politicians, I finally hear back from Social Services of San Diego. A gentleman by the name of Rick Palentino spent an hour composing a fifty-page deposition for me. Rick promised that I would not have to appear in court, that he would go on my behalf... and he kept his word.

Months passed. The phone rings at Henson Aviation. I pick it up reciting my usual enthusiastic greeting, "Good afternoon... Henson Aviation. This is Jeneen speaking."

"Hello, Jeneen. It's Rick Palentino. I'd like to speak with you. Do you have a minute?"

"Yes... Could you please hold on?"

"Joy, it's Rick Palentino from social services. Could I use the conference room for some privacy?" I ask.

"Sure... absolutely. Go for it!"

I make my way into the meeting room, "Rick, go ahead. What was the outcome?"

"We got it closed down because Victory Christian Academy is unlicensed and the building is not up to fire code standards."

"So what about the child abuse, Rick?" I ask, completely baffled that the real crimes were not addressed.

"Nothing on that," he replies.

"Are you kidding me? This *preacher* has abused so many girls and now he'll just continue somewhere else. What about my statements and all of the other survivors', I didn't know, from several years prior that had similar accounts? I don't understand how these people can get away with abusing children. Is it because they hide under the mighty flag of religion? QC also mentioned that if the state closes him down, he would just open another one in Florida. Apparently, these types of *schools* are unregulated by the government," I shout, outraged at the end result of the court's decision.

"You can always file a civil suit," he says, giving me another alternative.

"Would I see QC in court?" I ask, terrified to be in the same room with my worst nightmare.

"Yes," he answers.

"I cannot bring myself to do it," I respond, feeling helpless.

Not only do I feel threatened by QC, I am still brainwashed enough to believe I would go to hell for getting money from a preacher. *I've done all I can.*

Rick sent me articles in the mail from the *Los Angeles Times* regarding Victory Christian Academy. He also interviewed my parents and told them about the abuse. That is the first time my parents had a glimpse of what happened to us. I'm not sure what their reaction was because I don't speak to them at all. They don't have my phone number and have no idea where I live.

It's a shame it most likely took articles in newspapers of other girls' stories for them to believe any of it. It makes me so angry they didn't trust that I was telling them the truth about everything, however, when other children give their testimonies... In spite of the tangible evidence presented by social services, it would not surprise me if they still turn a blind eye. It doesn't matter anymore. They can think whatever they want. I've moved on.

Every morning, the catering truck would come by Henson Aviation and we would get breakfast during our break. I have to limit this to once a week, though, because I am on a tight budget. I usually *brown-bag* it. It is, however, one of my highlights. We would grab something to eat and then congregate in the break room to talk.

While I am out getting my breakfast burrito, a twenty-seven-year-old, darkhaired, lanky male approaches me.

"Hi, my name is Paul Reynolds and I work for the moving company next door.

I couldn't help but notice how beautiful you are," he says, smiling.

"Thank you," I respond appreciatively, offering a smile of my own.

Paul and I became friends rather quickly, and soon, he occupies most of my free time. Our relationship is non-romantic and we enjoy a strong friendship.

We would take our lunches together frequently. One day, out of the blue, he told me that he just accepted a job at Pepperdine University.

"That's great news, although, I'm going to miss our lunches," I express sadly.

"Don't worry, we'll still meet after work like we usually do," he says, reassuring me.

Paul spent the next month excited about his new position as a mover. "The university is on a hilltop, overlooking the ocean and I love the environment. It really makes a difference, since we spend most of our time at work." He sounds a lot like he's trying to sell me something…

"You know, there is a position opening in the Huntsinger Academic Center. I helped them move their office this week. The position is a word processing specialist and it requires a Bachelor's degree, plus experience. I think you should just go for it! I know

Susan Barringer, who is in charge of hiring. I can get you the interview but I can't get you the job. The rest is up to you," he says, determined to have me try for it.

"Isn't this a Christian university?" I ask, dragging my heels. All I see are red warning flags. Although I kept my spiritual faith, I remain apprehensive about organized religion.

"It's a non-denominational campus. It will be fine. They are not in your face about religion. They are non-judgmental and make an effort to have a team-oriented work environment. It's positive." He throws another blanket of reassurance over me.

"This sounds like an interesting opportunity and I believe I have enough experience to pull it off. The downside is my lack of education. At the interview, I am going to have to lead with all my positive accomplishments and downplay my educational gaps.

Okay, Paul... Let's set up the interview. Thank you so much!" I respond.

The interview went well. I used my work experience at Henson Aviation as leverage. As for my missing Bachelor's degree, I didn't focus on that but instead emphasized the psychology classes I am currently taking at Moorpark College. Susan is getting her PhD in psychology. As soon as I heard her goals, it seemed like the right time to bring up my interest in the subject. I wasn't going to allow my lack of a degree block my way through this door of opportunity.

I was completely honest regarding my lack of knowledge of DOS, DBase 4 and MS Word 5.5 (which they were in the midst of switching to from Word Perfect). Instead, I brought to the forefront my experience working on terminals connected to a server and my use of the company program for invoicing. I incorporated my excellent public relations skills into our conversation as well. I expressed how eager I am to learn new programs because I embrace change and am excited about the latest technology.

"Do you understand what this job entails, Jeneen? You will not only have to learn and know these programs proficiently but you will be trouble-shooting with faculty and staff and helping them resolve issues. You will be an *information resource* in person and over the phone. In between all of that, you will be preparing memorandums, tests, letters of recommendations, faxes, photocopies, formatting, labels, mail merges and dictation with deadlines. Do you think you can handle a high pressure job like this?" she questioned, trying to catch her own breath.

"There isn't anything I can't handle," I responded, with hard-won confidence pulled from the depths of my personal life. *If only she knew the half of it.*

I must have called once every two weeks. I expressed how much I would love to work in a learning environment and how much value it would add to my resumé.

I was up against over one hundred candidates. The race eventually dwindled down to two candidates, plus myself. Two months later, I finally receive a call from Susan…

I look out the window and catch a glimpse of students climbing up the steps. I notice a young girl, around my age, carrying a backpack. The young scholar has dark-brown hair, and if the sun catches it just right, her ringlets have reddish highlights. Her faded-blue, denim jacket is wrapped around her waist. I carefully study her demeanor. She is communicating with other classmates. Perhaps they just attended a book signing at the Payson Library. One cannot miss her excitement at being at this institution of higher education. Seeing my reflection in the window and the laughter I hear reminds me that…

My Diary Exists in My Soul

I no longer possess any of Drake's meticulously folded love letters. There were so many poetic messages in that old shoebox that I lost count. Between all of my moves, they were somehow lost, along with the beautiful necklace he gave me. My mother confiscated my three diaries when she locked me up in Victory. She read my private thoughts and then burned them, or so she told me.

All I have is my memory, my hard drive, so-to-speak. Now it's presented to you, my dear reader, in this book. I am the only person who has control of my soul and no one can destroy my fiery spirit. After spreading my wings, I can now soar freely through the sky, like a great and glorious eagle. There will always be associations that will lead me back to the days of butterflies and turmoil but they no longer have power over me. They are a part of my story — which is still being written.

Epilogue

MY EXPERIENCE AT Victory has changed my life's course. The aftermath has left me with anxiety, depression, fear of being alone, panic attacks, rage, PTSD (Post Traumatic Stress Disorder) and exercise anxiety (when I am in a class). When there is a change in my environment or when I fear abandonment, I wet the bed. I have suffered from sleep disorders.

I still have insecurities about not feeling loved and need reassurance. Instead of feeling bad about myself, I assume that others do not like me.

I have searched for validations from older men because of their education and greater experience; their opinions seem to hold more clout and are often more penetrating.

PTSD pops out of nowhere and is triggered by an association. For example, if I hear a Christian song on the radio, a preacher giving a sermon or someone talking about Jesus, it drags me back to Victory. I start to visualize the torture and then a flood of memories come rising to the surface. These play in my mind like an ongoing nightmare.

One time in a kick boxing class, I had a panic attack. I had a doctor run an EKG on me and he said "Your heart is fine. It could be exercise anxiety." I laughed. Moments later, I thought about Victory. It was the fear of not being able to keep up with the group and having the instructor (a student-*Helper*) call me out on a mistake that triggered the episode.

I wake up in a panic when I try to sleep. Everything is fine during the day but I can't shut down when it's time to retire. When I finally fall asleep, the slightest noise awakens me. I am often enraged to the point where I physically push someone away. I have thrown my iPhone against the wall numerous times, during the writing of this book, *Pieces of Victory*. I'm astonished that it still functions. Kudos to Apple!

I have impulsively walked out of prestigious jobs without giving notice. I would feel that no one liked me or that they thought I was incompetent. The *Victory* ruckus in my head would override my logic.

I have walked away from potential relationships, sabotaging them first before anyone had a chance to leave me.

As of the present time, I do not speak to my parents. I have forgiven them for Victory and attempted many times to just move forward but their abusive behavior continues. I refuse to be in the line of fire and won't allow their dysfunction to affect me negatively.

During the course of writing and editing *Pieces of Victory*, I took three bottles of prescription sleeping pills. I took one pill every night. When I ran out, I would be wide awake for twenty-four to forty-eight hours at a stretch.

On the other side of the spectrum, I choose to be empowered by my experiences. Currently, I do not take any medication, opting instead for the holistic approach. I focus on exercise, massage, being productive by setting goals and reaching out to help others.

I did seek out counseling, thanks to encouragement from my friends the Poserinas and *Drake McCallister*.

I am currently a massage therapist in the Las Vegas area. This career change has been therapeutic for my clients, as well as myself. When giving a massage, I get in tune with our energy, creating an inner peace for both of us. Like many others in my profession, I am a conduit for healing.

I am also volunteering in Las Vegas for Survivors of Institutional

Abuse (SIA), helping survivors cope with the aftermath of abuse. Jodi Hobbs, the founder of this organization, is also a survivor of Victory Christian Academy. A donation of 10% of each book will be contributed to SIA-Now.org and Help4Teens.org. James Swift is the founder of Help4Teens.org and proceeds will go towards building a shelter for teens on the streets. Thank you!

Quantum Touch

Quantum touch therapists work with energy as a means of healing others on all levels — physical, emotional and spiritual.

In the midst of writing this book, everything came up to the surface. I relived the good memories and the terrible. Although it has been extremely cathartic for me, my PTSD and sleep disorders increased tremendously. I reached out for energy healing.

A friend of mine who is a self-taught quantum touch therapist, guided me through the pain of my emotions and helped me allow them to dissipate into nothing.

He asked me what made me feel unloved. I told him, "My mother." I cried.

He asked me what I felt when I thought about her. I said, "Shame."

He asked me what made me feel loved. I immediately said, "Drake." I giggled.

He wanted me to go to my *happy place* and I did.

I closed my eyes and fell into a deep meditation.

My spirit is skimming across the ocean and I feel the fabric of a blue evening dress. I touch the soft material. The ocean mist sprays on my face and revitalizes my soul.

The stagnant piano has come alive and the sound of a Bach prelude is rising in the air. The chains around my heart have been released and I am free of the heavy weight I carried on my shoulders. Peace touches every part of my body and I can breathe. I can feel the energy of love coursing through me. **Finally VOICING everything that I had been suppressing was the most liberating moment of my life.**

The broken pieces of my soul, once scattered, are now mended. I feel whole. I am one and I celebrate my own victory.

A friend of mine once told me, "Victory Christian Academy is the work of Satan!" My response is, "Why would you want to give something negative that much credit?" I truly believe this was my mission in life. I had to endure this tragedy to want to help children — to make a difference — to take a stand. Pay attention to the hardships in your life. They may be the key to something greater. The universe may have a plan for you that doesn't make any sense, until viewed in retrospect. In the end, your puzzle will snap together, creating a beautiful and complex picture of your life. I chose to write this book so I can encourage, love, share and have a sense of compassion in order to reach my hand out to someone in need. My mistakes and my pain are lessons for us all. If I had an option to change my past, I would not. It makes me who I am today. I am a strong, determined woman. I am a fighter against child abuse.

We can be conduits for bad or for healing. We have the option to channel love through us. We just have to choose to do it.

To prevent child abuse in teen programs, we need oversight. Make a difference today and take action!

Come and share my mission in life by visiting my website: JeneenMiller.com

In Memory of Michele Ulriksen

THE AUTHOR OF "Reform at Victory", Michele Ulriksen, unfortunately died in March of 2011 from a drug overdose. I am in shock because I saw what a strong leader she was for survivors. I let it slip by me, for a second, that the PTSD and anxiety caused by Victory Christian Academy could penetrate a solid rock like Michele. I should have known better and I feel a sense of responsibility that I didn't reach out to her more. I'm going to do it now by promoting her book and taking action by spreading awareness like wildfire. I will take a stand in her name.

I was devastated when I found out Michele left this earth. I cried for days. She was proof that the abuse was real. She was on a crusade after QC and countless others like him. He has disciples, you see... There are other abusive facilities out there and she was on a mission to stop them all.

I am wondering about our legal system in America... Why is it that someone can have allegations of child abuse and rape leveled against them and continue to run an unlicensed facility without being prosecuted? He was allowed to close this school down, rebrand it calling it the Light House, and move to the state of Florida. It was open for over two decades. As long as he had girls' parents feeding him money, he was able to keep things running. If it weren't for Alexandra Zayas and Jodi Hobbs, founder of SIA-now.org, girls would still be abused by him today.

Michele was a beautiful soul who was tormented by QC. I know this because we've lived parallel lives. You see, we both were sentenced for a crime we didn't commit. We both have struggled with the aftermath of Victory's damage: PTSD, abandonment, not feeling *good enough,* fear of being alone and insomnia. Neither of us could wall ourselves off from the after effects of torture and emotional manipulation.

We need to wake up, America. Don't let Michele's death be in vain. Help me change the legal system. We need to put a stop to the *QCs* that, in surprising numbers, do exist in this nation. This could have happened to your child. Help me pave the way to a better future.

My courageous Michele wrote a book to spread awareness. Please visit: Reform at Victory

For more information on other survivors who are making a difference, please visit: JeneenMiller.com

CPSIA information can be obtained
at www.ICGtesting.com
Printed in the USA
BVHW070313240720
584448BV00003B/6

9 780692 539021